Louise Erdrich is one of the most critically and commercially successful Native American writers, securing prestigious awards and an international readership with her debut novel, *Love Medicine*. This book is the first fully comprehensive treatment of Louise Erdrich's writing, analysing the textual complexities and diverse contexts of her work to date. Drawing on, and taking to task, the critical archive relating to Erdrich's work and to Native American literature more broadly, Stirrup explores the full depth and range of her authorship, charting common themes in her writing and interrogating positive and negative critical responses alike.

Louise Erdrich

MANCHESTER
1824

Manchester University Press

Contemporary American and Canadian Writers

Series editors:
Nahem Yousaf and Sharon Monteith

Also available

Passing into the present: contemporary American fiction of racial and gender passing   Sinéad Moynihan
Paul Auster   Mark Brown
Douglas Coupland   Andrew Tate
Philip Roth   David Brauner

Louise Erdrich

David Stirrup

Manchester University Press

Manchester and New York

distributed in the United States exclusively by Palgrave Macmillan

Published by Manchester University Press
Oxford Road, Manchester M13 9NR, UK
and Room 400, 175 Fifth Avenue, New York, NY 10010, USA
www.manchesteruniversitypress.co.uk

Distributed in the United States exclusively by
Palgrave Macmillan, 175 Fifth Avenue, New York,
NY 10010, USA

Distributed in Canada exclusively by
UBC Press, University of British Columbia, 2029 West Mall,
Vancouver, BC, Canada V6T 1Z2

British Library Cataloguing-in-Publication Data
A catalogue record for this book is available from the British Library

Library of Congress Cataloging-in-Publication Data applied for

ISBN 978 0 7190 7426 4 *hardback*

First published 2010

Typeset
by Florence Production Ltd, Stoodleigh, Devon
Printed in Great Britain
by the MPG Books Group

Contents

Series editors' foreword

This innovative series reflects the breadth and diversity of writing over the last thirty years, and provides critical evaluations of established, emerging and critically neglected writers – mixing the canonical with the unexpected. It explores notions of the contemporary and analyses current and developing modes of representation with a focus on individual writers and their work. The series seeks to reflect both the growing body of academic research in the field, and the increasing prevalence of contemporary American and Canadian fiction on programmes of study in institutions of higher education around the world. Central to the series is a concern that each book should argue a stimulating thesis, rather than provide an introductory survey, and that each contemporary writer will be examined across the trajectory of their literary production. A variety of critical tools and literary and interdisciplinary approaches are encouraged to illuminate the ways in which a particular writer contributes to, and helps readers rethink, the North American literary and cultural landscape in a global context.

Central to debates about the field of contemporary fiction is its role in interrogating ideas of national exceptionalism and transnationalism. This series matches the multivocality of contemporary writing with wide-ranging and detailed analysis. Contributors examine the drama of the nation from the perspectives of writers who are members of established and new immigrant groups, writers who consider themselves on the nation's margins as well as those who chronicle middle America. National labels are the subject of vociferous debate and including American and Canadian writers in the same series is not to flatten the differences between them but to acknowledge that literary traditions and tensions are cross-cultural and that North American writers often explore and expose precisely these tensions. The series recognises that situating a writer in a cultural context involves a multiplicity of influences, social and geo-political, artistic and theoretical, and that contemporary fiction defies easy categorisation. For example, it examines writers who invigorate the genres in which they have made their mark alongside writers whose aesthetic goal is to subvert the idea of genre alto-gether. The challenge of defining the roles of writers and assessing their reception by reading communities is central to the aims of the series.

Overall, *Contemporary American and Canadian Writers* aims to begin to represent something of the diversity of contemporary writing and seeks to engage students and scholars in stimulating debates about the contemporary and about fiction.

Nahem Yousaf
Sharon Monteith

Acknowledgements

I am grateful to the series editors, Sharon Monteith and Nahem Yousaf, and to colleagues at MUP, for both their unswerving patience and careful guidance. By the time my first deadline came and went I was working – or rather not working – under the cloud of serious family illness. My thanks too, in that respect, to the Oncology unit at Kent and Canterbury Hospital.

Very early research on Erdrich's work was funded by the British Association for American Studies and more recently I must thank the British Academy for funding to research both this and another project. Thanks too to Colin Calloway for pointing me in the direction of Elaine Jahner's papers, and to Peter Carini and Sarah I. Hartwell in the Rauner Special Collection at Dartmouth for their help.

I am ever grateful to Mick Gidley and other former tutors; readers and mentors; colleagues and friends all; and my family for their support and encouragement. For advice and critique my thanks to Dave Murray, David Herd, James Mackay, Maureen Kincaid Speller, and to Kimberly Blaeser, among many others. None of these people are remotely responsible for my errors!

To Jo, Florence, Ottilie

List of abbreviations

Throughout I use the following parenthetical abbreviations for Erdrich's books, full details of which are located in the bibliography.

AW	*The Antelope Wife*
B&I	*Books and Islands in Ojibwe Country*
BBH	*The Birchbark House*
BD	*Baptism of Desire*
BJD	*The Blue Jay's Dance: A Birth Year*
BP	*The Bingo Palace*
BQ	*The Beet Queen*
CC	*The Crown of Columbus*
FS	*Four Souls*
GS	*The Game of Silence*
J	*Jacklight*
LM	*Love Medicine*
LR	*The Last Report on the Miracles at Little No Horse*
MB	*The Master Butchers Singing Club*
OF	*Original Fire: Selected and New Poems*
PD	*The Painted Drum*
PoD	*The Plague of Doves*
PY	*The Porcupine Year*
ST	*Shadow Tag*
T	*Tracks*
TBL	*Tales of Burning Love*

1

Native American literature: authorship and authority

A review of Louise Erdrich's *Four Souls* (2004) in the *Christian Science Monitor* speaks, albeit somewhat glibly, to the centrality of her position in the general public's reception of modern Native American issues: '[f]or better or for worse, most white people have two popular avenues of contact with Native Americans: casino gambling or Louise Erdrich. My money's on Erdrich, with whom the odds of winning something of real value are essentially guaranteed' (Charles 2004).[1] Carelessly, perhaps unconsciously, Charles rehearses one of the major controversies surrounding Erdrich's work. He elides the stock of questions and anxieties that accompany its popularity. The notion that the Native American 'experience', however this might be constituted or perceived, is 'diluted' and unrealistic, for instance, or that the Native American 'angle' is thematised – a conceit, a device, or a token to attract a particular readership – are common concerns around Erdrich's work. So too is the sense that the accessibility and/or popularity of the work (comparable to Toni Morrison, Amy Tan, or Anne Tyler) either causes, or illustrates, its apoliticism, making it 'unuseful' to Native American political issues. Clearly these anxieties cannot be ignored, and I will return to them at the end of this chapter. But Charles's emphasis on questions of race and 'access' to culture overshadow a far simpler yet significant point: that in reading Erdrich, 'something of real value is essentially guaranteed'.

That 'something of value' is, fundamentally, literary. In his provocative *Native American Fiction* David Treuer closes his searching – and at times scathing – critique of critical approaches to *Love Medicine* (1984; 1993) by asserting that Erdrich's first novel is 'so beautiful, so powerful, and so new, it is hard not to try and beatify it. But to make it divine . . . is to destroy its humanity. To treat it as culture is to destroy it as literature' (2006: 67–68). The power of Erdrich's writing is, ultimately, what has garnered her numerous awards, including the National Book Critics Circle Award (for *Love Medicine*, 1984); an honorary doctorate from her alma mater, Dartmouth College (2009); the Anisfield-Wolf Book Award and a shortlisting for the Pulitzer Prize (for *The Plague of Doves*, 2009); and, most recently, the Kenyon Review Award for Literary Achievement (2009). In conjunction with the latter, *Love Medicine* became the subject of a number of events around *The Big Read Knox County* in October and November 2009. This culminated in numerous seminars and lectures on and around the book at the Kenyon Review Literary Festival, 4–7 November 2009, at which Erdrich gave the Denham Sutcliffe Memorial Lecture.

That kind of currency – the continuing significance of *Love Medicine* and others of Erdrich's works – is also demonstrated in the critical archive, which continues to devote a deal of attention to her work. A glance at the programmes for the 2009 Native American Literature Symposium (Chicago, 26–28 February) and the 2009 meeting of the Native American and Indigenous Studies Association (Minnesota, 21–23 May), records five individual papers, more than any of the other 'majors' in Native American literature – N. Scott Momaday, Leslie Marmon Silko, James Welch, Gerald Vizenor (whose work was the subject of a special panel at NAISA), Louis Owens, or Sherman Alexie. There are many reasons why critics might be choosing to stay away from any of the more widely written about figures, of course, and two conferences in a single year hardly provides persuasive statistics. My point is simply this: that Erdrich's writing has commanded, and continues to command, an abundance of critical and scholarly, not to mention commercial, interest.

Beyond the problematic layers of appeal implicit in Charles's comments, Erdrich's prose in particular has long elicited abundant praise. A recent review of *The Plague of Doves* declares: 'Of all the fictional hamlets American writers have planted, from William Faulkner's Yoknapatawpha County to Garrison Keillor's Lake Wobegon, the most complex, luminous place yet might be a little town called Argus, North Dakota' (Freeman). Comparisons with Faulkner in particular are common and, although Erdrich's prose can be prone to decadence at times, not unwarranted. Her fiction's lyrical qualities and richly textured characters and textual landscapes are the dominant objects of praise, in recognition that here is a body of literature that combines irony and pathos, complexity of plot and sophistication of language, deft narrative turns and searching philosophical and ethical conundrums. Many critics have declared her to be among the most important late twentieth-/early twenty-first-century Native American writers, while P. Jane Hafen (Taos Pueblo) comments that her work manifests 'a Chippewa experience in the context of the European American novelistic tradition' (1999b). It is ultimately that ability to depict what many understand as 'Chippewa experience', while innovatively embracing the 'European American novelistic tradition' – to successfully navigate the 'betwixt and beween' – that is at the root of her success.

It is, however, not simply Erdrich's prose that impresses, and not merely the subject matter of her work that crosses 'boundaries'. Indeed there are few prominent Native American writers who have con-fined themselves to single genres within their writing. James Welch (Blackfoot) springs initially to mind, but then he, a highly significant novelist who inspired many including Erdrich, was also a poet. D'Arcy McNickle (Flathead) is as renowned for his political work as his fiction. N. Scott Momaday (Kiowa) and Leslie Marmon Silko (Laguna Pueblo) are well known for combining genres. The intermixing of poetry and prose, oral tales, fiction, autobiography, and photography enhances the essential drama of their work. Sherman Alexie (Spokane/Coeur d'Alene) is as prolific a poet as he is a successful prose writer, and has more recently ventured into screenplay and film direction. Paula Gunn Allen (Taos Pueblo) and Elizabeth Cook-Lynn (Dakota) are poets and, along with Louis Owens (Choctaw), academics and novelists; fellow scholar Craig Womack (Creek/Cherokee) followed up his incisive study of tribal literary nationalism, *Red on Red* (1999), with a novel, *Drowning in Fire* (2001), dramatising at least some of the critical work's key concerns.

Erdrich is comfortably at home in this list. She is also situated in a rich and vibrant tradition of Anishinaabe writing. Like a number of fellow Anishinaabeg – Gerald Vizenor, Kimberly Blaeser, David Treuer, Gordon Henry, Jr. to name a few – she is equally productive, her output impressively diverse, although unlike them she has not ventured into the world of scholarly criticism. In her novels, in the stories that were their genesis, and through her poetry, children's fiction, memoirs, and prose essays, Erdrich has been both commer-cially *and* critically successful since the first publication of *Love Medicine*.[2] Just as she refuses to be confined to genre in her practice, the critical domain seems equally at ease approaching Erdrich's fiction from a variety of angles, and with multiple perspectives and conclusions. This book is an attempt to engage with the full span of that output. Drawing out historical and culturally specific readings through the theoretical methodologies offered by both indigenous and postcolonial theories; the apparatus of feminism, postmodernism, and, in a minor way, regionalism, this chapter will very briefly map out the critical platform upon which the scholarly archive relating to Erdrich's work is built. In doing so, it will consider Erdrich's work in relation to Native *and* American concerns, and in relation to the multiple influences Erdrich has both drawn from and created in her own writing. These various themes and contexts are often inextricable; to take them together is invariably to consider what it means to understand Erdrich, in her own words, as an *American* author.

A 'Chippewa landscape'?

Legally designated as Chippewa in the United States, the word 'Ojibwe' is a term that has been used at least since the early nineteenth century and is variously interpreted as referring to the 'peculiar sound of the *Anishinabe* voice' according to Henry Rowe Schoolcraft (Vizenor 1993: 133); to the puckered seam of the Ojibwe moccasin (Vizenor 1998a: 18, qty Copway); to the practice of torturing enemies with fire – literally, roasting until puckered (Warren 1984: 36); and to the practice of lodge building (Pheasant 2007). Both Vizenor and Warren recount the first three possibilities, while the former also suggests 'Chippewa' is, ironically, a mishearing by a US official of that first misnomer. The historical term of self-definition among the Ojibwe is Anishinaabe, true also of their close allies the Ottawa and the Pottawattamii.

Much criticism focuses on those geographical, cultural, and environmental factors that most clearly and vividly inform Erdrich's ideas. In this respect, a consideration of Erdrich as a Midwestern writer is a striking absence in Erdrich scholarship, and will be touched on in later chapters. Native 'reinvestment' of territories resists and even unbinds the archetypical narratives of the Midwestern canon, challenging its pastoral nostalgia with a far deeper sense of emplacement.[3] Importantly, Foster (Anglo-Creek) defends the possibility of reading *both* within tribal specific *and* regional frameworks, particularly where that combination stands to alter those conventional concepts of region that serve the US national narrative (2008). Through most of Erdrich's oeuvre, the converging and conflicting historical and contemporary narratives of Natives and settlers are played out against the localised landscape of the Great Plains. As Foster argues: 'historically and theoretically astute regionalism . . . allows us to mediate and engage the claims of . . . very different speakers and their positions against and in dialogue with one another. Thus engaged, we can understand the relation between *Native* and *America* in a way that privileges the local and the tribal' (2008: 268). *The Chippewa Landscape of Louise Erdrich* (Chavkin 1999), in title and in spirit, gestures towards such tribal, regional, and national paradigms. However, such treatments often seem to forget the *constructedness* of that 'Chippewa landscape', presenting a limiting, at times phantasmal, view of tribal culture and skirting around the transposed cartography of its evolution. Beyond avoiding their own function in the abstraction of cultural material to mapped space, they often also fail to take account of the historical processes that differentiate the Plains Ojibwe (or Bungee) from other groups, while ignoring the fact that Erdrich's reservation is not, for instance, a singular representation of the Turtle Mountain Reservation (see e.g. Maristuen-Rodakowski 2000). It is in fact an amalgamation of the geography, demographics, and histories of several North Dakotan and Minnesotan reservations (including Turtle Mountain, White Earth, and Leech Lake), while the landscape Erdrich describes is highly evocative of the landscape of western Minnesota, around Little Falls, where she was born. Foster's model surely demands the full exploration of such nuances.

A number of critics explicitly make this connection between the landscapes, peoples, and memories portrayed in Erdrich's work and the work itself. Hafen, for instance, writes that 'Erdrich has created a vision of the Great Plains that spans the horizon of time and space and ontologically defines the people of her heritage' (2001a: 321). This 'vision' is one that finds its origins in the 'Ojibwe country' of the Great Lakes region, particularly in Madeline Island on Lake Superior (*The Birchbark House, The Game of Silence, The Porcupine Year* and *Books and Islands*) before tracing the remapping of Ojibwe territories on the plains through serial political historical processes. Not the least of these was the appropriation of land and the corralling of Native peoples on reservations, throughout the course of the eighteenth and nineteenth centuries.

Larson refers to the 'eighty-six million acres of North American real estate' appropriated by successive US governments, particularly through the Dawes Severalty (or General Allotment) Act (1887), described by Theodore Roosevelt as 'a mighty pulverizing engine to break up the tribal mass' (Larson 1997: 567, 573). Allotment was one of the most effective post-reservation mechanisms for containing the threat of tribal sovereignty and delivering land to settlers. Hastened by the Nelson Act (1889), it divided Native lands into parcels of up to 160 acres handed out to individual enrolled members of reservation bands and initially placed in government trust for twenty-five years. The general aim – to encourage individuals to farm, eventually removing the need for reservations and smoothly assimilating these communities into hegemonic society – also created vast areas of unattributed land ripe for settlement. Adding insult to injury, the Clapp Rider, Steenerson Act (1904) and second Clapp Rider (1906) removed many of the trust restrictions on sale of resources for mixed-bloods, especially timber.

Erdrich's chronologies begin in *Tracks* in the post-reservation moment at the close of the nineteenth century, thrusting us into the consumption epidemic of 1912. Following on from 'spotted sickness' (smallpox) this episode of 'sweating sickness' (consumption, or tuberculosis) coincides precisely with the end of the initial twenty-five-year allotment period and its varied legacy (Onion 2006). From the liquidation of forestland, a modern history of timber scandals on reservations, through the wholesale loss of tribal landholdings (from 138 million acres to 47 million acres across the US between 1887 and 1934), to factionalism and displacement, allotment tore great holes through already severely diminished homelands (Debo 1995: 330). The White Earth Land Settlement Act (WELSA) of 1986, which retroactively approved what many activists such as Winona LaDuke still hold to be illegal land sales, merely ensures the persistence of White Earth members' struggles to reclaim reservation lands (see Suzack 2008).

The outcome of a treaty of March 1867, White Earth is the most notorious of Ojibwe reservations in relation both to its establishment and historical conflict within its population. Serious opposition to the desire to concentrate Minnesota Ojibwe at White Earth came, among others, from the Pillagers of Leech Lake, a conservative people who, in 1898, instigated the last uprising against government policies (Vecsey 1983: 18).[4] They did eventually relocate, settling on the outer edges of the landbase, but factionalism indirectly became characteristic of the early reservation, with widely dispersed and relatively disparate communities forming throughout the territory (Meyer 1994).

Adaptation of cultural practices included the influence of Christianity, and with the establishment of missions and churches in the area, the most influential of which were the Roman Catholics and the Episcopalians, denominational conflict was initially a characteristic of the developing factionalism. While councils democratically made decisions, there existed no coercive control on the reservation:

> ethnic differences marked the genesis of community relationships at White Earth as reflected in settlement patterns, social and religious affiliations, household sizes, and surname frequency. The terms 'mixed-blood' and 'full-blood' were used to distinguish between ethnic groups and became politicized as disagreement over management of reservation resources escalated. (Meyer 1994: 5)[5]

Complicit in reinforcing 'ethnic' difference, allotment provided the test case for the development of blood quantum, a means of assessing validity of individuals' claims to tribal membership. McNally notes:

> A particularly insidious aspect of White Earth's dispossession was the prominent role played in it by the nation's leading physical anthropologists. In the 1910s, Ales Hrdlicka and Albert Jenks were summoned to settle investigations of fraud in land sales by scientifically determining the blood quantum of White Earth residents . . . Equipped with samples of hair and calliper measurement of skulls, the scientists dismissed half the fraud claims, determining that four hundred claimants had been of 'mixed blood' after all and therefore were unprotected by the trust clause of the legislation. In many cases, these findings completely disregarded the testimony that claimants themselves made concerning their family trees. (2000: 85–86)

Successful mixed-blood farmers and merchant traders such as Gus Beaulieu were set to make a fortune at the expense, many thought, of the conservative Anishinaabeg who began making moves to remove mixed-bloods, and their trade, from the reservation.[6]

Dispossession also came to the Turtle Mountain Band of Chippewa. Having already ceded 10 million acres of wheat land to the federal government, the reservation was 'cut in 1884 to two six-mile square townships of untillable brush-covered hills' (Debo 1995: 354). Allotment led to serious overcrowding and poverty: despite the dispersal of lands throughout the Dakotas and in Montana the people did not want to leave. Movement to the plains occurred around the turn of the eighteenth century when, benefiting from their close relationship with French and British fur traders, the Ojibwek were able to use guns and horses in the taking of territories and monopolising of trade in these areas. From the Pembina settlement on the Red River (North Dakota), large groups of Ojibwe hunters used the river network to clear the land of game. By around 1807, the land depleted, most of these Ojibwek returned eastward, with the exception of the Mikinak-wastsha-anishinabe, a band that chose instead to remain in the Pembina area and eventually to settle in the Turtle Mountains.

Turtle Mountain Reservation was established as a community of Ojibwe, Cree, and Métis, already in turmoil, and already suffering from poverty and harsh conditions:

> In the mid 1880's, there were severe winter storms and summer droughts. This harsh weather caused many pioneer farms to fail in the Great Plains areas. The influx of Métis from Canada following the second Riel Rebellion caused an overcrowding of the two townships. These circumstances took their toll and in the winter of 1887–88, 151 members of the Turtle Mountain Band of Chippewa starved to death. (Turtle Mountain Chippewa 1997)[7]

Undermining the hereditary chief, Little Shell III, the McCumber commission of 21 September 1892 oversaw the cession of land at 10 cents an acre with insufficient provision made for food and education; the result of a power struggle between Little Shell and the government-appointed Red Thunder (Turtle Mountain Chippewa 1997).[8] The residents of Turtle Mountain were also as susceptible to national and international events as any rural community. Despite its isolation, the reservation provided soldiers in the First World War, for instance. Under Franklin Roosevelt's presidency the Indian Reorganization Act (1934) restored a certain level of self-governance to tribes, while the Works Progress Administration (1935), established to rebuild communities stricken by the Great Depression, brought renewed hope:

> Accustomed to continuous poverty, struggle, and hunger, the impact [of the depression] on Turtle Mountain was not as severely felt. Hard-working and resourceful people, the Chippewa adopted farming and gardening. . . . [The WPA] program offered many economic options for the Turtle Mountain Band of Chippewa. . . . Some felt the depression was a blessing for tribal members because it opened up job opportunities through the WPA. (Turtle Mountain Chippewa 1997)

Among other effects, the Indian New Deal and the WPA brought many of the tribal members who had left after allotment back to the reservation, although the seasonal nature of the work gave rise to periods of severe hardship.[9]

The historical metanarrative is of Ojibwe dispossession and dislocation, furthered by the processes of termination that threatened many tribes between 1945 and 1960 (including the Turtle Mountain Chippewa specifically), and relocation, which lead to significant numbers heading for towns and cities for promised work. But paralleling this of course is the tribal story itself, one of migration, adaptation, and survival. Tribal history holds that the Anishinaabeg were led from the Atlantic to the St. Lawrence River and on to the Great Lakes by seven prophecies, each of which was validated by the presence of the sacred *miigis* shell, or cowrie. By the late eighteenth century the Anishinaabeg were in large numbers in present-day Ontario and Michigan, from which point trade, settlement, and disease encouraged further westward migration into the lands of the *abwenag*, or Sioux. Intermarriage with French and British fur trappers, traders, and voyageurs, and 'a little bit of Cree, a little bit of Ottawa; and also a little bit of Assinboin [sic] and Sioux' was common (Gourneau 1971: 5). Gourneau refers specifically to the Pembina Chippewa, also known as the Plains Bungi (or Punge) who settled in present-day North Dakota in the eighteenth century:

> With the westerly progression of the fur trade by establishment of trading posts farther and farther west, groups from different Ojibway bands followed in its wake. When trading posts were finally established on the Park and Pembina Rivers, in what was to become the state of North Dakota, groups from different bands of Ojibway and few members of other tribes as well, combined to form what was to become known as the Pembina band. By this time these migrants from the woodlands had successfully changed their culture from one developed to fit lake and forest regions to one very well adaptable to life on the Plains. (1971: 5–7)

The process of adaptation to which Gourneau refers includes the adoption of the tipi (as opposed to the birchbark lodge), the horse and travois, the buffalo hunt, and the hard-soled moccasin, while Erdrich herself specifically draws on the adoption of plains ceremonies such as the sun dance (the Ojibwe thirsty dance).

The result, though briefly glossed here, is a richly textured cultural (including Christian) mix. This is reductively identified as cross-cultural dilution or fragmentation by histories that focus on broken ties, eliding that story of continuity and adaptation, and recuperation and appropriation in the service of sovereignty. Nowhere is this more palpably figured than in the treaty document itself – source document of colonial delimitations *and* testament to the negotiated rights of indigenous peoples. These two reservations tell a story generally familiar to residents and reservations elsewhere in the USA, but it is against this specific backdrop that Erdrich writes. Because it is that historical backdrop I am addressing, this overview itself remains backward-looking. It must be noted that the reservation communities touched on here, although not without their trials, are thriving and successful, constitutionally organised communities with significant systems of self-governance. For a clearer picture of the vital present, see *Anishinaabeg Today*, Belgarde et al. (2007), and *DeBahJiMon*, publications of White Earth, Turtle Mountain, and Leech Lake Reservations respectively, and the bilingual journal, *Oshkaabewis Native Journal*.

Thematic frameworks

The matter of mixed-blood heritage – recast by Christie as 'plural sovereignties' (2009) – is rarely below the surface of Erdrich's work, whether explicitly in the performed identities of characters themselves, or implicitly in the juxtaposition and interweaving of apparently discrete categories: 'traditional' and 'modern', Native and Euroamerican, hyphenated-Ojibwe and full-blood, for instance. To read this in the simplistic terms of fragmented identity, however, is to emphasise the static narrative of the vanishing American. Even if, as I do throughout this text, we take the theme of 'splitting' to be a central concern, it is with the understanding that this is but a chance moment in a process; that just as it acknowledges the moment of rupture – too readily diagnosed as the death of culture – so it signals the far harder, but ultimately more significant, work of healing. The moment of splitting (the *daashkikaa*, or 'cracking apart', of Blue Prairie Woman's people in *The Antelope Wife* (1998)) is a vital narrative catalyst in the conversive patterns of contact, conflict, exchange, and continuance: splitting, in other words, opens up a potentially transformative space.[10] Certainly, my drawing attention to this moment here is intended to focus attention on its service as literary device rather than to assert the primacy of colonisation as the ground on/against which contemporary Native literatures are constructed. As a moment of transition, the space between splitting and healing is a necessary stage in the consolidation of individual and community identity. The 'split' itself requires a response and the writer's gaze lingers on the ways individual characters respond to injustices, conflicts, contingency, loss, love, and law, and other demands on them as individuals, as representatives, as members, as outcasts, and as observers and participants. To prioritise the principal themes of splitting and balancing in Erdrich's work, therefore, is not to focus on represented angst or neutered agency, but rather on the exploration of the complexities and contingencies of Native (and other) identities in the late nineteenth and twentieth centuries. Erdrich's narratives generally begin in, or proceed through the facility of, the moment of encounter – a postcolonial model, perhaps, read as interventions into historicity. This does not mean, however, that the colonial moment is the overwhelming focus. Even where 'encounter' establishes the ground on which some stories are built, narratives of recuperation and continuity emerge alongside depictions of the ways Euroamerican attitudes do not simply *constitute* the 'new' moment but are themselves modified by that contact, implicit in a *Native* narrative of the late nineteenth and twentieth centuries.

Stripes calls *Love Medicine*, *The Beet Queen*, and *Tracks* 'interventions in the writing of tribal histories,' suggesting they 'inscrib[e] revisionist histories of the cultural borderlands' (1991: 26). As he demonstrates, the key symbol of the tree is deeply integral in Erdrich's writing, a generic motif but absorbed and implicated in the service of the above history. This multiple resonance sees the tree as natural motif and metaphor in the claiming and 'taming' of the lands and peoples of North America, and symbolic of the paper trails that leads Nanapush to declare them a 'tribe of pressed trees' (*T* 225), developing what Chadwick Allen identifies as 'treaty discourse' in *Tracks*. Allen notes that Nanapush's 'articulation of this treaty context provides an important tool for interpreting the novel's powerful ending', while 'Throughout the novel, Erdrich associates the Chippewa with the trees standing on their remaining land. Their systematic and violent removal, by Indian as well as by white loggers, is metonymic of the Chippewa's dispossession' (Allen 2000: 76–77). The tree ultimately becomes a critical metaphor for the undermining of sovereignty, and an emblem of endurance, survival, and resistance. Stripes notes ironically that 'Native Americans were reinscribed as part of the landscape in 1849 when the Office of Indian Affairs was transferred from the Department of War to the newly created Department of the Interior; for the federal government the status of Indians went from that of enemies to that of trees' (1991: 31). Readdressing the processes of colonial inscription, geographical delimitation, and psychic – *imaginative* – containment, Erdrich's treatment of the land through such metaphors speaks boldly to those political histories of Native–European relations, addressing not only the histories but the historiography itself.

At a metaphysical level, Erdrich notes:

> although fiction alone may lack the power to head our government leaders off the course of destruction, it affects us as individuals and can spur us to treat the earth . . . as we would treat our own mothers and fathers. For once we no longer live in the land of our mother's body, it is the earth with which we form the same dependent relationship . . . helpless without its protective embrace. (2001b: 50)

Abstracted and romanticised, this sense of land-attachment and responsibility nevertheless attests to a sense of the temporariness of human societies that figures prominently in other indigenous writing about land. In *The Antelope Wife* Erdrich notes of *Gakahbekong* (Minneapolis), 'Although driveways and houses, concrete parking garages and business stores cover the city's scape, that same land is hunched underneath. There are times, like now, I get this sense of the temporary. It could all blow off' (*AW* 124–125). On the one hand, such descriptions evoke the opening of Cather's *O Pioneers!*, whose frontier town of Red Cloud sits cowering in the vast expanse of the Nebraska prairie: it speaks to the impermanence of human presence, the power of the natural world, and to the recurrence, in much regionalist writing, of the transitional. On the other, at odds with regionalist nostalgia, it speaks directly to the construction of colonial worlds on indigenous lands, to the broadly dialectical assertions of land as property and nature as active collaborator, and to the abiding presence of the natural world, hunkering down within the concrete and steel, long-memoried and biding its time.

If the fictional geographies, genealogies, and cosmologies of Erdrich's communities exceed multiple attempts to narrow them down it is because they speak clearly to a dual commitment: to the centrality of the relationship between communities, their lands, and the *geni loci* that inhabit them; and to the necessity to resist the fixity of colonial cadastres. Land, in this sense, both forms and mediates relations, becoming the locus of personal, family, and community identity and values. In this vein, Erdrich's own sense of community, evident in her fiction and poetry, and explicit in her memoirs, is of a place that has been 'inhabited for generations', and where 'the landscape becomes enlivened by a sense of group and family history' (2001b: 43). Again, we find echoes in the more ideologically driven assertions of tribal nationalism, where:

> Indigenous nationhood is more than simple political independence or the exercise of a distinctive cultural identity; it's also an understanding of a common social interdependence within the community, the tribal web of kinship rights and responsibilities that link the People, the land, and the cosmos together in an ongoing and dynamic system of mutually affecting relationships. (Justice 2008: 151)

Notwithstanding criticisms of Erdrich's political commitment and veiled accusations of commercial opportunism, I will argue that Erdrich's work recognises the ethical imperative of sovereignty. In doing so, it forces her readership to recognise it too, even as it explores 'community' in its dysfunction as well as its coherence; and in its capacity to do damage under the pressure of both external and internal imposition as well as its capacity – through kinship – to restore and endure.

The relationship between people, place, and politics is deeply implicit in Erdrich's representations of community. Those representations of relationality are constructed through a variety of tropes. The tree/paper trails mentioned above are one clear means by which relations between people are both defined and, through the highly complex and confusing genealogies of Erdrich's fiction, ironically subverted. Gish addresses another metaphor, the hunt, to delineate a process of reciprocity, which subtly modulates the Manichean allegory and demonstrates the ways in which both hunted and hunter are implicated in, and changed by, the process. Gish privileges the hunt as metaphor for crucifixion-resurrection, a reflexive paradox. Similarly, the co-dependency of many of the antagonistic relationships in the fiction might take up that same metaphor, whether in Nanapush's humorous attempts to seduce Rushes Bear, Pauline's sly attempts to match Sophie and Russell, or Gordie's dark fear of having killed June when he runs over a doe. Elsewhere, even close relationships within families, and successful hunts such as Eli's moose-kill in *Tracks*, depend on aspects such as chance, respect for relations broadly speaking, and recognition of common bonds and divisions. Frequent examinations of such themes as bloodlines (Van Dyke 1992), adoption

(Wong 1991), sisterhood (Stokes 1999), and women's community (Tharp 1993) draw all these themes of kinship and community together while attesting to the ubiquity of relationality and belonging in Erdrich's work.

Both of Erdrich's memoirs, *The Blue Jay's Dance* and *Books and Islands in Ojibwe Country*, deal explicitly (but not exclusively) with the relationship between mother and child. Emphasising the influence of her own maternity on her work and thought, and the centrality of maternity to other creative acts, Erdrich provokes thought about creativity as it is constituted in the fiction, about the generative potential of storytelling, and about the socially determined act of raising children. In *Books and Islands* she recounts a 'border-incident' in which she is quizzed over the maternity of her infant child. It is a paradigmatic instance of a specific microcosm – the mother–child bond, the male guard stopping a Native woman who is then combatively quizzed by a female guard – occurring against a macrocosmic politically fraught backdrop, addressing the failures of the US government to observe the Jay Treaty (1794) which assured Native peoples free passage; the contemporary problem of illegal trafficking; and the oppression of (indigenous) women by patriarchal systems. This incident situates Erdrich in many ways alongside many other women, particularly women from ethnic minorities or other 'border' communities in the United States, for whom motherhood, and gender more generally, can be especially politically fraught.

In *Borderlands/La Frontera: The New Mestiza* Anzaldúa offers a 'treatise that is "above all a feminist one"' that 'opens up a radical way of restructuring the way we study history' (1999: 2). While Erdrich is not so radicalised, and as Riley Fast notes, the notion that '"border writers ultimately undermine the distinction between original and alien culture" is . . . contrary to the practice of most contemporary Native writers' (1995: 511), there are aspects of Anzaldúa's testimony that are pertinent to Erdrich's fiction and poignant in such accounts as the border-crossing experience above. 'I am a border woman', writes Anzaldúa, 'I have been straddling that . . . border, and others, all my life. It's not a comfortable territory to live in, this place of contradictions' (1999: preface to first edition). Such a complexity defies stasis; it requires the construction of new ways of looking at, thinking about, and above all writing about, gendered and racialised experience. Anzaldúa's suggestion that 'Living on borders and in margins, keeping intact one's shifting and multiple identity and integrity, is like trying to swim in a new element, an "alien" element' speaks evocatively to the conflicted experiences of characters like Lipsha Morrissey, while Anzaldúa's insistence that 'Books saved my sanity, knowledge opened the locked places in me and taught me first how to survive and then how to soar' (1999: 3) is echoed in Erdrich's delight in textuality, including those cultural texts that the petroglyphs in *Books and Islands* represent.

Native women are carriers of culture. This truism has echoes in Chicana writing, and in the female-centred writing of women of colour such as Toni Cade Bambara or Audre Lorde (see Anzaldúa and Moraga 1984). Truism or not, '[a] common phrase heard at Indian women's gatherings is this: "We are the carriers of culture." This belief may provide Indian women a mandate to transmit cultural viability, engendering a sense of identity with a unique and satisfying cultural group' (Medicine 1987: 171). The comparison extends of course to the fiction, where the power of motherhood is not merely inherent in what is passed on but also in what is denied. With motherhood comes an awesome responsibility, expressed in *Love Medicine*, for instance, in June's decision to throw Lipsha into a slough to save him from the life she herself is leading (see Tanrisal 1997). This is political, without necessarily being polemical or propagandist, and sits in creative tension with Erdrich's own view of herself, where she says: 'I am on the edge, have always been on the edge, flourish on the edge, and I don't think I belong anywhere else' (Chavkin and Chavkin 1994: 111). While this clearly explains the basis for Erdrich's marginal characters, it also speaks to the innately 'political' position of the interstices. Written from this place, Erdrich's representations of marginality cannot help but hold some power, whether it resides in transforming infrastructures, or in offering transformative potential to those who recognise themselves or their predicaments in her characters. Being on, but not bound by, that 'edge' is intrinsic to those explorations of relationality, of the ability to resist containment and transcend boundaries.

The creative role of motherhood, then, is both metaphor and paradox. As metaphor for culture, motherhood is a centre, an originary force. However, the creative function in Erdrich's work is also about finding one's way back in. There are two key examples: in *Books and Islands* it is at least partly through the exploration of her daughter's patrimony that Erdrich finds her own way back into her Ojibwe heritage; and in her fiction, Nanapush takes on a (pro)creative function through his role as storyteller. As a trickster figure, his role is creative, or salvific. For all his flaws the culture hero Nanabozho is central to Ojibwe creation myths and integral to the power of storytelling. Nanapush's role, like Nanabozho's, is both one of 'creating' the world through story, and of saving individuals with the power of the spoken word. In *Tracks*, for example, he constructs Lulu's reality through the stories he tells her of her mother, her family, her tribe, and the dangers that face her in the future: in doing so, he literally ensures her survival, simultaneously ensuring the survival of the stories and memories he shares with her, *re*centring her in relation to her people.

Nanapush himself identifies what is most significant about his role. '[M]any times in my life,' he tells Lulu,

> as my children were born, I wondered what it was like to be a woman, able to invent a human from the extra materials of her own body. In the terrible times, the evils I do not speak of, when the earth swallowed back all it had given me to love, I gave birth in loss. I was like a woman in my suffering, but my children were all delivered into death. It was contrary, backward, but now I had a chance to put things into a proper order. (*T* 167)

His presence as nurturer, carer, and progenitor to some of the present-day larger-than-life characters of the fiction is crucial, his lineage remarkable: from Gerry Nanapush to Lulu herself, Nanapush has a hand in most families' lives.[11] In this concretization of genealogy through story, naturally enough, is also the key to belonging, to home and place as central facets of individual identity: as can be seen throughout Erdrich's work, those characters who fail to reconcile all of these elements and establish, or are denied, that connection to place and family are those who remain most dislocated. For the discarded, such as Pauline, dislocation produces a state of perpetual outside-ness. For the claimed, such as June Morrissey, marginality appears to lead to a transition into power-through-myth.

Story, as is the repeated testimony of Native literary criticism, does not merely represent, it creates, alongside other traditional modes of expression, the contemporary world that Native people inhabit:

> indigenous traditions are fundamentally concerned with the transformative powers of performative language, art, and thought. That is, when properly performed under the right conditions, ceremonies, songs, sounds, gestures, and dance steps do not merely give expression to the inner matters of feeling and meaning but are believed capable of transforming the self, the community, and the cosmos. (McNally 2000: 16)

The transmission of such practices and processes has, of course, a dual function for writers such as Erdrich:

> Traditional oral narratives, song, and prayers can be used to present an emotional structure derived from a particular way of life. As novelists give expression to the contemporary meaning of these emotional structures, they parallel the role of the ancient storyteller who tells the people who they are. (Jahner 1993: 11)

Erdrich has herself mentioned her pride when told by Native people that she managed, in *Love Medicine*, to finally present *their* reality, *their* modes of speech. Sarris notes of *Love Medicine*, 'Gossip. Jealousy. Drinking. Love. The ties that bind. The very human need to belong . . . This is the stuff, the fabric of my Indian community' (1993: 117). Stopping short of Jacobs's later claim (which I shall return to below) that Erdrich *is* a tribal storyteller (Jahner's 'parallel' is instructive), the Native American novel nevertheless performs in the world.

Two dense areas of Erdrich criticism focus, in different ways, on those questions of Indian identity with which this introduction began. The first, prioritising questions of Christianity and/versus Ojibwe spirituality and cosmology, often coincides and intersects with the second, concerned with narrative and with the relationship between the modernist/postmodern tradition in which Erdrich's fiction is often placed, and the oral tradition, from which it is often claimed to hail. Echoing the degree to which Erdrich undermines false binaries in her work, the majority of the critical writing seeks, more or less sensitively, to interrogate the nuances, rather than posit binary structures, in even the most oppositional portrayals. Stripes once more exemplifies this shift. He begins with a reductive statement of opposition: 'Historical dialogues regarding assimilation are refigured in the contrast of the parallel spiritual autobiographies of Pauline, Sister Leopolda and her daughter Marie Lazarre (Kashpaw) and with the stories of cultural survival of Nanapush and Eli' (1991: 26). The essay that follows this statement, like many that seek to explore these aspects of the work, recasts that model with greater complexity, going on both consciously and unconsciously to reveal the complicated negotiations and multiple inflections of even the most straightforward seeming characters.

Nevertheless, these oppositional readings are abundant in the scholarly archive, resting on the assumption that the 'natural' reading of Native American literatures will pay heed to distance, division, and conflict over proximity, syncretism, or healing. The first triad is incontestably present in Erdrich's writing. That it supersedes or overwhelms the second, however, is a harder position to defend. The fact is Erdrich's writing admits of both, allowing apparently incompatible states and attitudes to co-exist, sometimes harmoniously, sometimes in uneasy but necessary balance. It works repeatedly, in other words, towards an understanding of Native identity and indigenous sovereignty enacted within and through the post-contact contexts, embracing its essential pluralism and examining the myriad inflections of conflict and complementarity, and seeking to understand the politics of identity as much through affiliative as through filiative mechanisms. Although some of her characters are more 'real' than others, few are one-dimensional. Even Nanapush, preserver and protector of certain traditions, is ironically empowered by his Jesuit education. More to the point, he speaks 'the white man's way', using a mixture of 'the lumberjack and whiskey-trade slang Nanapush had picked up in his life' (*T* 144) that clearly, and perhaps ironically, affronts Pauline, though Stripes notes that 'he aligns himself with the traditional values of the Anishinaabeg, albeit speaking in ways which reflect Western autobiographical conventions' (1991: 27). For Stripes, this fact establishes his cultural 'authenticity' in that 'like his namesake Naanabozho, his disruption of conventions establishes and maintains traditional values' (1991: 27).

More apposite is the issue of agency that dictates both Nanapush's 'alignment' and his disruptions: as Rainwater makes clear, Nanapush chooses his own track on more than one occasion (1990). Although it can be argued that Pauline's choices are far more limited, that the forces that act on her life are harder for her to resist, nevertheless she also expresses a choice, a desire, to belong. In other words the conflict between them is never fully accepted as an essential or absolute opposition but is always understood to be an artificial stand, as dependent on performative as biological identity; on contingency as much as clear-cut 'roles' and paths; and on choice as well as coercion. It is, perhaps, Nanapush's 'training' in the ways of Christianity that enables his performance, while Pauline's zealous devotion to the forces that 'cannibalise' her people come at least partly out of *their* rejection of the orphaned misfit. In both cases, the performance is one of taking on masks and of mimicking – more or less earnestly – cultural roles. For Clute, 'they gaze at opposing vistas; but . . . they are of one body' (1995: 128). The semiotic coda become deeply complicated in the postmodern turn that Erdrich's writing takes.

The paradox of the splitting-healing power, or of the re-membering of the moment of encounter and its subsequent plurality, is resoundingly central. For Ferrari, this scenario leads to another kind of paradox – the border site as both container and site of imaginative reinvention. For others it becomes a useful strategy for the 'renegotiation of historical discourses'; or for addressing, by 'attending to the [novels'] silences . . . their postmodern use of "representation itself to subvert representation, problematizing and pluralizing the real"' (Ferrari 1999: 144, qtg Peterson and Castillo). Ferrari's own position has echoes in Owens's notion that Native literatures are a 'frontier' discourse, playing again at a paradoxical site 'wherein discourse is multidirectional and hybridized' (1999: 26). More recently Womack's 'reclamation' of hybridity discourse is both a useful rejoinder to the 'mixedblood' as constructed by Owens and others, and a reminder of the *possibility* inherent in that same model. Michelle Henry notes:

> Womack is true, in a literal sense, to the idea of 'hybridization' that is so much in vogue among a number of scholars in Native literature, but he challenges the notion of hybridization as a state of limbo between two cultures with no coherent identity in either space. Furthermore, he challenges the notion of hybridity used simply as a tool by which to bridge the gap between Euroamerican and Native American cultures, thereby subverting the dominant culture. (2004: 34)

This specific tension within Native Studies speaks to those tensions in methodological approaches outlined above. The power of multiplicity implicated in the semiotic and category slippage at play in all of this is intimately related to the creative. As text, Erdrich's writing repeatedly insists on its own hermeneutics; as 'response' in the terms Brant uses (see her *Writing As Witness*, 1994), it evokes a powerful resistance to containment, either in rhetoric or in governance. Indeed, as Ortiz notes, 'the indigenous peoples of the Americas have taken the languages of the colonialists and used them for their own purposes' (1981: 10); written in the service of a tribal nationalist call, the evocation of postcolonial models of 'writing back' and taking control of the 'enemy's' language is palpable.

As playful as it is, theory is most useful where it brokers a negotiation between aesthetics and politics. The collective authority implied by 'inscribing the oral' speaks to what Silko calls the 'web-like' structure of Laguna narrative, while Gunn Allen compares the non-linear, accretive, achronistic, and non-rationalist modes of Native literatures to their 'opposites' in western tradition, attesting to active, vivacious, community-producing utterance (see Silko 1996 and Gunn Allen 1996). Similarly, Wong (2000) and Sands (1986) note the 'community cohering' effects of gossip and anecdote, the apparently fragmented narrative of *Love Medicine* drawing the reader into a participatory role. Comparisons with William Faulkner's Yoknapatawpha County are ubiquitous. Few other authors have so convincingly, so intricately, constructed a community of characters rooted in a geophysical landscape that is at once stable and unsettling, and that is regularly expanded through repetition and relocation. It constructs community, creates familiarity with scenery, characters, and even events, whereby one text modifies or informs another, enhances our understanding of occurrences, and fleshes out the fuller 'picture' of life on the plains that Erdrich is depicting. It is also unsettling, perhaps for similar reasons, in that such repetition and revision inevitably alters our understanding of the apparently familiar.

This highlights the true (post)modernism of Erdrich's art as it emphasises the individual perspective-led constructions of historical action; a regionalism predicated on tribal grounds; and the problematic nature of perception and self-perception in relation to those tangled questions of self and identity. Vizenor claims that the various forces at play in the tricksy 'postmodern' strategies he (and, in part at least, Erdrich) employs, which he calls 'trickster discourse', can bring reader, text, and writer into communion. Beyond the thematic, in other words, the stylistic and aesthetic choices of Native writers are inherently, abundantly, performative and, in light of Erdrich's own historicism, essentially political. The literary landscape Erdrich has constructed is one that is fundamentally oriented towards community. Not necessarily to 'the' community in the way Cook-Lynn demands but to community in the abstract, to the nexus of relationships and connections, fragile and often dysfunctional, that hold people together – allied in affiliation or through a mutually sustaining and constructing enmity. Her contribution, catalyst to the continued development of Native American fiction, places her in a richly textured history of US literatures in which the small-community scene speaks volumes about both local/regional and national conditions. Where earlier writers, such as Welch and even, in their ways, Momaday and Silko, had navigated the isolation of individuals and, in the latter cases, their return to community, Erdrich's work takes a turn to representing, and negotiating the terms of, community itself. Attuned to the highly politicised nature of some indigenous experience; to the assertion of, and challenge to, sovereignty; to the myriad influences of Ojibwe heritage and European and American culture; to the celebration of American immigrant experience and Euro-indigenous exchange; the literary product is no manifestation of conflict between the many strands of Erdrich's resources – another plight narrative after all. Nor is it the easy consolidation or explanation of any singular or collective understanding of identity – a romance that threatens colonial imposition every bit as much as ignorance; and nor is it the mediating bridge between discrete cultures, with all the accommodationist rhetoric that might imply. Rather it is as part of a process of negotiation of severalty and pluralism, the re-membering after rupture – a rupture that absorbs as much as it implicates the colonial; that critiques as much as it derives from cultural imposition; and that appropriates and manipulates as much as it resists and regrets that imposition, that we might most fruitfully understand Erdrich's project.

The three As: authenticity, authority, agency ... and aesthetics?

Introducing an interview with Ahtna Athabaskan poet John Smelcer, Dale Seeds writes: '[p]erhaps the most contentious issues center on our notion of the "Indian author" and how this authorship is validated as being "authentic"' (2002: 133). He rehearses an argument that has both shaped and dogged Native American Literary Studies. The now somewhat hackneyed debate over authenticity and the canon – just what *is* Native American literature, where does it belong, who qualifies to write it, and who gets to say? – is deeply stratified. From the status of transcribed oral tales, songs, and speeches, through the authority of the collaborative 'auto'-biography, to the contested position of the mixed-blood author, attention has long focused on matters of 'adulteration'. Turning increasingly to vital, if vexed, questions of cultural and intellectual sovereignty, and literary nationalism, Native American literary scholarship continues to define its own parameters according to, and often in tension with, more or less 'European' or 'indigenous' methodologies. Teuton (Cherokee) identifies three key modes of critical discourse, which exemplify the shifting ground since the early 1980s. Grounded in anthropological discourse, mode one follows the authenticity model; mode two 'allows its discourse to be determined by that which it would argue against'; while mode three 'bypasses questions of representation to theorize how academic work can be made accountable and put in dialogue with Native people, communities, and nations' (2008: 201). He also notes, significantly, that single pieces of criticism often include the full range of modes of critical discourse (2008: 201). Rejected for their tendency to obscure the *literary* in Native American literatures (D. Treuer 2002) and berated for their tendency to obscure political realities, claims to authenticity have proven consistently problematic when used to 'validate' literary sources and tribal voices.

And yet this issue will not go away, as Womack notes:

> When discussing authenticity most critics simply throw up a theoretical wall and back away, claiming the topic as impossible. In conversations with classrooms full of Native students, however, I have learned that while a definition that *fixes* a notion of authenticity in a static, timeless vacuum is impossible; nonetheless, the *process* of thinking through issues of Native authenticity and even searching for forms of viable Native nationalisms are unavoidable in Indian country . . . We need a critical space where Indians can imagine forms of Indianism. (Warrior et al. 2006: 123)

If Womack is right, picking a path through the thorny trail of authenticating claims and exotic romances of the American Indian storyteller towards an ethical, 'responsibility'-led understanding of the social and political role of Native American literatures will be a considerable task. Erdrich's work has often been found at the centre of claims both for and against representativeness. It is impossible to begin a discussion of that work without acknowledging the prevalence of celebratory claims for its cultural 'performance' or insight. Often well-intentioned, these readings tend to draw on a host of assumptions embedded either in the anthropological underpinnings of early (1970s) Native American Studies; or in the stock of romance narratives, from the Noble Savage to the New Age shaman, that snap at the heels of America's 'Indians'.

Ron Charles's review of *Four Souls*, with which this chapter began, is a case in point. His review, as noted, effortlessly assumes an essential 'access' to culture through literature that all too frequently ignores the *literary* and elides the real presence of Native voices for what Vizenor has long called a 'hyperreal simulation' of '*indianness*' (1999: 4). This is not to suggest Charles is complicit in these deficiencies, though he *has* isolated the problem for many of Erdrich's harshest critics, keen to point to the fact that the author has lived little of her life at the absolute heart of tribal community.[12] The location of the review itself may be another source of discomfort in that it illuminates the degree to which Erdrich's books, held by many to offer insight into Native experience, are being read in isolation from those contexts. It attests, in other words, to a host of prior assumptions about Native American literature and its relation to culture. The casual use of the word 'essentially' in Charles's review also prompts thought about what, exactly, a reader will get from Erdrich's work, and what, exactly, a writer *can* transmit about a culture or experience that would or even could meet the optimistic agenda of the reviewer's comments, which unwittingly occludes politics and aesthetics from the cultural gaze, anticipating 'an entree into Native culture . . . into a hidden world of tribal wisdom' (Warrior et al. 2006: 2).

In recent years, concerted efforts to elucidate the tribal-specific qualities of Erdrich's work in particular have replied, albeit indirectly, to these accusations. In the opening paragraph to *The Novels of Louise Erdrich*, Connie Jacobs declares her focus to be Erdrich's 'place in the Native American Literary Renaissance and American Literary Canon as well as a study of how her North Dakota novels plus *The Antelope Wife* reflect Erdrich as a contemporary tribal storyteller' (2001: 1). While the compass of Jacobs's study is compelling, acknowledging tribal specificity and the power and function of story as the primary contexts for genuine understanding of Native literatures, her claim also deserves some complication, not least because it elides the role of Erdrich's late husband Michael Dorris, editor, collaborator, and teacher. Of course that particular connection provides yet another blind alley that requires a brief aside.

While it is not the intention of this book to delve either into biography or scurrilous conjecture, the couple's admission that the act of writing was a collaborative effort has long attracted considerable speculation into their working relationship. It provoked both suspicion as to who, really, was the driving force behind their work, and adulation as the ideal literary marriage. The latter notion was shattered in 1997 when Dorris ended his own life in a New Hampshire motel. This event revealed a stark hinterland of troubles: a year's separation only later admitted by Erdrich; accusations of child abuse by their estranged adopted son Jeffrey in 1995; one failed extortion court case against their son; long-term depression on Michael Dorris's part, doubtless fuelled by the apparent deterioration of his family; and further (unsubstantiated) claims of child abuse by one of his daughters. An earlier tragedy, meanwhile, had seen one of their adopted children, Reynold Abel, killed in a car crash in 1991. Reynold Abel, or 'Adam', was the subject of Dorris's impassioned account of foetal alcohol syndrome, *The Broken Cord* (1989), which itself caused some controversy within Dorris's 'field'. As has been well documented, apparent calls in that book and in Erdrich's foreword for the incarceration of pregnant alcoholic Native women drew ire from figures as significant as Gerald Vizenor and Elizabeth Cook-Lynn, who both contrasted their solution (an 'autocratic salvation for the moral crimes of a nation' (Vizenor 1999: 31)) with autonomous community-centred programmes. They lived, relatively speaking, in the limelight, and speculation about Dorris's suicide and the state of the couple's marriage has been played out publicly, both through choice and through the inevitably endless enquiry into personal issues that celebrity attracts. All of which has little to do with the act of literary criticism.

To return to tribal specificity, however, Jacobs also intriguingly notes that 'rather than sitting around a campfire throughout the winter months . . . we as readers can pick up her novels and read them at any time, not heeding tribal taboos of storytelling outside of the traditional storytelling season' (2001: xii). This, clearly, is problematic for its too-easy conflation of oral and written narrative and its elision of the considerably different circulatory cycles of both; tribal storytellers, for instance, have traditionally worked within, and with the general endorsement of, the tribe. Far from investing the modern moment in tribal storied traditions, Jacobs's move risks reinforcing the 'colonial divide' between precolonial (pristine) and postindustrial (tainted) culture. As with Charles, there seems to be an implicit expectation of 'insider information' rooted in a romantic sensibility; in Jacobs's argument, this would seem to undermine its own assertion for tribal-centred criticism. Berninghausen takes a less ideological positition, for instance, when he asserts:

> The ideal of the traditional storyteller forms an important context for understanding Erdrich's fiction . . . though she is quite conscious that in her own novels she is not a traditional storyteller. Her works are published, not oral, performances, and her audience encounters her stories as new experiences, not as the frequently repeated myths of their culture. (1998: 190–191).

The unsustainability of claims like Jacobs's – which become, most importantly, an unjustifiable burden on the Native author[13] – increases their problematic nature, advancing a theoretical strategy rooted in the epistemological traditions of a tribal people, but also implicitly promoting a sense of precolonial culture trammelled by, but reclaimed from the clutches of, colonisation; it teeters, treacherously, on the brink of the anti-modern.

Even though 'story' – and more particularly the desire to make the story 'heard' in the reading – is at the centre of Erdrich's work, it is all too simplistic – idealistic even – to assert 'tribal' storytelling as the principal means of her literary identity, notwithstanding her own opinion that *Love Medicine* 'reflects "Chippewa story telling technique"' (qtd. in Treuer 2006: 33). Regardless of Treuer's persuasive deconstruction of such claims, there is, more simply, a significant difference between 'reflecting' something and acting as its representative, and an equally significant difference between what Erdrich seems to be doing and what critics consistently claim on her behalf. Although in recent years Erdrich has run an annual writers' workshop with her sister Heid at Turtle Mountain and although, as will be explored in Chapter 5, her latest memoir returns us to the primacy of her Ojibwe heritage, she also acknowledges that this is a learned inheritance, a strand – albeit an important strand – of a multivalent legacy. She has said the Germans in the family told the stories, though she also notes that she does 'not feel that much part of a German community' (Rolo 2002: 38). Her second memoir, *Books and Islands in Ojibwe Country*, in particular, suggests she is as much writing *into* as *out of* Ojibwe culture. This is by no means to deny that aspect of Erdrich's provenance, central as it is to her writing, or to second-guess her reception by Ojibwe readers. Nor is it to diminish the importance of that work which, to borrow from Christie, becomes in its inception a contribution to Ojibwe patrimony (2009: 33). What is truly problematic is that claims like Jacobs's tend to lead to equally oversimplified rebuttals, of which this may well be one. And, of course, in objecting to Jacobs's formulation I am ever conscious of my own outsider position. I do not seek here to make definitive or intentionally limiting statements about Erdrich's role but rather to enter into dialogue with others, many more highly informed than I, and I hope that any errors or presumptions I am guilty of will find their correction elsewhere. A minor lament concerning the secondary protagonist of *Shadow Tag*, artist Gil, might stand here for the author's own stake in this conversation:

His technical mastery had pushed his painting past the West and
Southwest . . . and then at last into New York, but he had not made the
big leap. He was still classified as an American Indian artist, or a Native
American artist, or a tribal artist, or a Cree artist or a mixed-blood artist
or a Metis or Chippewa artist or sometimes an artist of the American
West, even though he lived in Minneapolis. (ST 37–38)

The irony of these lines will not be lost on readers of the Erdrich
criticism, and they certainly carry the echo of Erdrich's own desire to
be seen as an American author, to be let loose of categories and boxes.

What is lost in all of this is the authenticity of experience in favour
of the authenticating 'label'. To interrogate such claims is not to
reinvent the authenticity wheel. It is to assert that such significant
terms are rigorously tested in the light of tribal realities and to
acknowledge that arguments about Erdrich's role reflect the most
fraught of debates around the place and function of Native American
literatures and literary criticism. On the one hand, Erdrich's friend
Mark Anthony Rolo notes, 'The great thing about Louise, . . . is that she
lives in a Native community in town. And her family is well rooted in
her community back home. She is not the Jane Austen of the Native
community looking out a window at the industrial plight of her people'
(Olson 2001a).[14] Elsewhere, however, Rolo describes her in her own
terms as 'a woman from a modest Midwestern town who loves words'
(2002: 37). Meanwhile, fellow mixed-blood writer Louis Owens,
drawing on Edward Said's notion of the strategic location of the author
to their material, declares about himself: 'My strategic location . . . may
be found in what I think of as a kind of frontier zone, which elsewhere
I have referred to as "always unstable, multidirectional, hybridized,
characterized by heteroglossia, and indeterminate"' (2001: 11). That
question of *strategic location* recurs in many senses throughout the
critical archive: in Cook-Lynn's accusations of the inadequacies
of Erdrich's sense of place (1993); or, in opposition, Hafen's sense of
Erdrich's *emplacement* (2001a); in the various postcolonial paradigms
brought to bear on Erdrich's characters, such as hybridity and colonial
mimicry; in the narrative analyses of Erdrich's work as postmodern,
carnivalesque, tribal, feminist, and so on; and in the more general
commentary on where Erdrich – and by implication writing by other
mixed-blood writers – belongs.

Tribal specificity is clearly the key contextual framework in the
development of Native American Studies. In this, Jacobs's study is
certainly instructive. Methodological alternatives, such as postcolonial,

cosmopolitan, and even 'ethnocritical' turns taken by major figures such as Arnold Krupat are increasingly rejected either wholly or in part by Native writers and scholars. The principal dangers of such readings are, as Thomas King (Cherokee) points out, that they assume the 'starting point for the discussion is the advent of Europeans in North America' (qtd in Schorcht 2003: 4). Beth Brant (Mohawk), for instance, claims: 'Our writing is, and always has been, an attempt to beat back colonization and the stereotyping of our Nations. But the writing is *not* a reaction to colonialism, it is an active and new way to tell the stories we have always told' (1994: 40). Such a position is not restricted to critical discourse, however, but is repeatedly engaged in in Erdrich's nuanced narratives. Nevertheless, Barak notes that 'Whether or not Native American literature is technically postcolonial, Native American writers still deal with issues of identity and cultural (re)construction that are central to other postcolonial literatures' (2001: 5). Notwithstanding Brant's position, Barak asserts as primary the relationship between Native writing and the colonial condition. Certainly some strategies in postcolonial writing – such as Chinua Achebe's creation of a 'usable past', Ngũgĩ Wa Thiong'o's notion of 'decolonisation of the mind', and Gayatri Spivak's justifications of 'strategic essentialism' – have corollaries in indigenous methodologies. Where postcolonial strategies often fall short is in an insistence on prioritising 'usefulness' of application, or scope, above specificity and tribal sovereignty, leading to a tendency to reinscribe colonial discourse on Native literary production.

As Blaeser argues, the study of Native texts requires a tribal-centred starting point. She insists on 'a critical voice and method which moves from the culturally-centered text outward toward the frontier of "border" studies, rather than an external critical voice and method which seeks to penetrate, appropriate, colonize or conquer the cultural centre, and thereby, change the stories or remake the literary meaning' (1993: 53). Ruffo (Ojibwe) concedes that we can 'begin to recognize the limitations of the aesthetics of postmodern and semiotic theory' in light of the overwhelming arguments for cultural and political particularity (1995: 153). It is not so much 'theory' that is under fire here, as it is the imposition of western theory as a mechanism to silence the Native voice. Blaeser elsewhere notes that 'Because aesthetic systems originate in cultural systems, any discussion of tribal literary forms must inevitably engage Native beliefs' (1997: 557). Her own position does not *exclude* but rather *embraces* theory as a 'positive alternative to the social/anthropological approaches which to date have dominated discussions', quoting Vizenor's belief that ' "structuralism, structural linguistics and various semantic theories reveal more about trickster narratives . . . than do theories in social science . . . that have dominated the academic interpretations of tribal cultures" ' (Ruffo 1995: 136).

The *boundaries* of the social scientific theories that Vizenor et al. object to are imposed, largely, by the ideological imperatives of political agency. While authenticity frequently implies 'insight' and beds authors and texts into what King sees as a precolonial fixity, similarly it often signifies legitimacy, an equally confining imposed coda. As is further considered in Chapter 3, Leslie Marmon Silko and Elizabeth Cook-Lynn demand a political engagement that they find lacking, particularly in *The Beet Queen*. That expectation, born of the 'direct connection between political and cultural sovereignty' that Cook-Lynn draws and the desire to 'protect and nurture "the myths and metaphors of sovereign nationalism," which need to operate as "the so-called gold standard against which everything can be judged" ', is in itself laudable if ultimately untenable (Murray 2001: 81). Cook-Lynn's objections to cosmopolitanist criticism are themselves rooted in mistrust of the strategic modes of postcolonialism and multiculturalism. Erdrich and Dorris are at the heart of her rebuke when she refers to 'The American Indian Fiction Writers' whose representations of Native life portray 'gatherings of exiles, emigrants, and refugees, strangers to themselves and their lands, pawns in the control of white manipulators, mixed-bloods searching for identity – giving support, finally, [to] the idea of nationalistic/tribal culture as a contradiction in terms' (1993: 86).[15] Murray among others draws attention to the potential circumscription of this position, noting that 'Cook-Lynn's stubborn drawing of lines can be seen as an insistence on an irreducible difference' (2001: 83). Such reservations are echoed in more recent developments of tribal nationalism, where Justice notes 'Cook-Lynn's focus on a purity/ assimilation binary and conflation of multiraciality with lack of national spirit seems counterproductive' and her 'focus on mixed-bloodedness as *the problem* draws attention away from the colonial powers that turned intermarriage into a colonizing state' (2008: 162).

If this position is problematic in relation to the fiction, risking as it does another kind of authoritative delimiting, enfolding those same fraught questions of authenticity and inclusion, it becomes more manageable in critical terms where the lines of battle are arguably more clearly drawn. Where many, particularly early, studies of Erdrich's work prioritise ideas of fragmentation, isolation, and dislocation, others attempt to navigate more empowering perspectives. This will be explored more specifically in Chapter 3 but it is important to note the ways in which these shifts echo the broader movements of Native American Studies. Bird (Spokane) speaks to the 'decolonisation of the mind' in Native texts and, by implication, through sympathetic scholarship. Rather than simply dwelling on a history of pain, Native writers must go further by identifying and isolating the source of the pain, to overcome its power (Bird 1998: 30). 'Victim' is not a useful term here, just as notions of assimilation and acculturation merely advance the cause of 'critical colonialism'. Simon Ortiz (Acoma Pueblo) writes of 'the creative ability of Indian people to gather in many forms of the socio-political colonizing force which beset them and to make them meaningful in their own terms (Ortiz 1981: 8). Deliberately shifting focus away from 'binary conceptions' of Native cultures, he continues: 'And because in every case where European culture was cast upon Indian people of this nation there was similar creative response and development, it can be observed that this was the primary element of a nationalist impulse to make use of foreign ritual, ideas, and material in their own – Indian – terms' (1981: 8). These latter ideas have been developed further by Craig Womack, Robert Warrior (Osage), and Jace Weaver (Cherokee), who respectively (and collectively) elaborate the terms of Native Literary Nationalism, indigenous intellectual histories, and 'communitism'.

But what of the relationship between the political ideal and the literary aesthetic? Notionally at least the aesthetics of tribal literary nationalism derive from their social and political – tribal – contexts. Critical reception of Erdrich's work populates the entire spectrum of approaches, from the paradigms of western literary theory, through cosmopolitan and postcolonial 'dialogues', to Anishinaabe-centred analysis; there are also analyses that use Erdrich's writing as a vehicle for dialogue between these various processes. Most recently, Christie's *Plural Sovereignties* (2009) proposes a means of reconciling the above poles, asserting 'not the subordination of sovereign indigenous traditions to the English language as such, but its adumbration' (6). Erdrich herself counts Shakespeare, Flannery O'Connor, J.E. Powers, Toni Morrison, and Philip Roth among the authors she most enjoys (2002: 37), while elsewhere she cites Linda Hogan, Amy Tan, Jeanette Winterson, A.S. Byatt, James Welch, Joyce Carol Oates, and Margaret

Atwood as writers she admires, and Angela Carter, Gabriel Garcia Marquez, Willa Cather, Jean Rhys, Adrienne Rich, and Jane Austen, alongside Faulkner, Morrison, and many others, as direct influences (Chavkin and Chavkin 1994: 221–222, 232–233). Unsurprisingly, that the literary tastes and influences of an Ivy League college-educated, acclaimed international novelist are diverse and multiple reveals only that her tastes are *literary*. This knowledge contributes little to the tension between those readings that explore the literary strategies of Erdrich's writing and those that seek cultural explanations. Her repeated assertions, however, that she be read as an *American* writer, now recently modified by her implicit claim, through her comments on Anishinaabemowin in *Books and Islands*, that the *American* writer needs to be able to apprehend the landscape through indigenous languages, is significant in the contexts of the methodological debates within Native American Studies.

In that same text she concedes that her language skills are limited; so, if her attempts to raise her youngest child to speak and understand Anishinaabemowin can be seen as responsive, that prior claim to her role as 'tribal storyteller' remains, at best, a construction. It authenticates the value of the writing as something more than, or other than, the sum of its influences and the lived experience that informs it. Through all of this and, indeed, long before David Treuer accused Erdrich (and her critics) of a form of cultural nostalgia (2002), Erdrich had identified an 'unziemliches Verlangen' – unseemly longing – in her practice, rooted in German Romanticism and driven by a desire to 'resolve' the 'awful mix' of her French/Cree/Ojibwe, German/Jewish/Catholic heritage (qtd in Pearlman 1994: 152). As Lischke and McNab note:

> While Erdrich's family history forms the point of departure, the raw material and stimulus for her writings, her ultimate aim is to expose and possibly resolve the tensions between wandering and immigrating on the one hand, and between settling and 'being' (between foreign and native, European and (native) American) on the other. (2006: 192)

Indeed, Lischke and McNab have begun to mine this specifically German/émigré background, which has largely been neglected. We must note, too, that while many critics have isolated specifically 'Chippewa' themes, Erdrich's work has always navigated the broader cultural mix of Cree/Ojibwe/Métis heritage; even Fleur Pillager, that most 'traditional' of stalwarts, is of French-Ojibwe derivation. This is, at the very least, a reminder that Erdrich neither presents nor seeks to represent an idea of 'pure culture'. Rather, she invariably explores contemporary Ojibwe experience in its diversity, and the 'contact zones' *within* Ojibwe identity that reflect 'her fluid and split self – the European and the Indian' (Lischke and McNab 2006: 196). In so doing, it is precisely in the complex interchanges and exchanges, and the refusal of delimited identity, that Erdrich's work most explicitly and actively engages with questions important to Ojibwe community specifically, and that her work becomes community-serving and community-producing more generally.

Controversial for its dismissive air, Treuer's rebuke nevertheless echoes the tone of other scholars, not least Cook-Lynn's castigation of the 'mixed-blood' topic of 'the connection between the present "I" and the past "They," and the present pastness of "We"' (Cook-Lynn 1996b: 67), and it might be that many critics and readers are guilty of 'championing intent over product, desire over language' (Treuer 2002: 60). Unlike Treuer, Cook-Lynn is not concerned about *literariness* being compromised by the persistence of cultural readings (and writings) but rather the political agency of Native peoples held in check by problematic representations. There is, paradoxically, a danger of calls for 'political' prose turning in on themselves, of her criticisms of mixed-blood writers for representing from 'outside culture' leading to a new generation of insider informants – the very thing Treuer opposes. What is clear, however, is that the problematic nature of the label *Native American literature*, and the contests over cultural and political sovereignty as they pertain to literature, will not go away as long as the commercial enterprise thrives on that general confusion between cultural artefact and literary trope. These arguments amply demonstrate the problematic intersection of identity construction, authorship and its 'authority', and political and literary representation. The ultimate balancing act, this arena is all too easily thrown into principled battles that often threaten to obscure both the literary aesthetics *and* the political demands of any so-called Native American text.

Notwithstanding these caveats, Erdrich's explorations of 'an "unseemly desire" to belong to the peoples who populated America before the European conquerors, colonists and settlers arrived' (Lischke and McNab 2006: 192) do centre predominantly on a tribal people, and, more specifically, 'recast the domain of contemporary indigenous sovereignty "that revises, modifies, or rejects, rather than

accepts as a model, the European and American nation"' (Christie
2009: 5, qtg Womack). One feature of the authenticity debate is its
circularity – but if the rebuttal of Cook-Lynn's anti-mixed-blood
argument, let's say, is simply its inverse, we are at a stalemate. As
Justice notes, it is possible to be on the edge of tribal community but
fully participant in its discourses, and as Womack argues, claiming
tribal identity and investigating, even embracing, hybridity, not as a
pejorative or angst-ridden 'state' but as one of many strands in
'process-oriented intellectual sovereignty', are not mutually exclusive
(Justice in Acoose et al. 2008; Warrior et al. 2006: 124). To understand
Erdrich's work within a tribal-specific context, then, is not to ignore
or underplay the other contexts of her birth, her upbringing and
education, or even her literary status. Indeed, it is to understand
all of these contexts as mutually informing and constructing
Erdrich's explorations and even negotiations of personhood; and the
examination of nationhood that such explorations inevitably entail.

Notes

1 Erdrich is an enrolled member of the Turtle Mountain Band of Chippewa.
   Still legally designated 'Chippewa' in the USA, Ojibwe in Canada, tribal
   members often self-identify as either Ojibwe or Anishinaabe. Erdrich was
   once identified most commonly by the term Chippewa, though she tends
   now to use Ojibwe almost exclusively. For this reason I will refer to the
   Ojibwe in the immediate contexts of her work and Anishinaabe more
   generally. Native scholars are identified according to their tribal affiliation
   at first mention throughout this book, as is common in Native American
   Studies. I repeat this practice to reflect the range and diversity of
   indigenous cultural and intellectual production in North America.
2 Erdrich's first book, *Imagination* (1981), was a children's textbook that is
   now very difficult to obtain and unknown to the majority of her readers.
   Many of the bibliographies of Erdrich's work that abound on the internet
   incorrectly identify this as a book of poetry.
3 Elsewhere, Anderson asserts the strategic 'undoing' of Southern
   regionalism in Native texts (2007).
4 Their name is literal, as the band, who had taken possession of Leech Lake
   by 1781, became known as *Muk-im-dua-win-in-e-wug*, or 'men who take by
   force' (Warren 1984: 256).
5 Despite this distinction, it is my understanding that the terms used here
   are reasonably fluid rather than universal. They refer, strictly, to those
   open to market capitalism, and those opposed to what they perceived as a
   threat to traditional lifeways, but are not necessarily all-inclusive. Meyer

establishes a strict bifurcation that ought perhaps to be understood as a simplification of the reservation society, more socio-economic than ethnic in division. Having said this, the denominational conflict lessened after 1889 as missionaries found themselves ministering to congregations largely divided along the ethnic lines described.

6 Although initially successful, the 86 mixed-blood members removed in 1911 were reinstated in 1916. Throughout I use variations of the term 'Mixed-blood' to refer to authors and characters known for, or otherwise characterised by their mixed Native and European heritage. Later, the term Metis is used for its specific reference to people descended of French and Cree/Ojibwe intermixing, particularly in the Midwestern USA and Canada. The latter term is occasionally used more generally to refer to Native people of mixed descent.

7 Louis Riel, of French and Chippewa descent, was hanged at Regina (Saskatchewan) on 16 November 1885 for attempting to establish an independent government in midwestern Canada.

8 In 1980 the U.S. Court of Claims awarded a judgement of $52.5 million to the Pembina band for over 8 million acres of land ceded under the McCumber agreement.

9 These brief snapshots deal with what was a very troubled period; it is, of course, only one version of the history and I would direct readers to the very positive work of Anishinaabe activists and advocates performing roles ranging from the organisation of community activities (Laduke and the White Earth Land Reclamation Project, for instance), through simple acts of continuity, to radical attempts to revisit these moments of federal imposition and reclaim sovereignty.

10 'The term *conversive* conveys both senses of conversion and conversation in which literary scholarship becomes a transformative and intersubjective act of communication' (Ramirez 1999: 1).

11 The poignancy of this scenario is that by the time of the mythical Nanabozho's birth, according to Johnston, he had been abandoned by his spirit father, his earth mother was soon to die, and he would be raised by his grandmother (1990: 17).

12 Stookey notes Erdrich's relationship with her maternal grandfather Patrick Gourneau, a tribal chairman at Turtle Mountain Reservation; Rolo speaks of her more recent involvement in writing programmes on the reservation and the urban Native community in Minneapolis as examples of her engagement with these issues.

13 As Appleford notes, 'All too frequently, Aboriginal artists are viewed (by Aboriginals and non-Aboriginals alike) as impersonal explicators of truths about their culture' (2005: 85).

14 Perhaps Rolo means Elizabeth Gaskell? Austen is not generally noted for industrial plight narratives.

15 Dorris was roundly accused by Cook-Lynn of assuming an unwarranted capacity to speak for tribal people and Erdrich is possibly tainted by association.

2

'I thought I would be sliced in two': towards a geocultural poetics

The depth and richness of Erdrich's canvas is in full view in her poetry, which has nevertheless suffered relative critical neglect. While analysis of the work within the wider contexts of Native American and American poetry would be timely, this chapter will attempt to address that neglect by largely foregoing a contextual analysis in favour of an investigation into several significant themes and a close analysis of a selection of representative poems. Like much Native American poetry, Erdrich's work tends towards the personal-political, reflecting on aspects of space, place, and the individual, through such themes as Native ('Pan-Indian' and Ojibwe) cosmology, cultural and multiple heritage, spirituality in all its forms, family and community, claimed and contested identities, and the geographical and political landscape. Largely, though not exclusively, focusing on those poems that deal with spiritual and religious imagery, this chapter endeavours to illustrate the complexity and importance of Erdrich's symobolism – an aesthetic that sets her, and many other Native poets, apart in contemporary Anglophone poetry.

Criticism has made much of the bicultural nature of Erdrich's fiction, despite what Vine Deloria Jr. (Lakota) sees as its potentially damaging tensions for those living with its connotations.[1] The dichotomous aspect of biculturalism – that resultant idea of being something of two cultures and not quite of either – is explored repeatedly in Native American literatures, not least by Erdrich. Indeed, P. Jane Hafen notes that 'the ritual recounting in "Jacklight" intimates that, as cultures change, the complexity of the universe becomes both more enlightened and more shadowed' (1996: 152), giving body to this ambiguous cultural space. In distinction to the cultural-anthropological diagnosis of 'in-betweenness', however, Hafen believes:

Such criticisms frequently focus on anthropological evidences in American Indian literatures, are bound in an absolute past, and fail to acknowledge contemporary peoples and their adaptive modes of cultural survival. Nevertheless, all factors of Erdrich's background, including mainstream/American/Western Civilization and Chippewa culture contribute to her source material. (1996: 148)

In a sense, Hafen is arguing that in Erdrich's work 'bicultural' is a watchword for multifaceted and multivalent; that the poetry responds to what may be described as a geocultural influence, which is an ever-adapting amalgam of cultural traditions from that German-Chippewa background, the French-Cree aspects of the Turtle Mountain Chippewa, and the geographies and communities of North Dakota and Minnesota especially; and that these contexts *inform* rather than confuse her cultural identity.[2] These influences range from the attachment to land and local geography of both her Ojibwe ancestors and the small immigrant farming communities of the Midwest, to the urban influence of Minnesota; the oral stories she grew up with and the academic education she grew into; and her continuous development as mother, wife, reader, writer, bookshop owner, to name the most 'public' of her many roles. None of this is monolithic or static, and the readings that follow are not intended to be taxonomic or delimiting; my interest lies not in any determination of cultural singularity but in close observation of the play, the interchange, the struggle, and the celebration of *all* of these strands.

The resounding link between the poems is an exploration of the ways in which we are caught between individuation and communality. In other words, Erdrich repeatedly explores the gap between self-identification and identity-by-association (whether by gender, ethnicity, nationality, or religion), and her poems are often acts of *re*pairing or healing, purging or curing. In this vein, Erdrich's poetry is punctuated with dichotomous imagery, combining apparent binaries or opposing forces, and highlights the tensions of love, life, and identity. Within the larger context of the relationship between the individual and the communal, Hafen notes, 'ritual effaces differences in a society, it establishes community or oneness. Erdrich's poems manifest the paradox of individuation occurring within and being defined by communal and tribal relationships' (1996: 148). This 'ritual' prominence, the performative nature and role of Erdrich's poetry is, at the very least, an optimistic view of the role and nature of Native American writing. It is a view that envisages the author (as individual) within both real and imagined community: the community from which the author emerges, and the readership community into which she enters. It also places emphasis on the piece of writing as participant *in* community, theoretically assuming and practically enacting the role of the traditional oral story in a ritual context. With such connotations of community participation and community-building, this notion is also foundational to investigations of the role of religion or spirituality in a more general sense, which is rarely absent from Erdrich's poetry and prose. Depictions of freedom and enclosure and the double paradox of freedom in enclosure, and entrapment in the open spaces of the plains and the imagination, are integral to these linked themes.

Erdrich's first book of poems, *Jacklight*, was published in 1984, the same year as *Love Medicine*. The majority of the poems, which establish many of the major concerns of her fiction, were written in 1977–1978, before Erdrich completed her MFA at Johns Hopkins. Even so, the poetry has many analogues in the fiction to come – most strikingly in the treatment of her German ancestors, particularly the experiences of her paternal grandparents, who shadow the butcher shop sequences in *The Beet Queen* and, of course, alongside the mysterious 'Step-and-a-Half Waleski', *The Master Butchers Singing Club*. The prevalent imagery of transformation, metamorphosis, and the figurative (and real) blendings of 'natural' and human worlds draws, of course, on Ojibwe and Plains Indian cosmology, and recurs in various ways throughout the fiction, most notably in Fleur Pillager's character and in *The Antelope Wife*.

Baptism of Desire, published in 1989, essentially consolidates the need to see Erdrich as a poet in her own right, not just a novelist who writes poetry, despite her prior assertion that she would not publish more poetry, finding it too personal, too intimate (Rader 2004: 103). Although the earlier concerns of *Jacklight* still echo in this volume, there is a far greater weight to the religious and mystical, a more rarefied thematic, and a greater distance from the patterns of the fiction. The Catholic material under scrutiny in these poems is present in later novels, particularly in the development of Leopolda's character through *Tracks* and *Last Report on the Miracles at Little No Horse*. Erdrich has not again captured the intensity and intimacy of the poetry, and yet the powerful emphases on memory and maternity that lend it much of that intimacy are continuous through her oeuvre. That her third and to date only other collection, *Original Fire: New and Selected*

Poems (2003), contains only a small selection of new poems, very much in continuity with that earlier work, suggests either that the prose fiction now thoroughly dominates Erdrich's writing, or that that earlier sense of the overt privacy of her poetry has increased with time.

The poetics of space

Comprised of four main sections – 'Runaways', 'Hunters', 'The Butcher's Wife', and 'Myths' – *Jacklight* introduces readers to the major concerns of her work. Navigating questions of encounters, belonging, gender, place, family, and community, it engenders a lyrical passage through the literal and spiritual geographies of the Great Plains in general, of Turtle Mountain reservation and its environs more specifically, and North Dakota/Minnesota more broadly. Drawing clearly from both her German-American and Ojibwe/Métis heritage, the book's essence is encapsulated in the nuances and intimacy of its final poem, 'Turtle Mountain Reservation'.

'Turtle Mountain Reservation' (82–85) presents a signature multivalent image in its opening lines, the half-rhyme of 'cross' and 'compass' arresting attention:

> The heron makes a cross
> Flying low over the marsh.
> Its heart is an old compass
> Pointing off in four directions.
> It drags the world along,
> The world it becomes. [3]

The biblical suggestion of the heron's cross is counterposed by the heart-as-compass motif, evoking the sacred compass or hoop celebrated by many Native cultures. Indeed the cross itself, while Christian in connotation, is also symbolic of the fourth degree of the Midé, the Ojibwe Medicine Society (Erdrich 2003c: 55).[4] Simultaneously, it evokes the compass of western appropriation, a geographical as much as spiritual marker of the four directions and a signifier of the flawed 'discovery' of 1492.[5] Such careful juxtaposition of the sacred and the secular is not accidental: an intricate dialectical play results from what superficially appears to be a straightforward combination. It is echoed in the pairing of the flying heron (air) with the marsh over which it flies (earth and water), which in itself enmeshes another superficial binary in the transcendent quality of flight and the earthy, perhaps even stagnant, quality of the marsh.[6] Theresa Smith notes, however, that the dualism of sky and earth or water 'is but one movement in what [she] would call a complicated dialectical dance' (1995: 2). Focusing on the animate spirits of the 'complex' and 'fluid' Ojibwe cosmology, Smith continues:

> It is my contention that the Thunder and Underwater manitouk are determinative beings and symbols in the Ojibwe world and that their relationship inscribes a dialectic that both reflects the lived reality of that world and helps to determine the position and existence of the human subject therein. In other words, the human person is suspended between heights and depths both literally and figuratively. (1995: 2)

In the poem, the heron flies low – is both free of, and in proximity to, the earth – evoking the suspension Smith claims, and drawing together ground and air as if suggesting itself as common denominator between the two. Further, the stanza closes with the pairing of past and present, of agency ('it drags the world along') and passivity ('the world it becomes'), again of grounded certainty and of freeing or frightening uncertainty. From another angle, the sense of motion or process is juxtaposed with the static because, as centre of the sacred hoop, the heron *is* the world: or, with the compass a technological sign of progress, of mapping and boundary-laying, it drags the world along, consuming it, *becoming* that world as it does so. Like Christ's cross and the sacred hoop, this ritualised moment offers a point of connection between the flesh and the elements: the earthly and the spiritual, the known-experienced and the unknown-yet-to-come and, finally, between fact and faith.

The heron – clan totem of the Be-nays on Erdrich's maternal side (McNab 2004: 34) – is the ideal bird to carry this mythicised burden, not least because it is a recurring motif in Erdrich's poetry, but also because it engenders an ancient, mysterious quality in its solitariness and silence. That the compass and its contexts are also suggestive of aerial mapping increases the symbolism. Erdrich's play with time and space in this opening stanza means that the heron encapsulates the idea of openness *and* enclosure. It *en*compasses, just as its ancient quality does the same with time; the present tense is imbued with an awareness of historic and mythic time. The heron, more than any other bird, retains a hint of the triassic in its flight, so the image conveys ancient time collapsing into the present, fraught with the weight of post-contact history. The dedication to Pat Gourneau,

Erdrich's grandfather, similarly evokes an awareness of generation that the remainder of the poem develops. Ultimately, the spiritual resides in the geographical in this poem for several reasons: in the 'organic' mapping of the heron's flight and metaphysical journey; in the compass as centre of the sacred circle; and, paradoxically (conflictingly) in the 'godly' enterprise of Columbus's expedition and the later concept of Manifest Destiny. A grating juxtaposition, nevertheless the tension is creative. Erdrich constructs a poetic scene that carries connotations of the cultural encounters from which her heritage stems, without quite letting either touch the earth and claim the terrain. The metaphysical sense of that 'becoming' world prevails.

This opening stanza, at once expansive yet simultaneously pointing to the specific geography of the Turtle Mountains, opens a poem that intimately navigates the local spaces of self, home, and family relations:

> My face surfaces in the green
> beveled glass above the washstand.
> My handprint in thick black powder
> on the bedroom shade.

The active/passive shift of the first stanza remains; the poet observes herself and the marks she leaves on her immediate environment with a detachment perhaps born of overfamiliarity. There is something both comforting in this familiarity, yet also sinister in the imagery it invokes: the face 'surfacing' in the mirror becomes almost ghoulish in its detachment, the handprint on the shade connoting both ownership and *evidence* – the 'traces' of presences both comforting and disquieting. In the next four lines, the notion that home is something the poet could 'drink like thin fire' is powerfully evocative of the *desire* that Erdrich deals with elsewhere – the knowledge, or longing, that both comforts and destroys, that is 'heart's armor'. Then the final image's sense of memory of home 'that gathers/like lead in my veins/heart's armor, the coffee stains', which subtly refuses chronologic time references, similarly encapsulates tensions between the familiar comfort of coffee rings on a favourite table, the immovable stain, the liquid that can be both fortifying and damaging, and the life measured out and quantified by the marks of habitual activity. 'Turtle Mountain Reservation' highlights the modernism of Erdrich's poetry. Although the foregrounding of daily or seasonal cycles concurs with non-western modes of timekeeping, the image of coffee stains nods notionally towards T.S. Eliot's coffee spoons – 'I have measured out my life in coffee spoons' ('The Love Song of J. Alfred Prufrock'). I would suggest, though, that the thematic comparison between Erdrich and Eliot probably stops here, for while Prufrock identifies the apparent emptiness and hollowness of these ritualised cycles, Erdrich's poetic voice finds ground through just such observations. Here, the temporal becomes spatial metaphor.

The poem repeatedly touches on these themes of multiple influence. For instance, the poetic voice juxtaposes Theresa in stanza three, a vivacious representative of self-aware beginnings ('one frail flame eating wind' who rides 'a blue cricket/through the tumult of the falling dawn'), with Grandpa, whose presence is anticipated with another 'ancient' bird: 'At dusk the gray owl walks the length of the roof,/sharpening its talons on the shingles'. Having introduced the grey bird, significant to Ojibwe cosmology,[7] the poem then introduces Grandpa himself, leaning back 'between spoonfuls of canned soup' and repeating to himself 'a word/that belongs to a world/no one else can remember'. This link between past and present is immediately followed with a link to a third sphere – the mythical:

> The day has not come
> when from sloughs, the great salamander
> lumbers through snow, salt, and fire
> to be with him

The euphony of the 'lumbering' salamander enhances the weight of the mythical, imprinting Grandpa's age and memory in that realm. Yet the relentlessness of the mixture and merging of signifiers in this poem is not abandoned in this figure, for later in the poem, Grandpa is characterised as mad, a view apparently opposed to the wisdom and assuredness that his memory of old times and his connection to the mythical might imply. There is an out-of-placeness about him. While Theresa goes to bars to be fawned over by men, Grandpa 'walks from Saint Ann's, limp and crazy'. There is a further juxtaposition in the poem between the way Grandpa is described and the third and final character, Uncle Ray, a drunk, 'looking up/dark tunnels' of the sleeves of the nuns who, presumably, raised him.

While Theresa retains her earthy vitality ('She smells/like a hayfield, drifting pollen/of birch trees') and Grandpa, going homeward from the Bingo, clearly inhabits a world that is outside the sight or experience of those around him, Ray occupies a familiar space, disturbing only for the fact that it no longer disturbs:

The latch
is the small hook and eye

of religion. Twenty nuns
fall through clouds to park their butts
on the metal hasp. Surely that
would be considered miraculous almost anyplace,

but here in the Turtle Mountains
it is no more than common fact.

These nuns are no less spectral than the inhabitants of the convent in
Erdrich's prose. Their apocryphal story here, implicated in Raymond's
delirium, returns us to empire, not religion, which resides rather in
Theresa's near-mystical ephemeral beauty ('Her hair steals across
her shoulders/like a postcard sunset') and Grandpa's proximity to
myth/death – 'The Ping-Pong balls rise through colored lights,/brief
as sparrows/God is in the sleight of the woman's hand'. The poem's
act, or, after Hafen, the poem's ritual enactment, is in drawing all of
these strands – the universal and local geography, natural resources
such as 'the stones that line/the road and speak/to him [Grandpa] only
in their old agreement', youth and age, spirituality and materiality –
into the Gaussian blur of the face in the washstand mirror and the
handprint on the shade. The poem closes by returning to an image of
biblical and cosmological import, with a description of Grandpa's
hands: 'Hands of earth, of this clay/I'm also made from'. By implication, of course, this clay is also the source material for Theresa and
Ray, and the poem, in encapsulating (even encompassing) these
multiple events, personae, and experiences, works towards a catharsis
that ties metaphysical to ontological being, self to relations, relations
to one another, and the total to the land and environment within which
they reside.

A number of Erdrich's poems invite similar readings, perhaps the
most significant being 'Whooping Cranes' (J 73). Again, Erdrich
connects the locally specific to the universal, beginning the poem:

Our souls must be small as mice
to fit through the hole of heaven.
All the time it is shrinking
over Pembina.

Another metaphysical double image, this hole of heaven refers to the
entrance to the world in many Plains origin myths; it is the hole

through which the first grandparents descended. It also evokes the Romantic entrance of Wordsworth's Immortality Ode, new souls 'trailing clouds of glory', the hole of heaven an entrance through which the souls of newborns must squeeze. Then there is the deft juxtaposition of 'souls small as mice' with the internal rhyme and wordplay on the '[w]hole of heaven' that suggests an indivisibility between states of nature and divinity, tiny souls becoming the very substance of heaven.

And finally this universal state is linked to the local, as the hole shrinks 'over Pembina', a city on the North Dakota/Minnesota/Manitoba border, almost literally a crossroads, both edge and centre, and as liminal a site as the space occupied by the orphaned newborn of the poem, found in a ditch and later to join the cranes in flight:

> This boy grew
> strange and secret among the others,
> killing crows with his bare hands
> and kissing his own face in the mirror.

As Hafen elaborates, the boy in this poem is clearly in a 'mythical realm', even though the physical chronotope – the narrative itself, whose space and time occupies a recent past – is relatively contemporary. Alluding to Greek myth (Narcissus), there are also intimations of deicide here if the crows the boy kills are read as trickster figures. All of this mixes native story with evocative religious symbolism, where '[t]he boy, born of elements of Chippewa mythology and ascending with images of Christianity, becomes the intermediary between the two cultures' (Hafen 1996: 151). Just as the boy and cranes mediate the division between earth and sky as the hole closes behind them, the poem itself mediates the division between myth and 'reality', between past, present, and future, and between the loss of myth and venerable traditions in the face of other cultural codes (Hafen 1996: 151),[8] or what Joseph Bruchac (Abenaki) describes as a 'cross-fertilization of past and present in legend' (1994: 98).

Baptism and desire

Baptism of Desire (1989) focuses even more intensely, and intensively, on material religion, although it plays forcibly on aspects of desire, passion, and fecundity that the volume title both evokes and, in its

Catholic context, seems to resist. 'In Catholic doctrine,' writes Jaskoski in an early review of the volume, 'Baptism of Desire has a rather technical meaning: a person who is unable to manage conventional baptism of water can, by earnestly and truly wanting to be baptised, gain the benefits of the sacrament . . . Longing and will may serve where form and ritual are impossible' (1991: 55). Although, as Jaskoski notes, this element of doctrine is not a pivot, but rather a departure point for the collection, the first section contains ten poems that directly concern religion.⁹ Of these the most prominent is 'The Sacraments', a poem of seven sections beginning with a list of sacraments – '*Baptism, Communion, Confirmation,/Matrimony, Penance, Holy Orders, Extreme Unction*'.¹⁰ The implication that each of these corresponds to each of the numbered sections is made explicit in the *Original Fire* (2003) reprint, where each section is sequentially subtitled with both number and name of the sacrament.

The first section, baptism, conveys violence imitative and evocative of Christ's passion. Just as baptism is a rising again with Christ to rebirth, this section describes symbolic death and rebirth, a rewriting of Christ's sacrifice that involves suspension of the flesh in a ritual of *humilitas*:¹¹

> As the sun dancers, in their helmets of sage,
> stopped at the sun's apogee
> and stood in the waterless light,
> so, after loss, it came to this:
> that for each year the being was destroyed,
> I was to sacrifice a piece of my flesh.
> The keen knife hovered
> and the skin flicked in the bowl.
> Then the sun, the life that consumes us,
> burst into agony.

The sacraments in Catholic practice are moments at which God's purpose and design is most clearly revealed. Equally, they are points at which we are made most receptive to divinity – the efficacy of *humilitas* that opens the sun dancers up to the presence and entrance of a divine being. This intensity of purpose is emphasised through consonance, the 's' sound broken – punctured even – only by the harder edges of 'keen knife . . . skin flicked'.

The irony of placing the plains sun dance within a Catholic sacramental framework is conspicuous. In this instance, it is not God who enters the supplicant but rather a bird (the eagle, a mediator between man and the supreme being), whose 'wings closed over us, her dark red/claws drew us upward by the scars,/so that we hung suspended by the flesh'. Imagery of ascension is ironically juxtaposed with what must be seen in biblical terms as satanic imagery of the red bird – doubtless an eagle – pinning flesh; yet the image is nevertheless transcendent, combining flight and descent as Christ died, rose, and was reborn.[12] The resultant state also parallels the sacramental purpose of baptism:

> As in the moment before birth
> When the spirit is quenched
> In whole pain, suspended
> Until there is no choice, the body
> Slams to earth,
> The new life starts.

The bird imagery, needless to say, is not demonic, but, like the sun dance itself, belongs to a different epistemological and cultural tradition. Erdrich is not merely making comparisons here. It has been argued that, 'Through poetic imagination and linguistic play, Erdrich ... create[s] a "third space" for religious experience ... And in doing so unsettle[s] radical oppositions both within Christianity and between it and tribal religions, turning these differences into what Native theologian George Tinker calls "reciprocal dualisms"' (Hughes 2001: 60). Hughes's use of the phrase 'third space' here invokes the interstitial, playing again on that idea of in-betweenness. Yet the central idea she draws from, the notion of reciprocation, so vital according to Tinker to what is, in one sense, the cornerstone of a Native metaphysic ('theology in community'), prevails upon the individual to view themselves as a 'vital part of a community' that includes all 'createds': implicitly, these different cultural and religious forces must seek not to displace one another, but to reciprocate (Tinker 2004: 113 and *passim*). This is not simply a matter of syncretism or synthesis, but rather of ways in which both cultures from which Erdrich's poetry derives respond one to the other – *trans*culturation as opposed to *en*culturation, as both the sun dance and the baptismal rite each draw on the imagery of the other. In this instance, Erdrich represents a changing world, and again a dualistic image of two cultural traditions interacting, presenting an environment, as distinctly plains-derived as elsewhere in her oeuvre, touched by traditions that adapt and mould themselves to and through the landscape's populace.

Feminism and ethnicity

This dense, intense relationship between the land, people, and rituals is equally evident in the poem that lends this chapter its title. 'Captivity' (J 26), a touching, mildly sardonic meditation on the Puritan Mary Rowlandson, sees the captive at once appalled and intrigued by her captors and their way of life, speaking quite differently to those questions of freedom and entrapment and the collision of Christian and indigenous 'perception'. Just as Rowlandson's classic American captivity narrative (1682) reveals some sense of discomfiture between her role as member of the pious elect and her reality as a woman amidst an unrecognisable (to her) version of humanity, 'Captivity' expresses a split based in desire for and repulsion of the other. The epigraph characterises her fear: '*He (my captor) gave me a bisquit, which I put in my pocket, and not daring to eat it, buried it under a log, fearing he had put something in it to make me love him*'.[13] Investigating the possibility this fear of love represents, the poem teasingly suggests that fear of desire implicitly reveals a yearning for the freedom from restraint that desire represents. It opens, '[t]he stream was swift, and so cold/ I thought I would be sliced in two'.[14] This physical fear embodies the psychological impact of encounter, an experience that the Rowlandson persona longs to explain in providential terms ('I hid my face in my dress, fearing He [God] would burn us all'). Yet she is unable to entirely resist the humanity of her captors, despite her attempts to persuade herself and her readers that 'There were times I feared I understood/his language, which was not human'. Her fear of being sliced in two is *both* a fear of her own degeneracy and a fear of her captor's humanity – for if the 'Indians' are not being destroyed by God it either questions the beliefs of the Elect in their own Irresistible Grace or, as the original narrative suggests, it makes them agents of God, placed before the Puritans as judgement for their turning from the true path.

Either way, her captors appear the more blessed and the Rowlandson persona is forced to embrace that split she first feared, allowing that:

> Rescued, I see no truth in things.
> My husband drives a thick wedge
> through the earth, still it shuts
> to him year after year.

As the earth refuses to yield to his violent stroke, so she is haunted by her exclusion (from both societies): 'And in the dark I see myself/

as I was outside their circle'. The contrast to Rowlandson's original narrative unsettles and destabilises its cultural and theological authority. No longer inside either 'circle', her closing expression of desire becomes a plea *both* for rescue from the situation this night-time memory describes *and* from her current situation, a literal and figurative liberation. Joining their ritual performance, she seeks to emplace herself where her husband seeks to impose himself:

> They knelt on deerskins, some with sticks,
> and he [her captor] led his company in the noise
> until I could no longer bear
> the thought of how I was.
> I stripped a branch
> and struck the earth,
> in time, begging it to open
> to admit me
> as he was
> and feed me honey from the rock.

It is not entirely clear whether 'the thought of how [she] was' refers now to the degrading circumstances of her captivity or to the remoteness from the earth her thoughts have suggested. The essence of the poem is epitomised by that very ambiguity, the outcome of what Riley Fast sees as a 'dialogic discourse' between poem and narrative (1999: 83). True enough, rather than resolving, consolidating, or reconciling the resisted historical narrative, Erdrich's poem opens up that authoritative space to indeterminacy, to conjecture, to conversation; where the traditional captivity narrative is one of return and redemption, in 'Captivity' Erdrich presents a scene of disorientation that foregrounds a decisive shift in settler, not Native, stability.[15]

Liminality here ironically marks Rowlandson as Other to her captors. It draws a key correspondence between the liminal status of racial and gendered otherness, infusing those poems that might be considered feminist first and foremost. Many of the poems, for instance, deal with women as childless mothers ('Mary Kröger' *BD* 29), as unstable and potential murderers of their children ('Poor Clare' *BD* 31), as spectres ('Manitoulin Ghost' *OF* 23, originally published as 'Bidwell Ghost' in *BD* 34), as 'prey' ('Jacklight' *J* 3), as nuns or saints ('Saint Clare' *BD* 5), or more straightforwardly as outsiders ('Here Is a Good Word for Step-and-a-Half-Waleski' *J* 50). Balanced by the centrifugal force of motherhood, the poems are also balanced, often internally, by imagery of women as carers and healers, as stalwarts or keystone figures, and as sirens. To say that these figures are often liminal is by no means to suggest they are submissive, passive, or subject to male design. Rather, their characterisations serve either to represent an exploration of self or space, or womanhood, combining, as Rader suggests, the various forms of woman, Native, and animal (2004: 107); or they serve to destabilise those dominant masculine discourses that 'Captivity' reconfigures in *its* evocation of a narrative that subtly negotiates such discourses. In the terms applied to American women's poetry by Adrienne Rich, 'Captivity' 're-visions' the anger and frustration of women in narratives written and/or controlled by men. Re-vision is 'the act of looking back, of seeing with fresh eyes, of entering an old text from a new critical direction – is for us more than a chapter in cultural history: it is an act of survival' (Rich 1972: 18). Erdrich's narrative not only 'revisions' that patriarchal 'myth' but also reinvests the colonial (particularly the Puritan anti-Indian) narrative with the more explicit gendered nuance buried deep in the original.[16] Rich writes of the 'split' between the 'girl who wrote poems, who defined herself in writing poems, and the girl who was to define herself by her relationships with men' (1972: 21–22). In 'Captivity' perhaps, the 'split' that the Rowlandson persona fears – evocative of Anzaldúa's 'Staking fence rods in my flesh/Splits me   Splits me' (1999: 24) – is that between a self-defining agency and living as a wife, woman, Puritan Goodwife; between the 'opposition of [the] imagination . . . [and] life-style' (Rich 1972: 22). This idea also connects to the 'transformational power' of Erdrich's women, characterised by Van Dyke as a rejection of the 'cultural bifurcation of Native American women' (1999: 130). In interview with Bruchac, Erdrich declares in Rich-like tones: 'we are taught to present a demure face to the world and yet there is a kind of wild energy behind it in many women that *is* a transformational energy' (qtd in Van Dyke 1999: 131). In 'Captivity' perhaps Erdrich's Rowlandson is coming to know the discombobulating force of that 'wild energy'.

'Jacklight' (*J* 3–4) also draws several of Erdrich's principal themes into a single multivalent space. Apparently describing a deer hunt from the perspective of the deer, 'Jacklight' presents a forest space, out of which these figures emerge: 'We have come to the edge of the woods,/. . . where we slept, unseen,/out of knotted twigs, out of leaves creaked shut,/out of hiding'. The repeated movement outwards suggests something both vulnerable and peripheral: the transformational possibilities of emergence are evoked alongside the threatening realities of deforestation, or the 'uncovering' of pristine nature it implies. The poem also represents a quiet confrontation between female and male, specifically male aggression and its capacity to separate or make vulnerable:

> At first the light wavered, glancing over us.
> Then it clenched to a fist of light that pointed,
> searched out, divided us.
> Each took the beams like direct blows the heart answers.
> Each of us moved forward alone;

It represents a comparison between intuition and surface fact ('We smelled them behind it/but they are faceless, invisible./We smell the raw steel') and the single-minded impersonality of the hunt (as male) with the intimacy, instinct, and inquisitiveness of the prey (as female):

> We smell their mothers buried chin-deep in wet dirt.
> We smell their fathers with scoured knuckles,
> teeth cracked from hot marrow . . .
> We smell their minds like silver hammers
> cocked back, held in readiness
> for the first of us to step into the open.

Finally, inverting the scenario, and realising the potential of that opening movement, Erdrich represents the seduction of that 'male' type by the female:

> It is their turn now,
> their turn to follow us. Listen,
> they put down their equipment.
> It is useless in the tall brush.
> And now they take the first steps, not knowing
> How deep the woods are and lightless.
> How deep the woods are.

Here, the deer hunt is transformed into a moment of feminine seduction. The vulnerability of the deer/women on the edge of the treeline is inverted as they draw the hunters inside. Erdrich has reflected that 'the woods to me have always been a place of mystery, shelter. That's where we have to go to find each other' (qtd in Barak 1996: 49). It is no coincidence that the forest here is a traditional site of seduction by natural forces in American literature; we have only to think of Nathaniel Hawthorne's *The Scarlet Letter* (1851) to *feel* the force of the 'primitive' and 'feminine' wilderness.[17] This, of course, points also to the virgin land that tempted the first pioneers, creating a matrix of metaphors of conquest and seduction. The poem's epigraph, from Dunning's *Social and Economic Change Among the Northern Ojibwa* (1959), explains much: 'The same Chippewa word is used both for flirting and hunting game, while another Chippewa word connotes both using force in intercourse and also killing a bear with one's bare hands'. Reading the hunt as metaphor for seduction is relatively simple but not simplistic – in fact it is a commonplace of lyric poetry but effortlessly inverts the denial of Thomas Wyatt's 'Whoso list to hunt', a sixteenth-century sonnet regretting the unavailability of Anne Boleyn. Erdrich captures the latent violence of the latter half of the quotation from Dunning, while simultaneously transferring the bravery of the bear kill to the calm, strong sensuality and sexuality of the women who, having 'come here too long', ensnare their would-be killers/captors.

The masculine overtones of that word, and its place as metaphor in discourses of dominance, are appropriated by a feminine interpretation of stealth, guile, and irresistible calm. That these mysterious women/deer 'know', by smell, the danger they face, indicates both their sensitivity to the natural incongruity of the hunter-aggressors and the obstacle *they* pose to the huntsmen's ambitions. 'Jacklight' subtly challenges the patriarchal order. But this is not all. The intimacy is both deeply sensual and implicitly sexual. In a more subtle reading of the poem, we might explore not only that confrontation between male and female that both the hunt and the courting scenario enact, but also a natural 'unfurling' (after winter, for instance, or even in puberty), beautifully described in the first stanza ('out of brown grass where we slept, unseen,/out of knotted twigs, out of leaves creaked shut,/out of hiding'). In this way, the poem becomes not merely an act of destabilising but a true act of emergence, celebrating womanhood, sensuality, and female sexuality.

These various connotations are explored elsewhere, most markedly in 'The Woods' (*J* 23), where once more the anthropomorphism of the forest is explained as a merging of the feminine voice of the poem and the natural world. It is also characterised as a trickster-like transformation between states, a performative mediation between mortal and divine, from ambivalent to malignant being:

> At one time your touches were clothing enough.
> Within these trees now I am different.
> Now I wear the woods.

I lower a headdress of bent sticks and secure it.
I strap to myself a breastplate of clawed, roped bark.
I fit the broad leaves of sugar maples
to my hands, like mittens of blood.

Here the seduction goes beyond the inherent risk of pursuing desire, to the absolute death of submersion in another: 'When you lay down in the grave of a slashed tree,/I cover you, as I always did;/this time you do not leave'. The connection between woman and nature is made axiomatic. This return to nature, its ironic freedom through immersion, also speaks powerfully of the self-abnegation in imagination of the poet (the 'I' that dissolves into camouflage), and the escape from the confinement of language, that recurs throughout twentieth-century American poetry, from Robert Frost to the aforementioned Adrienne Rich. In Frost's 'A Dream Pang', for instance, the poet '[withdraws] in forest, and my song/Was swallowed up in leaves' (*A Boy's Will*). Torn between the temptation of the mystery of nature and the reality of flesh – the 'muse' of language and the imagination – the poet withdraws: Erdrich's persona, Daphne-like, transforms herself, but far from becoming subsumed by Apollo's love, the result of Eros' malice, *she* possesses her lover.

More ambiguous but highly suggestive in Erdrich's poetry is the connection between woman and death, where sex is frequently cast as a (self-)destructive act and birth repeatedly echoed in death. Those connections are implicit across much of Erdrich's poetry, and explicit in the theme of motherhood – indeed, some of her most powerfully personal poems, appearing first in *Baptism of Desire*, were written 'between the hours of two and four in the morning, a period of insomnia brought on by pregnancy' (2001a: 48). The life-giving forces of childbirth and the necessary conflicts it produces are subjects shared with many female poets, not least Erdrich's sister Heid, whose recent book of poems, *The Mother's Tongue* (2005), takes the procreative figure as a locus for meditation on motherhood, language, culture, and more. However, while many of the poems that are explicitly about motherhood are tender, there is a stark supernal force to 'The Woods' that is also brought about by the influence of the divine parent represented here by nature, and by the trickster-like transmogrification of the speaker into a tree. Not only is this highly evocative of the cycle of life and death, and return to nature, it is also a mystical metamorphosis that crosses the boundaries between these various realms, playing on and subverting other versions of the same. Nevertheless,

the liminality of the image – which here *expresses* a transformative state
and elsewhere expresses the *potential* for transformation – is best
encapsulated in motherhood poems, such as 'Birth' (*OF* 132):

> When they were wild
> When they were not yet human
> When they could have been anything,
> I was on the other side ready with milk to lure them,
> And their father, too, each name a net in his hands.

In 'Birth' mediation between realms or states, and the incarcerating
language of luring and netting, describes the same tensions between
freedom and desire, life and death, and the individual and communal
explored in 'The Woods'.

Seduction is even more strikingly explored in 'Mary Magdalene' (*BD*
16), where the double sense of Christ's favourite as both victim and
agent tessellates between two triads of devotion, desire, passion, and
lust, self-destruction, self-immolation. 'I wash your ankles/with my
tears', the Mary persona declares; 'I cut off my hair and toss it across
your pillow'. 'I will drive boys', she concludes, 'to smash empty bottles
on their brows', a destructive power that goes beyond the temptation
of 'Jacklight' to the full extreme of revenge:

> I will pull them right out of their skins.
> It is the way that girls
> get even with their fathers –
> by wrecking their bodies on other men.

This allusion to the Electra complex has as much to do with religion as
it does the earthly relationship between the sexes. The father with
whom Mary is getting even might equally be a divine presence, or more
appropriately, the church to which her relationship is one of submission. While Christ selected Magdalene for special recognition, His
church, as the poem subtly suggests, has historically overwritten her
favour as pity, her passion as lust, her devotion as dedication to self.

Erdrich's own ambivalence towards the Catholicism of her upbringing is well documented and readily apparent – not an ambivalence that ignores but one that explores. 'Saint Clare' (*BD* 5) is one
such exploration of the relationship between a woman and God,
nature, the church, her sister, and her mortal family. The poem tells
the story of Clare Scifi (St. Clare of Assisi), who, inspired by Francis of
Assisi, took a vow of poverty and formed the Poor Clares order. Having
drawn her sister Agnes to her, Clare prayed to keep her when her

father's people came to take her home; her prayers rendered Agnes too heavy to remove and they returned to him empty handed. Erdrich leaves no ambiguity as to the nature of this story, beginning with an epigraph from Delaney's *Pocket Dictionary of Saints* (1983) that outlines the 'plot'. The poem itself, however, expands on this, delineating Clare's character and motives more finely, interpreting her actions as another of Erdrich's strong yet 'haunted' women, tied by the weight of family, duty, and 'density of purpose', and drawn by the 'ponderous light' of St Francis's sermon. In section one, 'The Call', the poem's eponymous narrator reveals:

> First I heard the voice throbbing across the river.
> I saw the white phosphorescence of his robe.
> As he stepped from the boat, as he walked
> There spread from each footfall a black ripple,
> From each widening ring a wave,
> From the waves a sea that covered the moon.
> So I was seized in total night
> And I abandoned myself in his garment.

This revelation, a first leap of faith, precipitates a material renunciation that recurs in three key elements of the woman's being. The first describes the rejection of her family's affluent status: 'The scales of my old body melt away like coins'. The second, transforming material loss into natural and spiritual gain, occurs in sections two and three, 'Before' and 'My Life As a Saint': first, 'The girdle of green silk, the gift from my father/slithered from me like a vine/. . . the skeins of hair /. . . were cut from my head'; and secondly, as Clare describes her observations of a nest of fledgling wrens:

> By morning, the strands of the nest disappear
> into each other, shaping
> an emptiness within me that I make lovely
> as the immature birds make the air
> by defining the tunnels and the spirals of the new sustenance.

That new sustenance is enabling, as 'no longer hindered by the violence of their need', the birds 'fling themselves deep into the world'.

This liberating tendency is both ironic and apt in view of the back story Erdrich evokes. With no equivalent of the Franciscan monastery for women, Clare was placed in the Benedictine convent of San Paulo and found herself fighting to maintain the original vow of poverty that her Franciscan devotion required before later establishing the order of the Poor Clares at the convent of San Damiano. The dream, or ideal, of liberty granted by bounds (a principle of the poetry *as* poetry) is echoed in the poem's closing lines. In this section, entitled 'Agnes', Clare, who predeceased her sister by a mere three months, describes her releasing of her sister in death, juxtaposing material weight and spiritual lightness in one further image of freedom in enclosure that is a simultaneous apology for the impossible example she set:

> That is why, toward the end of your life,
> When at last there was nothing I could not relinquish,
> I allowed you to spring forward without me.
> Sister, I unchained myself. For I was always
> the heaviest passenger,
> the stone wagon of example,
> the freight you dragged all the way to heaven,
> and how were you to release yourself
> from me, then, poor mad horse,
> except by reaching the gate?

As appropriate to the sororal relationship between nuns as the siblings' own relationship, 'sister' describes a gradual releasing and the ascent from the worldly to the celestial as the result of relinquishing material ties and duty.

The poem also describes the sacraments, through such imagery as the metaphorical baptism of hearing Francis's voice across the river; celebrating the eucharist by breaking her own bread to feed the wren's fledglings; the confirmation, matrimony, and holy orders of taking Francis's vow; the penance of giving up worldly goods, and the extreme unction implicit in the nurturing and loss of one of the chicks and in the image of ascent at the poem's close. All of this both draws and builds on the self-abnegating imagery of sacrifice, or giving oneself up to a higher essence. Hughes reflects on the symbiotic relationship between physical process and sacramental tradition: 'By insisting on both the ascetic and the sacramental Catholic traditions simulta-neously, Erdrich opens the door to a more traditionally tribal view of the spiritual reality and mutually regenerative power of the earth and the body – a view which also has specifically feminist implications' (2001: 60). Hughes argues that Erdrich recasts God in the image of mother, neither the 'traditional orthodox representation of God the father . . . [nor] an outright rejection of the Euro-Christian deity' (2001: 64). She also grapples with the cultural negotiations made in lines such as those that invoke the eucharistic cup: 'Then the cup was made fast/to the body of the tree,/bound with the silver excrescence of the spider' ('My Life As a Saint'). 'More than just a symbol for natural productivity, or even a feminist emblem of relationality', Hughes goes so far as to argue that 'the symbol of the spider signals an increasingly pan-tribal understanding of first creation and [our] on-going role in it' (2001: 62–63). The tree itself is both a Christian and a Native symbol of life, and the sacred significance of the four eggs the cup contains is doubly clear as both Native and Christian symbol: in the four quartiles of the sacred compass, the four points of genuflection, and the four extremes of the holy cross. The subtext of this poem is devotion, close to Erdrich's heart and central to her depictions of motherhood. Its depiction relies on a sublimation of self, but that sublimation, ironically, is also self-completing.

Identity politics and postcolonial poetics

The political import of Erdrich's poems is not, by any means, limited to gender politics. Equally attuned to issues surrounding Erdrich's Ojibwe heritage and in many senses the mythological or storied histories of her German background too, the negotiation of negative histories is recurrent in the poetry – whether they be women's histories or untold stories, or others of more or less universal significance. Indeed, while the feminist (or at least feminine) is implicit across Erdrich's oeuvre, there are a number of poems that explicitly stamp their mark on particular areas of Native American socio-political experience. These poems depart from the locally specific and touch on themes of loss and disaffection that most closely speak to the confusion Deloria sees in biculturalism. The first of these, 'Dear John Wayne' (J 12), is perhaps Erdrich's best-known individual poem. Appearing first in *Jacklight* in the section entitled 'Runaways', 'Dear John Wayne' is a relatively conventional lyric poem, describing a group of youths at a drive-in movie. A brief description of a mosquito attack gains ironic inflection later, when the closing line of the first stanza ('They break through the smoke screen for blood') picks up on several recurring motifs of the poem, including the 'whining arrows' of the Sioux ('or some other Plains bunch') attack on settlers, the 'thick cloud of vengeance' of Wayne's character's oath of revenge, and the disease with which the poem closes – the pathological inference of the blood referring not only to disease but also to the 'mark' of blood quantum that places the viewers 'back in our skins'.

The poem's true melancholy, however, is not merely in the ironic situation of a group of Native youths watching Hollywood's most beloved cowboy exacting revenge on 'Indians' – an example of double-consciousness, in which the viewers identify, for the moment of the film, with the white hero rather than the 'savage' Indians. It has equally to do with the simple notion that Wayne's character evinces: '*Everything we see belongs to us*' – a spiritual, ocular, as well as material possession. On one hand the reader will invariably be put in mind of Native Americans' historical reluctance to consider land as property; on the other, the reader will be alerted to the death-defying, desperate need for immortality that such a claim represents. The poem responds, '*The eye sees a lot, John, but the heart is so blind./Death makes us owners of nothing*'. Manifest Destiny becomes a grotesque caricature in Wayne himself: 'He smiles, a horizon of teeth/the credits reel over'. Those credits, of course, are also the 'credits' of history, the fictions of American settlement, sardonically highlighted in the lines 'and then the white fields/again blowing in the true-to-life dark./The dark films over everything'. Making a play on the word 'dark', the *white* fields obscure, where they should be obscured by, the 'true-to-life dark', creating a *darkness* that ultimately obscures light, or truth. 'Where the site of cultural imperialism and eradication in the nineteenth century was Sand Creek', writes Rader, 'in the twentieth century that space is the movie screen' (2002: 150).

The power of the movie is clear, although it is important to note that Erdrich makes no initial distinction between Native and non-Native audience, rather referring to the humbling power of the big screen for all: 'We get into the car/scratching our mosquito bites, speechless and small/as people are when the movie is done'. The penultimate stanza's final line, 'We are back in our skins', however, while reflecting back on the blood of the first stanza, leads on to the rhetorical question of the final stanza, which reinvigorates the American myth:

How can we help but keep hearing his voice,
The flip side of the sound track, still playing:
Come on boys, we got them
Where we want them, drunk, running.
They'll give us what we want, what we need.

The personal and the universal combine in this stanza, reflecting on the relationship between history and the present (implicit with the ongoing impact of expansionism), between audience and film, and between John Wayne and everything his films represent. Nowhere is the irony more powerful, or more personally inflected, than in the final two lines: 'Even his disease was the idea of taking everything./Those cells, burning, doubling, splitting out of their skins', referring to the cellular control of received history that the film represents as well as Wayne's cancer. John Wayne, whose face fills the screen with 'acres of blue squint and eye', occupies an apparently infinite space of mis-representation, his own body's 'assimilation' an apt metaphor for the assimilation of others, those who in death or self-denial find themselves 'splitting out of their skins'. Implying that the splitting embodies the struggle between submission to stereotypes or fight for recognition of one's (true) stories, the poem moves towards purg-ing, or revising, those negative histories. The mutually destructive movement of these relationships, explored further in later novels, is anticipated in that correlative image of consumption.

'Indian Boarding School: The Runaways' (*J* 11) and 'Orozco's Christ' (*BD* 15) also deserve mention in this context. The first is a simple narrative of escape and injustice, referring to the practice of sending children to residential schools that began with the found-ing of the Carlisle Indian School in Pennsylvania in 1879. The poem begins 'Home's the place we head for in our sleep', describing that initial separation, with home a far-off destination for dreams and memories. What is interesting is the geography of the dream's journey home:

> Boxcars stumbling north in dreams
> don't wait for us. We catch them on the run.
> The rails, old lacerations that we love,
> shoot parallel across the face and break
> just under Turtle Mountains. Riding scars
> you can't get lost. Home is the place they cross.

This is both somatic and psychological terrain, the scars are physical (body and earth) and emotional (mind and spirit) and vividly demarcated by the lexis left by the enjambement: dreams, love, shoot, break, scars; a semantic shift from naive idealism to traumatic realities 'dreamt' of in both senses of nightmares and longings. They repre-sent both the scarring of the earth, body, and mind in the coming of Europeans, their dominance, and their technology, and also the trail that leads back home, back through memory, the 'old lacerations' and scars fit for riding. The land, and the 'pathway' home, is absorbed and internalised, an interior landscape in which 'home', a distant dream, is encapsulated. In other words, the marks of destruction left by the dominant majority are simultaneously a means of escape; as the scars 'cross' home in a destructive sense, so they become paths that lead back there both literally and metaphorically.

The physical escape is short-lived. 'We watch through cracks in boards' it reads; 'We know the sheriff's waiting at midrun'. Having been returned to school in the sheriff's 'hostile' car ('it only hums/like a wing of long insults'), runaways are punished by scrubbing sidewalks wearing long green dresses, as stanza three describes:

> Our brushes cut the stone in watered arcs
> and in the soak frail outlines shiver clear
> ... things us kids pressed on the dark
> face before it hardened, pale, remembering
> delicate old injuries.

The shame of the punishment meted out to the runaways is offset here by the subtle suggestion of subversion, the marks made by the children on the sidewalks that remind them of these 'delicate old injuries', simultaneously leaving reminders of themselves. '[S]pines of names and leaves', then, like the scars on mind and landscape, become pictographic memory-trails, recorded histories, by the subjects, the subalterns, of those histories. Territory, power, the right to record, even the right to 'color' their own shame, get reclaimed within the poem.

In 'Orozco's Christ' a more general form of cultural politics is enacted. Hafen believes the poem is based on a fresco at Dartmouth College painted by José Orozco (1883–1949), who was influenced by the artistic traditions of Mexican Indians but a practitioner in the historical media of western conventions.[18] The poem, like the fresco, infuses Christ with an aggressive agency seldom encountered in western interpretations of His sacrifice:

> Who rips his own flesh down the seams and steps
> forth flourishing the axe
> who chops down his own cross,
> ...
> who stares like a cat,
> whose cheeks are the gouged blue of science,
> whose torso springs out of wrung cloth
> blazing ochre, blazing rust . . .

Orozco's Christ exerts an authority and exudes a will that refuses quiet
submission to fate. The poem offers a disquieting vision, including
an implied matricide, a patriarchy that ironically controls even the
subject's own father, and a scene in which aggression and rage establish the tone over the more serene traditions of passion and sacrifice.
This resurrected Christ is savage and defiant, managing his own
fate. Where Hafen rightly sees him as the figurehead of the 'savage
authority of Christianity' (1996: 150), it is worth noting too that he is
distant from contemporary Christianity and far closer to pre-Christian
culture heroes, a legendary Beowulf or Gilgamesh, returning one of
the originary stories of Christian culture to its mythological status.[19]
Clearly such rewriting is a political statement in itself, yet there
are two other points to consider. The work of art is a public statement
that beckons both interaction with the painting and response to its
presence. As such, the 'Dartmouth fresco mediates public and institutional space with the privacy of a poet's response to religious faith – or
challenge to that faith' (Hafen 1996: 149). Then, the poem represents
a personal interaction both with the painting and its subject matter
that enacts a further political comment on the relationship between
Christ the redeemer and Native culture heroes, who, as Rader notes,
need not be benevolent to be accepted and respected (2004: 110).
Indeed, Rader suggests, the placing of this poem alongside 'Christ's
Twin', which describes the Christian saviour's apotheosis, suggests a
fragile equilibrium, since twinship stories generally deal with opposites existing in creative tension: 'Uniting the two Christs reveals
an overarching desire for inclusion and significance that does not
subsume identity' (2004: 110–111). These blurring lines are integral
to understanding Erdrich's poetry, to seeking and finding that 'third
space' that Hughes sees as syncretic, hybrid; that Hafen sees in
terms of performative acts of mediation and transformation; that is
absolutely focal to Erdrich's destabilisation of monolithic interpretive
modes.

There are many examples of such synthesis. 'Hydra', for example,
(*BD* 41–48) draws on Greek mythology, brings in Christian symbolism
and references to *The Other Bible*, dwells on such themes as sex, sin,
and motherhood, and situates the poem's action between the mythic
realm and localities we are familiar with such as Wahpeton, North Dakota.
The command of multiple sources and subjects evidences not only
her reading but her modernist strategies, emphasising the layered,

mutually illuminating nature of cultural referents, and Erdrich's awareness of the cross-cultural transcendence of story. That Hydra's killer, Heracles, is one of many pagan gods believed to prefigure Christ lends the feminist inflections of the poem, with regard to paternalistic white hegemony, even greater power. In much simpler fashion, we see similar awareness in poems including 'Sorrows of the Frog Woman' (*OF* 135). Here the story 'Wampum Hair', told by Charles Kawbawgam, epigraphically announces a poem derived from European folk tales about enchanted frogs and princes. Alternatively, 'Night Sky' (*J* 33–36) merges Greek and Ojibwe mythology in the naming of stars and retelling of the bear driver myth (Arcturus, 'Bear watcher', being the principal star named). It is apposite, however, to turn to two poems that repudiate – insofar as the above 'celebrate' – the effects of cultural contact, addressing not transculturation but resistance to cultural destruction.

Appearing in *Original Fire* (2003), 'The Buffalo Prayer' and 'Rez Litany' (122 and 123) are also the most directly and fiercely political, satirising Catholicism by way of attacking the impact of America's colonial history:

> Our Lady of the Buffalo Bones, pray for us.
> Our Lady of the bales of skins and rotting hulk
> from which our tongues alone were taken,
> pray for us, Our Lady of the Poisoned Meat
> and of the wolves who ate
> and whose tongues swelled until they burst. ('The Buffalo Prayer')

The repetition in the poem is evocative of the repetition found in both traditional oral poetry and in Christian prayer and psalmody. In both instances it is key to the ritual nature of the incantation. Ironically, the prayer assaults the religious basis of the colonial enterprise:

> Our Lady of Destruction Everywhere
> our bones were ground into fertilizer
> for the worn-out eastern earth.
> Our bones were burned to charcoal
> to process sugar and to make glue
> for the shoe soles of your nuns and priests.

'For the shoe soles of *your* nuns and priests' figures an ironic division between the speaker of the poem, addressing 'Our Lady', and that speaker's alienation from the church's representatives who control the image of Our Lady. The Native speaker, presumably a woman, claims Our Lady as an image in which she can invest, thus wresting her, partially at least, from their control. Simultaneously, the very ambivalence of this criticism through invocation of one of the prevailing icons of the thing criticised emphasises the ambiguity of Native subjugation to Christianity. Elsewhere, Erdrich speaks of the *transculturation* between Christian and Ojibwe religions – her grandfather, for instance, combining ceremonies of both – which this poem both acknowledges and despairs of via the relationship between missionising and the imperial project of assimilation and religious suppression. 'The Buffalo Prayer' is an instance of both assuming *and* critiquing this position, picking a way through the contradictions of both resenting and aligning oneself with such power lines.

Even more directly focused on the colonial project, 'Rez Litany' uses the same form to attack the terms of white settlement:

> Let us now pray to those beatified
> within the Holy Colonial church
> beginning with Saint Assimilus,
> patron of residential and of government
> boarding schools, whose skin was dark
> but who miraculously bled white milk
> for all to drink.

Beginning with a reference to lactose intolerance, which, the poem claims, affects ninety percent of Native children, 'Rez Litany' runs through 'mistaken blood tests and botched/surgeries', praying to the 'patron saint of the Indian Health Service,/who is also guardian of slot machines'. Commodity food, the grand casino buffet, Saints Bloatinus, Cholestrus, Macaronia, Diabeta, Pyromane, Quantum, Bingeous, Odium, Tremens, Microcephalia, Primapara, Gravida, and Humpenenabackseat form a long line of aspects of Native health, social welfare, government programmes, and behavioural patterns that come under scathingly humorous attack. Taking on these subjects in the terms that, without overstating the case, are attached to intentions to *improve* the circumstances of the Native population engenders an attempt to deconstruct that position and thereby destabilise the dominant discourse of patriarchal, federalised, Christian governance. Erdrich infuses dominant epistemologies with criticism of the cultural determinism and arrogant superiority of those epistemic traditions.

'How long must we live in the broken figures':[20] resisting conclusions

In the first section of the poem, 'New Mother' (*OF* 133–134), the poet writes:

I am here to praise this body
On loan from the gods
By which we know the god in us
The god made earth,
Pulled out blue and stunned into the lights.

Here, the human body, itself a divine fact, is celebrated and recognised, its divinity affirmed in the act of creation. The ultimate mystery, and mystical connection with both the universe and universal humanity, is encapsulated by procreation. There is no avoiding that this prioritises feminine experience, but Erdrich's feminism stems, it is fair to say, from a female-centred epistemology, from a cultural origin that gives primacy to the relationship between life, earth, and mother as central to the complementary compact between all of creation. First female, unlike in western, Christian epistemic traditions, is accorded full prominence *alongside* first male, completing a symbiotic relationship between human, divine, and earthly. In the above instance, completion occurs through the sublimation of self to the larger cycles of the cosmos.

These ideas of sublimation of self to children, community, and landscape are central to an understanding of Erdrich's poetic concerns. As I suggested at the beginning of this chapter, such concerns reflect on ideas of individuation within the communal and on the paradox of community activity defining the individual by permitting them to find their place. The ritualistic allows what is performative about the poetry to be transformative; this potential in turn denies the fixity that more singular readings of Erdrich's poetry permit. Although I do not deal with the idea in detail here, Hafen asserts the ethnopoetic possibilities of the orality of Erdrich's poetry, outlining the main characteristics of ethnopoetry as key to those poems that allude to ritual. Hafen borrows from Michel Benamou and, while I will not rehearse her argument, I do want to reflect on two of these characteristics in so far as they reflect on the arguments I have outlined above: the reunification of both the poet and her audience with the 'human past', and reterritorial-isation of language, thus retotalising the human community (Hafen 1996: 148). This work of reterritorialising and retotalising is, of course, crucial to the negotiation and mediation of cultures that the 'spaces' of Erdrich's poetry access. Erdrich's poetics develop, then, within a nexus of exchange that draws from that multiple heritage. Rader notes that her poems 'underscore larger attempts of collaboration and trans- formation', rendering the ethnopoetic work that Hafen identifies not a retreat into an Ojibwe-focused cultural identity, so much as an exploration outwards, across and in spite of perceived 'boundaries' (Rader 2004: 107).

For some, the syncretic adequately defines this apparently hybrid space and yet the syncretic is a space in which cultures merge and neither remains intact, discrete. While clearly this describes the kind of transculturation present in Erdrich's fiction and is far more appropriate than any acculturative definition would be, there is still something dissatisfyingly restrictive – reductive even – about consid- ering Erdrich's treatment of religion and culture in these terms. When she describes her grandfather as having managed to consolidate *both* Christianity and the Ojibwe religion, it is with a sense of the two existing in complementarity, reconciled rather than fused, Gourneau mediating the contact. What Erdrich deals with is not merely the sum of the two parts *but also* the point of mediation between separate spheres that are continuously engaging and resisting one another.

This, perhaps more than anything, gives cause to reflect on the meaning of the title of such books as Treat's *Native and Christian* (1996). Native *and* Christian. Neither Native Christian, nor Native *or* Christian. The distinction is fine and the means by which we tread these parameters are invariably poorly formed, particularly for non- Native scholars. But that part of Erdrich's poetry that neither permits a bifurcation nor envisages a composite speaks to this notion of balance as opposed to separation or combination. That negotiation depends, clearly, on the acknowledgement and negotiation of multiple influences, voices, and constituencies. It wends its exploratory way through both Ojibwe and Christian understandings of individualism and communality, and versions of passion and desire, through the Ojibwe traditions of seeking connection with ancestral and cosmo- logical counsel, and the historic Catholic need for confession and self-denial; through both Ojibwe and Catholic means of achieving revelation, and the human need for self-reflection; and through both traditional oral and western orthographic modes of finding voice. 'Through poetry', writes Rader, 'Erdrich combines modes of cultural dwelling, enabling her to reside in two worlds at once' (2004: 102).

We find its choicest metaphor in 'The Sweat Lodge', section three of 'Asiniig', where the stones, describing the offerings made to them, declare:

> When we break ourselves open –
> that is when the healing starts.
> When you break yourselves open –
> that is how the healing continues. (*OF* 155)

The work of breaking and healing, then, is central to the treatment of religions and communities, individual identities and cultures with which Erdrich engages.

Notes

1 In *Custer Died for your Sins* Deloria notes that assertions of 'bicultural mediation' may be the single biggest barrier to personal development for Indian youth (1969: 83).

2 A number of Erdrich's poems were written in New Hampshire. The 'Geo' in the title of this chapter refers as much to the constant awareness of environment her poetry evinces as to specific localities.

3 Where poems appear in more than one volume, citations will be from the earlier text.

4 For more on the *Midéwiwin*, see, for instance, Hoffman 1891 and Landes 1968.

5 The compass was originally a Chinese invention thought to date back to the third century BC and known to have found its way to Western Europe some time in the twelfth century.

6 Similarly, it is no accident that this usually solitary bird, in the case of the great blue heron especially, nests in large colonies during breeding time.

7 As *Kokoko*, the owl is connected to dark desire, death, and bad medicine, another poem, 'Owls', hints (*BD* 75).

8 The above paragraph closely echoes Hafen's reading of 'Whooping Cranes' (1996), to which I refer the reader for the full development of the process of mediation Hafen describes.

9 The sections in *Baptism* are simply numbered.

10 Extreme unction, or the last rites, was replaced at the second Vatican council of 1962–1965 with the anointing of the sick. Erdrich is probably aware of this but the symbolic function of the last rites is of weightier import.

11 Humiliation – not just shame or degradation, but the act of giving oneself up to other powers or spheres (see Lincoln 1982). Here, it carries notes of both ritual humiliation – a matter of creating equality and receptivity – and the Catholic emphasis on humility.

12　The two principal totems involved in the plains sun dance are the buffalo and the thunderbird, often represented by an eagle.

13　Rader quotes Robin Riley Fast's insightful point that in reading this epigraph, we trust the legitimacy and validity of it in precisely the same way readers of Rowlandson's narrative would have presumed its authority. It is not, in fact, from the original text (2004: 108).

14　From Rowlandson's sixteenth remove, on wading over *Baquaug* river: 'the stream very swift, and so cold that I thought it would have cut me in sunder' (1998: 34).

15　In doing so, this 'narrative' echoes John Tanner's 'alienated position' as a white boy kidnapped by Indians who returned, in later life, to Anglo-American society (Sayre 1990: 481).

16　Many scholars have noted the double-voiced nature of Rowlandson's text, as the narrative shifts between observation and participation. Erdrich favours the latter, privileging an 'eye-opening' and influential engagement with the reality of Native community.

17　Hawthorne's novel is merely the most obvious example of a male American writer situating both gendered and racial 'others' as temptation within a forest setting, i.e. outside the sanctified social sphere. The poem also invokes Robert Frost's poems 'Stopping by Woods on a Snowy Evening' and 'A Dream Pang', not least in the syntax and sentiment of those closing lines.

18　Hafen suggests the painting is probably Orozco's *Cristo destruyendo la Cruz* (1932–1934). She also extends the connection between poet and artist by suggesting that Orozco's merging of cultural traditions is akin to Erdrich's (1996: 149). Rader seconds the title but seems to suggest it is not the one at Dartmouth but a different painting of the same name.

19　I cite these two in particular because, as very early examples of written epics (*Beowulf* a pre-1000 AD tale transcribed in Old English, *The Epic of Gilgamesh* from ancient Sumatra), they circulated first in oral traditions.

20　'I Was Sleeping Where the Black Oaks Move' (*J* 67–68).

3

Spatial relations: the *Love Medicine* tetralogy and *Tales of Burning Love*

Notwithstanding Womack's distaste for symbolist readings of Native Literature (2008: 7), Erdrich is, at least partly, a symbolist. *Love Medicine* begins with a scene replete with egg-related imagery. Explicit in Christian significance, the egg indicates the cycles of death and rebirth implicit in the Easter analogue of June Morrissey's 'transcendence'.[1] As many critics have noted, the eggs June shucks and eats while sitting in a bar; her sudden re-entry to the world when she exits 'Andy's' car; her death in the winter storm; the 'false homecoming' of its depiction; and her centrality to the rest of the novel, as friends and family remember her and reconcile that memory with their ongoing lives, are all evocative of a salvific presence in the novel:

> June had wedged herself so tight against the door that when she sprang the latch she fell out. Into the cold. It was a shock like being born . . . Even when her heart clenched and her skin turned crackling cold it didn't matter, because the pure and naked part of her went on.
> The snow fell deeper that Easter than it had in forty years, but June walked over it like water and came home. (*LM* 6–7)

Erdrich's use of egg imagery in this opening importantly includes intense focus on the shell specifically. 'Andy' peels painted eggs for June, watching as she gorges herself on the substance and sustenance beneath. She wears a 'shell', which is at once suggestive – 'it was no turtleneck. You called these things shells. He said he would peel that for her, too . . . and handed her the naked egg' (*LM* 2) – and indicative of her vulnerability:

> It was later still that she felt so fragile. Walking toward the Ladies' she was afraid to bump against anything because her skin felt hard and brittle, and she knew it was possible, in this condition, to fall apart at the

slightest touch . . . The pink shell was sweaty and hitched up too far
under her arms but she couldn't take off her jacket . . . because the pink
top was ripped across the stomach. (*LM* 4)

That fragility, her insubstantial 'shell' already pierced, compromised,
establishes her down-at-heel displacement.

This scene evokes the immanence *and* imminence of breaking
apart, through its emphasis on surface, at once brittle, fragile, and yet
revealing of heat and substance. Past, present, and future converge on
an always-already under-threat foundation. Secondarily, it anticipates
the contrast between the Williston-street dropout (June is quite
possibly a prostitute), vapour-thin, and the powerful 'substance' she
represents both for members of her home community and for the
novel as a whole. The further assertion that 'she knew that if she lay
there any longer she would crack wide open, not in one place but in
many pieces' (*LM* 6) confirms this sense of potential disintegration.
Jeanne Smith asserts a metaphysical cause: 'severed from her home,
she can no longer hold her body together' (1991: 14–15).[2] Through this
imagery of personal and social disintegration, set against a backdrop
that conjours and echoes such imagery – ' "When you're in the plains
and you're in this enormous space," Erdrich has stated, "there's
something about the frailty of life and relationships that always haunts
me" '[3] – Erdrich's characters begin the work of piecing those fragments
back together.

Cracking, splitting, falling apart, are metaphors returned to
throughout the novel: in the pies that are smashed later in the first
chapter; in depictions of what many see as community disintegration; in Henry Lamartine Jr.'s suicide; in Nector Kashpaw's senility; in
the dispossession of Lulu Lamartine, itself evoking the factionalism
mentioned in Chapter 1. The latter, grounding all this symbolism,
is itself figured in June's death, as if that death is an inevitable
consequence of earlier dispossession. As Albertine returns to the
reservation, drawn home by the belated news, she notes the 'joke' of
allotment, seeing 'how much of the reservation was sold to whites and
lost forever' (*LM* 12). It is returned to, as well, in later books: the
daashkikaa of *The Antelope Wife* refers multiply to the destruction of a
community, the severing of a family, the psychic disintegration of
several characters and, more profoundly, the mosaic-like distribution
of those resultant fragments through several generations of three
families. This simple image of broken surfaces reveals much of the

ground on which Erdrich's novels develop. Paradoxically it anticipates, for Jeanne Smith, the gathering sense of connectedness and *emplacement* in what she calls 'transpersonal selfhood' towards which *Love Medicine* at least navigates; it encodes the gulf between appearance and reality, the superficial and the substantial, emphasising particularly the transitional state; and, simply, the motif of splitting catalyses and then encodes the essential processes of personal survival and of negotiation between individual and community, of holding together the fragile shell. It is a metaphor for survival.

The novels

For all the nuances and diversions of the first five novels, these books are unified by both location, common characters, 'the intersection of Catholicism and the shamanistic religion of the Ojibwe' (Chapman 2007: 149), irony, and other elements to be explicated here that are explored to varying depths in each book. That location, a fictional 'non-space' resembling an amalgamation of several reservations and the landscape of (north)western Minnesota in particular, is firmly based around an unspecified reservation (presumably the 'Little No Horse' of the later novel), the border town of Argus, and the real cities of Fargo and Williston, North Dakota. The tetralogy, beginning with *Love Medicine* (1984; 1993), catalogues the lives and deaths of a number of individuals and families in a fictitious North Dakotan community. Erdrich charts the fluctuations of this community, its challenges and achievements, disasters and triumphs from a polyfocal perspective, through the eyes of various Euroamerican, Métis, and full-blood Native Americans. *The Beet Queen* (1986), *Tracks* (1988), and *The Bingo Palace* (1994) complete the quartet, although *Tales of Burning Love* (1996: *Tales* hereafter) also deals with many of the same characters.[4] A full summary of the events of five novels is untenable in this context but it is important to have a grasp of the main relationships that I will refer to in this chapter.

Tracks, the earliest chronologically (1912–1924), is alternately narrated by the old-time Ojibwe Nanapush to his granddaughter Lulu, and the abandoned Pauline Puyat, mixed-blood descendant of a forgotten clan of skinners. Nanapush, named after the trickster Nanabo'zho, represents (often ironically) an Ojibwe 'perspective', espousing the power and mystery of the shamanic Fleur Pillager and imparting the local legacy of consumption and winter deaths. Pauline, meanwhile, invests ever deeper into Catholic doctrine, seeking first sanctuary and then novitiate status at the local convent. As her ascetic fervour grows, she becomes an opposing force to Nanapush and Fleur and, later assuming the name of Sister Leopolda, comes, superficially, to embody a depiction of self-assured inviolability and violence in colonial missionary practice.

Love Medicine itself, arguably the best known of Erdrich's novels, is the most episodic of the quartet. Opening in 1981 the novel meanders its way back and forth through the fifty years between 1934 (the year of the Indian Reorganisation Act) and 1984. The 1993 reissue encompasses seven first-person and several third-person narratives across eighteen chapters, foregrounding three principal connected family groups: the Kashpaws, the Lazarre-Morrisseys, and the Lamartines, along with several members of more peripheral families including the Pillagers and the Nanapushes.[5] The novel begins, as above, with the death of June on her way home to the reservation. The narratives that follow offer alternative perspectives, insights, and snapshots relating to June's life and death, communal and individual struggles, and searches for emplacement in a changing world.

The Beet Queen, second in order of publication, covers a similar time span to *Love Medicine*, in this case 1932 to 1972, again achronologically. This novel deals principally with the Euroamerican Adare family and Adelaide's abandonment of her children, Karl, Mary, and a baby (Jude). While the baby is found and taken by a stranger, Mary and Karl find their way to the butcher shop run by their aunt Fritzie, her husband Pete Kozka, and their daughter Sita, in a small reservation border town called Argus. Karl runs away and is to make periodic reappearances in the novel, fathering Dot, the child of Mary and Sita's mixed-blood Indian friend Celestine (daughter of Dutch James and Regina Pillager), and conducting a love affair with the speculator Wallace Pfeff. Meanwhile the relationships between the three women, Mary, Sita, and Celestine, come under scrutiny as jealousy, the special interest taken in Mary by local nuns, and the challenging Dot – the misplaced Beet Queen – modulate their lives.

The Bingo Palace returns to the series' present, picking up in 1981 and culminating in 1995. This novel focuses closely on the individual struggles of the commercially minded Lyman Lamartine and his nephew Lipsha Morrissey, a young man on a spiritual (and sexual) quest. Both men struggle to find and consolidate their roles as mixed-blood Ojibwe in the modern world; they compete for the affections of the beautiful Shawnee Ray, and also over Lyman's plans to turn part of the reservation into a gaming complex. Characters come and go throughout the tetralogy, at times on the margins, at others as focal points. Events also repeat themselves, change with altering perspectives, are alternately clarified and obscured. Just as the tetralogy begins with the death of a dispossessed and disillusioned woman, it ends with the transcendent image of Fleur Pillager metamorphosing into a bear; it ends, in other words, in a new imagined beginning.

Picking up some of the threads of the earlier novels, *Tales* opens with a reiterative account of June's last liaison and her death in the blizzard. This time, however, the focus is on 'Andy', or Jack Mauser, the man she picks up in a Williston bar. Jack is a self-employed builder, a mixed-blood Indian passing as white, and general philanderer, who fakes his own death in a house fire as his business fails. He becomes the subject of stories told by his ex-wives, a survival technique when caught in a blizzard in the car that was supposed to be taking them from Jack's funeral. This novel is more immediately comical than the preceding four, with an 'unrealistically cheerful set of ending sequences' (Beidler and Barton 2006: 33), but it expands those narrative threads that lead to it from the tetralogy and that are reconnected in later novels.

Fragmentation and/or community: tribal nations, compromised states

The fragility of June's characterisation at the beginning of *Love Medicine* and in its revisited form in *Tales* is echoed throughout this series of novels. Many prominent studies of *Love Medicine* and the tetralogy more broadly, for instance, echo the titular claim of Larson's analysis of *Tracks*, 'The Fragmentation of a Tribal People'. That sense of fragmentation, encapsulated by tribal dissolution and familial dysfunction in the wake of the Dawes Severalty Act (allotment), is further reflected in the individual conflicts of the characters themselves, and in what Larson elsewhere describes as the 'liminality' of Erdrich's narrators (2000: 92).[6] Rainwater's earlier study, 'Reading between Worlds', supports this. 'Nanapush', she writes, 'grows up Christian in a Jesuit School, but later chooses life in the woods and Chippewa tradition', while Pauline 'is a mixed-blood raised in the Native American tradition, but she wishes to be white and eventually becomes a fanatical nun, constantly at war with the "pagans" who "had once been her relatives"' (1990: 405–6). This description both reinforces that claim for the marginality of the characters made by Larson and others, but often simplifies a more nuanced, possibly even contrapuntal, symbiosis[7] – a more positive understanding of Erdrich's early achievement, and the issues of transculturation and transformation she explores. Both Larson and Rainwater turn with great sensitivity to the interventions and exchanges of these novels and it is in that space somewhere between the representation of community fragmentation and the active reclamation of community 'participation' that our general focus on surface and substance, appearance and reality, will remain.

Individual challenges, such as Lipsha Morrissey's search for his parents and abortive attempts at traditional medicine practices (*LM*); or Jack Mauser's toothache (*TBL*), as the 'white' mud engineer of *Love Medicine* is revealed to be a mixed-blood man from June's own reservation; or Karl Adare's restless nature in *The Beet Queen*; function both microcosmically and metonymically in relation to those broader themes of fractured community, loss, dislocation, and oppression. Elizabeth Cook-Lynn's appraisal of this kind of representation, noted in Chapter 1, is damning. There is plenty to support such a reading – what she also calls a 'Christian-oriented apocalyptic vision' (1993: 30) – in these early novels of course. Lipsha's wandering, his dislocation from his people, his abandonment as a baby by his mother, June; the random appearances of his father, Gerry, a jailed activist; the drunken rages of June's ex-husband, Gordie, and their son, King; the vague ethereality of Indian presence in *The Beet Queen*; the ravages and conflicts of disease, allotment, and feuds in *Tracks*; all of these things speak, as a small selection of numerous examples, to that sense of disempowerment, even victimhood, that Cook-Lynn deplores. 'Tribe' in this context becomes little more than a collective – and collectively mismanaged – label for a group of misfits.

These same depictions, however, are means to address the very specific post-contact condition of Native, particularly mixed-blood, life in the United States. In *Other Destinies* Owens quotes an earlier work of postcolonial theory to address, and extrapolate from, the key concerns of John Joseph Mathews's novel *Sundown*:[8]

'A valid and active sense of self may have been eroded by dislocation, resulting from migration . . . Or it may have been destroyed by cultural denigration, the conscious and unconscious oppression of the indigenous personality and culture . . .' Like others in such a postcolonial drama, including nearly all Native Americans, Mathews's characters are beset by 'a pervasive concern with . . . identity and authenticity.' (Owens 1992: 50, qtg Ashcroft et al. 1989: 9)

Such themes are manifest in Erdrich's work too. In *Love Medicine*, Lipsha is beset by the need to discover his genealogy. Lulu Lamartine, abandoned by Fleur as a young child, is nurtured to a sense of her familial identity by Nanapush in *Tracks*. Nector Kashpaw, white educated and ambitious, having used his knowledge to better the situation of his family at the expense of the Pillagers, descends into blank senility (*Love Medicine, Tracks, Last Report*).[9] Henry Lamartine, Jr., a returning veteran from the Vietnam conflict, fails to refind his feet and ends his own life. These starkly individualised character-isations are common in Native writing, ubiquitous even, and deeply entrenched in the signifying phrase 'Native American literature'. The drifters, nomads, 'passers' (Nector in a sense, along with Jack in *Tales*), whether white or Indian, populate the pages of Erdrich's novels, while those characters close to the 'centre' of tribal culture such as Fleur and Moses Pillager, even Eli Kashpaw and, to a degree, Nanapush himself, are, with the exception of *Tracks*, frequently presented in peripheral terms, often uncomfortably close to stereotype: as woods-man (Eli), mad isolate (Moses), or fearsome mystic (Fleur).[10] It is not hard to see these characterisations in the light of Owens's analysis: but where *his* analysis is about reclamation and revitalisation, it is equally easy to understand Cook-Lynn's concerns about the persistence of colonisation in such representations of Indianness – not least in Owens's claim that these models speak to the concerns of '*nearly all Native Americans*'.

Such positions take account, inevitably, of only half the argument. Fleur Pillager, for instance, has become iconic for some for her strength in adversity, a woman who stands up to decreasing odds and refuses to be defeated. Nanapush lays claim to his white education in the service of his tribe when he runs for tribal council. Lyman Lamartine, despite his own defeat and the tragic loss of his brother, rises from the ashes of his own Bureau of Indian Affairs files to become an entrepreneur, although this, clearly, is problematic in light of the controversies surrounding the advent of Indian casinos and his own remorseless ambition. And then, when Lipsha brings his mother's car and his adoptive grandfather's ceremonial pipe home at the end of *Love Medicine*[11] and is 'rescued' by Fleur at the end of *The Bingo Palace*, it is difficult to see these homecomings as instances of negative or unreconstructed representation: the first is a return to centre, the second a suggestive legacy of one old-time healer to a new. Such representations are repeatedly explored, as in the contest between Lipsha and Lyman to take possession of Nector's pipe. Caught up in otherwise sympathetic arguments about his patrimony, indeed his identity, Lyman nevertheless repeatedly lowers his guard to reveal his quest for 'prestige' and his intention to '[p]ut it out where the public could see it, in a glass case maybe, right at the casino entrance', whereas for Lipsha it represents a present, active, spirituality rather than an historical artefact (*BP* 85–86). What is truly significant is not the either/or of the 'modern' and 'traditional' but the *process* of engagement whereby individuals, both with and despite their communities, respond to changing circumstances. The negotiation over the nature and function of the pipe – ostensibly also a tussle between free-market capitalism and what Christie sees as the 'post-capitalist' imperative (2009: 127–156) – opens dialogue, enlivening the space of sovereignty.

What is partly at stake is the viability of postcolonial strategies and paradigms, steeped as they are in European discourses, for under-standing Native American novels. Connecting the universalist para-digm of 'postcolonial theory' at large, through readings that focus on disarray, to an understanding that what Erdrich is doing offers insight into *Ojibwe* community is, in a very real sense, to ignore, if not occlude, the vitality of Ojibwe community more generally. One of the problems with the model that Owens identifies, founded at least partly on Erdrich's work, is that it becomes the archetype of *successful* Native literature, in other words those novels that have sold in significant numbers to white readerships, while fiction that sets out to empower specific communities and explicitly conduct the very real work of decolonisation, as both Cook-Lynn (1993) and Devon Mihesuah (2004) see it, goes largely ignored by mass audiences.[12] The field is developing rapidly, however, as scholars pursue ever more nuanced objectives. Of these, perhaps the most crucial is the further embedding of ethical, indigenist theoretical frameworks into the practice of Native Literary Studies. Alongside this, however, scholars need to rigorously interrogate the ways in which the likes of Owens and Arnold Krupat, in focusing on the mixed-blood question, have sought to *improve*, rather than simply *prove* those universalising frameworks already mentioned in relation to the diverse and (in comparison to ex-commonwealth and postcolonial states) intrinscially *different* experi-ences of the indigenous peoples of the Americas.[13]

Echoing the great white wail

Let's not denigrate the active work of disabusement manifest in
Erdrich's work, however, carrying as it does a different political
function to that advocated by Cook-Lynn et al. A prime example of the
above tension in the usable deconstructive work of Erdrich's texts can
be seen in an iconic moment in *Love Medicine*'s early stages. When
Nector is first introduced he is a senile old man. And yet his first
narration describes a young man at the peak of his vitality and in the
process of mastering his political identity. The Kashpaws had been
the 'last hereditary leaders' of the tribe yet he finds himself leaving his
1957 graduating class at Flandreau Indian School, South Dakota, for
the Hollywood Western set. To underline the irony, Nector is selected
for the 'biggest Indian part'. Being tall and lean he suits the producers'
vision of what a Native warrior should look like so gets the 'biggest'
role in both senses. His first scene turns out to be his only scene:
' "Clutch your chest. Fall off that horse," they directed . . . Death was
the extent of Indian acting in the movie theater' (*LM* 123).

A deeper satire of cultural representation follows, as Nector ends
up in Kansas, posing for a rich white female painter's masterpiece,
which would later hang in Bismarck, North Dakota. Having posed
semi-nude in her studio, he is later shocked when she shows him
'Plunge of the Brave'. 'There I was', he tells us, 'jumping off a cliff,
naked of course, down into a rocky river. Certain death' (*LM* 124). The
scene is straight out of a Fenimore Cooper novel – there is in fact a
similar scene in *The Last of the Mohicans* (1826) – and the imagery
of Cooper's constructed Indian, the noble savage, is clear. Pittman,
using a different American classic, suggests that this subversion of
canonical texts, as a reassertion of cultural tradition, is the principal
thrust of the scene:

> Nector is used again for a picaresque as well as postmodern engagement
> with the canon 'through a critical lampooning of some of [society's]
> favourite literature' – specifically *Moby-Dick*. By having Nector live the
> 'marginal man's career of deception' through his identification with both
> Ishmael and Ahab, Erdrich engages in a dialogue with the canon that
> subverts its power . . . When Nector tells his mother, Rushes Bear, that
> the novel is about a 'great white whale,' she wants to know what 'they
> got to wail about those whites'. (1995: 781)

Whereas in Cooper's version the Native presence is fleeting and
terminal, in this one it is the artist who disappears as Nector takes

off for pastures new. The painting, despite what it depicts, becomes a site of resistance to hegemonic narratives as the scene subtly, humourously, subverts the power dynamic, undercutting the romantic grandeur of the Cooperesque image. As a whole it undermines the stoical stereotype of the Hollywood death scene. Where the picture is supposed to be tragic, pathetic, nostalgic, bearing witness to the demise of the 'primitive', the narrative is comic: 'I was paid by this woman ... a round two hundred dollars for standing stock still in a diaper'.

It also plays on many of the tropes of American art – the Hudson River School and allegorical landscapes of the mid-nineteenth century and, of course, the constructed scenes of artists such as George Caitlin and later photographers like Edward Curtis, who found their vocation in visually documenting the 'Vanishing American'. The scene exposes the constructedness of such representations. As Nector insightfully notes, 'Remember Custer's saying? The only good Indian is a dead Indian? Well from my dealings with whites I would add to that quote: "The only interesting Indian is dead or dying by falling backwards off a horse" (*LM* 124). Even the misidentification of Sheridan's misquote is a pointed echo of the homogenisation and invention implicit in these various clichés; an image of what Vizenor calls the hyperreal simulation of the 'Indian'.

We are well used to the colonial narrative of brutalisation of 'virgin' territories: the pillaging by an aggressive patriarchy that in turn brutalises itself to the point of emasculation (a necessary oversimplification of a complex dynamic). In this scene, Erdrich inverts it. As Nector enters her studio, the artist 'put me on a block of wood and then said to me, "Disrobe"'. He pretends not to understand, until she eventually hollers, '"Take off your clothes!"' The semi-naked male model subjected to the dominant and domineering female gaze heightens the comedy and the subversion. By subverting expectations, this scene forces readers to address the issue of the objectification – indeed the fetishisation – of the other, as well as the prior oppression and exploitation that the scene references. Given that this scenario does involve a female agent dominating a male 'object' it is tempting to take a negative view: that this is an example of the emasculation or infantilisation of the displaced, dispossessed, Native man. But Nector/ Erdrich further undermines that possibility on two levels.

The first, as in Rushes Bear's mishearing of 'whale', 'calls attention to barriers between oral and written traditions' (Pittman 1995: 781). At the first command to disrobe, he pretends not to understand her.

' "What robe?" ' he asks, projecting his very real embarrassment on to her in a comedic act of defiance. The second is that he refuses subjugation, escapes the 'snaggle toothed old wreck of a thing' (a likely rendition of Britannia given the early republic connotations of the painting), and more importantly 'got out of the rich lady's picture'. So while the picture tells a nostalgic fantasy of romantic tragedy, the narrative confronts that grand narrative, resists its doctrine, and moves beyond it to a living present in which the Indian subject is recast as a Native agent who escapes and survives subjugation; the Cooper-esque construction escapes the page. While Pittman's assertions are apposite, there is a deeper significance here, in that the events almost literally thrust Nector, by stages, into political life, returning him both to the family 'tradition', to the centre of community life, and to the core of contests for political agency, however flawed, as the only way, long term, to truly defeat those key cultural traps.

This move is not, of course, unambivalent, returning us to Cook-Lynn's rebuke of Erdrich's 'anti-tribal' representations. Nector leaps out of the painting into modern tribal politics and his trajectory there results in betrayal, symptomatic of the factional feuds that thread through the tetralogy and presenting an image of tribal politics as a compromise, tainted by the mechanisms through which it must operate. While his penmanship as a youngster seems to indicate positive agency, it is later undermined by his willingness to pay off the Kashpaw parcel with the Pillager bond, leading to Fleur's exile. Nevertheless it forces said politics to the foreground as a running theme for those 'doomed' and ineffectual men, so that other than Nector, we also see Lyman pursuing his business ventures after the 'rebirth' he experiences following his brother Henry's death. Lyman is drawn from his grief by bureaucracy:

> Here, to my surprise, I had ended up a nobody. I could die now and leave no ripple. Why not! I considered, but then I came up with the fact that my death would leave a gap in the BIA records, my IRS account would be labeled incomplete until it closed. There would be minor confusion. These thoughts gave me a warm jolt. In cabinets of files, anyway, I still maintained existence. The government knew me though the wind and the earth did not. I was alive, at least on paper. I was someone. I owed cash. (LM 300–1)

It is ironic, but pertinent, that Lyman is revivified through the inability to find a paper clip, which would allow him to file, and therefore forget, an IRS notice.

Countering the negative edge of Nector's portrayal, the pursuit of
bureaucracy also preoccupies Nanapush towards the end of *Tracks*,
when, having earlier resisted Father Damien's urging to work *with*
rather than against the local Indian agent, he concedes:

> That's when I began to see what we were becoming, and the years have
> borne me out: a tribe of file cabinets and triplicates, a tribe of single-space
> documents, directives, policy. A tribe of pressed trees. A tribe of chicken-
> scratch that can be scattered by a wind, diminished to ashes by one struck
> match.
>
> For I did stand for tribal chairman, as you know, defeating Pukwan in
> that last year. To become a bureaucrat myself was the only way that I
> could wade through the letters, the reports, the only place where I could
> find a ledge to kneel on, to reach through the loophole and draw you
> home. (*T* 225)

Given the despoliation of Ojibwe lumber in Minnesota in the early
twentieth century, the figure of the tree here speaks immediately to
the wasting of vitality in the form of bureaucracy, and the myriad other
ways colonial and then American powers stripped the Ojibwe of land
and language. It becomes in Nanapush's hands, however, a means to
assert autonomy and, undoing a set of stereotypes in the process
(including the notion that Indians don't do politics), reassert control of
the figures and images, including releasing Lulu from residential
school. Most importantly of all, those documents – the maps and
treaties in particular – emblems as they are of imposition, become,
through the kind of advocacy Nanapush represents, means by which
sovereignty can be reasserted; an irony most deeply illustrated by
Fleur's cabin being lined with treaty papers.

The ongoing 'territorialisation' of Erdrich's fiction is arguably one
further facet of this whole argument. As critics seek to 'map' what is
often referred to as a 'Chippewa landscape', so the topography of
Erdrich's fiction resists such literal mapping. For Cook-Lynn this lack
of specificity is a deficiency but it can be read, in light of the issues
raised here, in more positive, more resistant, terms, following Maria
DePriest's recent reading of *Tracks*, as 'retriev[ing] the blank space on
the [colonial] map' (2008: 251). The psychic geographies the fiction
depicts are concretised through these documentary hooks while
simultaneously – through their fluid outlines – refusing to allow the
fiction to wholly consume realities on the ground as if Erdrich were
truly seeking to *represent* the Ojibwe. Reclaiming those narratives
(including cartographic narratives) of dispossession resists further

critical acts of *re*mapping; if the 'reclamation' is, as it may be, as much a matter of accident as strategy, it is, nevertheless, far from a 'vague' political failing.

Those readings that foreground tribal dissipation, nascent individualism, and the corruption of older systems and values – elements that reflect, and respond to, the metropolitan centre rather than stressing collective strategies of resistance – echo the ethnographic record, which focuses on atomisation (Hallowell 1947; Barnouw 1950).[14] Even as Hickerson showed the limitations of Barnouw's conclusions (arguing that the Plains Ojibwe adopted many plains customs, stressing transculturation and continuity in change (1962)), that prevailing sense, speaking as it did to the myth of the vanishing American and highlighting anthropological concern with how the Ojibwe *had* lived, rather than how they *do* live, drip fed into the popular imagination and into a casual misunderstanding of the nature of the relationship between the Ojibwe past and present.

Making a broader point about Native literatures, a critique that includes her own book *From the River's Edge*, Cook-Lynn notes: 'Seemingly overwhelmed by violence, self-hate, romanticism, blame, mournfulness, loss, or anger, the [American Indian] writers seem to suggest that there is little room for liberation literature, little use for nationalistic/tribal resistance' (1993: 85). Elsewhere, she more critically appraises Erdrich's early achievement in the following terms: 'In the 1980s, the . . . saga of an inadequate Chippewa political establishment and a vanishing Anishinabe culture suggests the failure of tribal sovereignty and the survival of myth in the modern world. Erdrich's conclusion is an odd one, in light of the reality of Indian life in the substantial Native enclaves of places like South Dakota or Montana or Arizona or New Mexico' (1996b: 125–126). Erdrich herself notes that the role of the Native American author is, '[i]n the light of enormous loss', to 'tell the stories of contemporary survivors while protecting and celebrating the cores of cultures left in the wake of the catastrophe' (2001b: 48). This sentiment, although potentially reductive in its implicit understanding of 'culture', nevertheless speaks positively to its survival and celebration, remembering Cook-Lynn's frequent emphasis on authorial intent. What cannot of course be accounted for is critical and public reception. Emphasis on 'catastrophe' pervades the criticism, indicative for McKinney of a 'cultural schizophrenia' in American society (1998).

Starkly at odds with Womack's assertive rhetorical question, 'Just what is there to write about that is more important than Native authors testifying to surviving genocide and advocating sovereignty and survival?' (2000: 7), such intense focus on loss fails in both the resistance work advocated by Owens and the decolonisation imperative of Mihesuah. Turning back to Larson, however, we might also be mindful of Sarris's insistence that Native writers and scholars need to open up to talking about pain:

> The erosion of social ties, in both mainstream U.S. culture and in Indian communities, and the elevation of individual autonomy and resentment of culture as essential conditions for achieving authenticity have promoted false or deficient sense of being, and this is the primary problem faced by both [United States and Indian] societies today. (Larson 2000: 76–77)

Such an implicit process of ressentiment leading to rapprochement is at the heart of Erdrich's work. It is indeed this very agenda that is central to her depictions of fragmentation. Erdrich's 'subtle fabric of alienation, deracination, and despair' speaks to this more universal canvas of 'tangled lives' (Owens 1992: 204, 205), refuting as it reworks the absorption and occlusion inherent in the 'plight' narrative. So Erdrich's work sits centrally in this ongoing contest. As one of the most prolific of Cook-Lynn's 'mixed-bloods' her work reaches possibly the largest audience of any Native writer; as one of Owens's 'mixedbloods' it speaks consistently to the issues of marginalisation and reassertion of Indian identity of which he speaks. For readers of both Erdrich and Mathews, and Cook-Lynn and Mihesuah; of both Krupat and Owens, and Womack and Warrior, Erdrich's work often compellingly becomes a site of contest over interpretive shifts and methodological models and it is this intersection, above all, that still awaits full and frank exploration. There are, however, key examples around and within the early novels that bring that need into sharp focus, not least the controversy sparked by Leslie Silko in her 1986 review of *The Beet Queen*.

The Silko controversy

Leslie Silko's review begins with a commendation of Erdrich's prose style ('dazzling and sleek . . . I call this "poet's prose"') that becomes an act of condemnation: 'Erdrich's prose is an outgrowth of academic, post-modern, so-called experimental influences . . . Self-referential writing has an ethereal clarity and shimmering beauty because no history or politics intrudes to muddy the well of pure necessity contained within language itself, (1986: 179). That the novel transmits a privileged perspective for Silko is palpable: 'In Erdrich's hands, the rural North Dakota of Indian-hating, queer-baiting white farmers, of the Depression, becomes magically transformed. Or maybe 'transported.' Rural New Hampshire seems a far more probable location for *The Beet Queen* and its characters, white and Indian, straight and gay' (1986: 180). What is at stake in this for Silko is not so much Erdrich's point of view as it is the occlusion of the *Realpolitik* in mainstream celebration of a 'representative' author:

> *The Beet Queen* is a strange artifact, an eloquent example of the political climate in America in 1986. It belongs on the shelf next to the latest report from the United States Civil Rights Commission, which says black men have made tremendous gains in employment and salary. This is the same shelf that holds the *Collected Thoughts of Edwin Meese on First Amendment Rights* and Grimm's *Fairy Tales*. (1986: 185)

In a note to the reprint of Silko's review, the editors of *SAIL* interestingly encourage readers to consult Rubins's positive review of *The Beet Queen* in the *New York Review of Books* for January 1987.[15] They go on, however, to note that 'It marks the beginning of a critical definition of Erdrich as something other than a fine "ethnic" or "Native American" novelist endeavoring to incorporate her into the fictional "mainstream"' (Silko 1986: 179). Silko's argument is clearly not that only stories that reinforce violence and difference can be told of Indian–white conflict. It does seem, however, that for her the novel's strange ahistoricism itself challenges sovereignty, not only relegating the Indians to the periphery but removing their agency, violence being implicit in any easy assimilation to the 'mainstream'. This makes the *SAIL* editorial seem all the stranger when they continue:

> This process seems an inevitable one . . . They, and we, will be required to re-imagine the nature and function of Indian literary art in contemporary society, not least through confronting the issue of whether 'Indian' is just another 'ethnic' group, or something distinctively and specially 'American.' (1986: 179)

Unlikely to alleviate Silko's unease, this anticipates the contest between 'cosmopolitan' and tribal nationalist modes of engagement.

Connie Jacobs accuses the critical response of fanning the flames (2001: 40) but actually the apparent divergence, described by Erdrich as a misreading of her novel, is instructive.[16] Key responses to Silko's review come in the form of a direct riposte by Susan Castillo (1991); several passing mentions by Louis Owens; a brief reinforcement by Cook-Lynn (1993); opposition by Vizenor, who rejected Silko's use of the word postmodern 'to mean separation from communal experience' (1989c: xii), and an essay addressing the 'Indianness' of *The Beet Queen* by Walsh and Braley (1994).[17] While these are not the only judgements of the novel and its subsequent review, they do serve to crystallise the issues at stake. Besides the narrative issues quoted above, Silko is most concerned with the absence of racially motivated enmity in the 1930s North Dakota of the novel, citing the friendship between Sita, Mary, and Celestine, and the static representation and marginalisation of Russell – and the reservation – as most problematic. Accusing Erdrich of 'swallow[ing] white sexist standards of beauty rather than challenging them' (1986: 182) and reflecting the implicit racism of the time and place without dealing with its explicit manifestations, she perhaps overlooks some of the work's subtler nuances.

Castillo, for instance, interrogates Russell's opacity:

> [S]urely it is significant that Russell is trotted out by the white Establishment of Argus to display his scars at patriotic parades . . . Silko herself has movingly described the figure of the Indian war veteran in her portrayal of Tayo in Ceremony; but it must be said that Tayo, like Russell, is somewhat unidimensional. As Marxist theorists like Pierre Macherey have demonstrated, a text is linked to ideology by its silences as well as by that which it explicitly states. Erdrich's silences are often very eloquent indeed, and are perhaps more politically effective than overt sloganeering. (1991: 288)

The silences Castillo identifies include the implicit sexism of both the narrative span (1932–1972) and the present (1980s/90s) in which the exclusion of Native women from mainstream anthologies may be attributed to 'her status as a woman, *or* a Native American, *or* both' (1991: 288, emphasis added). That coalescing of spheres of prejudice is also manifest in the general marginalisation of most of the characters – Wallace and Karl as homo/bisexual, for instance – that might, actually, *reflect* the political climate despite being attributed to 'internal psychological conflicts' (Castillo 1991: 288). Given that the novel is cast from the points of view of these liminal figures, attempting to deal with their own internal struggles, caught up in the stifling atmosphere of small-town community, the resultant myopia is effective. Given also that the novel deals largely with the immigrant/ Euroamerican community, the resultant ephemerality of the reservation – very much epitomised by the predominance of air and flight imagery – becomes a representation that is *reflective* rather than overtly demonstrative of the moment. Is Russell opaque, then, because we readers are on the border looking in and because that ready elision reflects disenfranchisement more generally even while it glosses over specific local circumstances? Such a depiction reveals, without necessarily condemning, the social/ethnic hierarchy.

As Castillo again notes:

> Paradoxically, the cultural ambivalence reflected in *The Beet Queen* may be mimetic in character, mirroring the fragmented ontological landscape in which many Native Americans exist today, shuttling between radically diverse realities. This diversity can be seen, however, not only as potentially alienating, but also as a source of creative ferment and positive historical change. (289)

Owens's early response reinforces this sense of the novel's political landscape: 'The story is one of men and women without reservations, hung out to dry on the flat, dull edge of the North Dakota-Minnesota heartland in a small town that could be anywhere or nowhere' (1992: 205). Later claiming an emphasis on *internalised* colonialism and racism (1998: 73), Owens notes that 'Russell's inarticulateness underscores his physical dearticulation by American culture', a 'hauntingly mute Indian presence' (1992: 206). Placing Russell alongside characters like Fleur and Moses Pillager and, to a lesser degree, Step-and-a-Half (*Master Butchers*), this speaks to a kind of survival unacknowledged by the mainstream. In Russell's case, it is only when he is in 'familiar' role – dead, dying, 'stuffed' spectacle – that he is recognisable to the white community. In subtle ways, *The Beet Queen* underscores the persistent discrimination against and disdain for Native Americans. As with Nector above, in Russell's character Erdrich both draws from and quietly undermines generic stereotypes.

None of this deals with Silko's major point about racism and racial conflict, of course. The reality of this situation was not atmospheric, it was real, it involved violence, but this depends on understanding the novel as a realist text. Robert Morace, by contrast, develops a reading directly through Mikhail Bakhtin's theories of the carnivalesque:

'Between the scenes of abandonment with which it opens and the complementary and rather conventional scenes of redemption with which it closes, *The Beet Queen* is a tour de force of comic grotesquerie' (Morace 1999: 48). Morace's reading draws in all of the early novels, highlighting the full range of the Bakhtinian carnivalesque: from the dialogic, comic, polyphonic and heteroglossic, through the intertextual, grotesque, chronotopic, to the close associations of sex, food, and death, and other features of Rabelaisian chaos. He echoes prior reference to Bakhtin and is echoed by others, such as Winter (2000) or Clarke (1992). Rainwater describes Karl Adare with reference to the Fool in a Tarot deck; like the joker in a pack of cards the jester image is a key motif of carnival (Jacobs 2001: 208 fn. 18). These readings, though, as Morace acknowledges in a swift rebuttal of Silko's 'more-Native-American-than-thou (and error-prone) review' (1999: 64 fn. 5), stand somewhat at odds with the Native political engagement Silko demands. Prioritising the postmodern literary technique over the historical moment, many readers question the efficacy – perhaps even the ethics – of such Euro-western theory-bound readings. Morace makes a clear and persuasive case, not least when he demonstrates the ways in which the literary techniques themselves engage in the political processes Silko expects, such as Lyman Lamartine's 'comic decrowning' in *Love Medicine* (Morace 1999: 41), a transient ritual dissolution of the economic hierarchy. In real terms, such moments serve to appraise, redefine, and confirm community – and, indeed, to provide some light relief. This is clearly highly pertinent to *The Beet Queen*, in which several of its narrative strands reach their denouement during the Beet Carnival.

Fundamentally, it is play itself – of language, of reference – that is at stake in such readings. That playfulness of reference is deeply illuminated by Morace: Argus, he points out, may be named for 'the hundred-eyed giant charged with guarding the heifer' (1999: 48), in which case might we understand the town as *both* refuge and danger? Carnival aside, the emphasis in this image on eyes (the creature, after all, is called Argus *Panoptes*) hints at the almost prying nature of small towns, wherein everyone knows everyone else's business. Erdrich does speak in interview of the discomfort of being different in the small-town setting but Morace misses a neat coincidence: one of the earliest newspapers to come out of North Dakota was called the *Argus*, predecessor to other Fargo-based newspapers.[18] Again, the invocation of a daily rag, whether intentional or not, speaks to that gossipy sense of community surveillance. It is precisely this kind of potential slippage in signification that both invites and resists straightforward literary taxonomy. If these apparent carnivalesque tropes in *The Beet Queen* teach us anything it is the dangers of easy categorisation.

But there are other ways of approaching the lack that Silko perceives. The first, prioritising Native-centred readings that engage such things as trickster narratives, is common and will be touched on later in this chapter. Indeed, Morace quotes Daniel Cornell, who draws the parallel between the carnivalesque and the trickster figure (1999: 37). In either framework, the subversive force of the humour in Erdrich's work is abundant. The second is far simpler: *The Beet Queen* participates in a broader arrangement of textual narratives than that contained within its covers. The community in *The Beet Queen* is an ephemeral lacuna, self-contained and united in its disunity. Argus, on the edge of the reservation, is a liminal state in itself. Peopled effectively by misfits, the novel narrates the larger than life 'near-misses' of its cast, encapsulated perhaps most brutally in the figure of Sita (Kozka) Tappe. Her warning to her once-friend Celestine, ' "You'll eat shit with the chickens someday too" ' (*BQ* 279) indicates her own sense of mortality, reflected in a psychosomatic loss of voice, an addiction to medication, and a compulsive-obsessive cleaning habit, all finally subverted by the black comedy of her suicide. *The Beet Queen* carries a sense of the same quirkiness as 'regionalist' classics like Sherwood Anderson's *Winesburg, Ohio* (1919). Its politics are deeply embedded in the tangled lives of its often strange inhabitants. Egalitarian in the sense that nobody, upstanding or otherwise, is too 'big' to caricature, it opens up small-town life to excoriating satire. What results is a darkly comic interlude of sorts between the intensity of *Love Medicine*'s narrative demands and the sombre depths of *Tracks*' historicism. Taking those more tribally focused narratives as 'first position', Foster has recently said, 'I see the connection of the tribal and regional to be acts pursuing the same project of knowing ourselves and the world' (2008: 270). In this context, the novel's relationship to the two that frame it is fundamental.[19] Exploring other relational dimensions of the Midwestern canvas might not be so inappropriate to the overall project after all. The novel contains thematic threads, alongside common characters, that pertain to all five of the early novels. Elements of *Love Medicine* – not least the presence of Argus as a spectral figure on the edge of the reservation – are explored through *The Beet Queen*. It is only in reading *The Beet Queen* within the whole of the tetralogy – a task aided by the publication of *Tales*, which reduces the anomalous sense of the Argus novel – that it fully coheres. As Clute notes, for instance, 'Both Nanapush and Pauline are necessary for the understanding of Argus in 1980' (1995: 128). Taken in sum, the series reflects the strains and strands of the parallel communities of Erdrich's multiple heritage, sometimes overlapping and enmeshed, sometimes jarringly discrete.

More concretely, the two later novels *The Bingo Palace* and *Tales* expand and modify the earlier narrative. In *The Bingo Palace*, for instance, we learn that Russell Kashpaw is a respected and productive member of the community. Following his return from Vietnam he runs a tattoo parlour and, significantly, rescues Lipsha from a beating (although even here Lipsha describes him as a statue, a 'native Paul Bunyan' (*BP* 66)). This view of him, located as it is within the reservation boundaries, is a somewhat different picture than that provided on the streets of Argus. Furthermore, that violence and the vandalism of Lipsha's van respond to the absence of racism in *The Beet Queen*. The exchange Lipsha has with one of the perpetrators, a cashier at an all-night gas station, is charged with racially bound hostility:

> 'Take the money,' I order him. 'Hand over my change and I'll be out of here. Don't make me do something I'd regret.'
> 'I'd be real threatened.' The guy turns from me, ringing up my sale. 'I'd be shaking, except I know you Indian guys are chickenshit.'
> As I turn away with my purchase, I hear him mutter something and I stop. I thought I heard it, but I wasn't sure I heard it. Prairie nigger. (*BP* 71)

That Lipsha's own aggressive-defensiveness is the catalyst for these events is indicative of the balance of cause and effect – without prescriptive judgement as to its historical causes – while his response to his own bravado is intriguing in light of Silko's specific criticism: 'It's strange how a bashful kind of person like me gets talkative in some of our less pleasant border-town situations' (*BP* 71).

Ultimately, the vengeful aspect of this collision is entirely contained by the white youths' willingness to pursue and harass Lipsha. This narrative, however, parallels a number of other 'internal' conflicts in the novel: June's abuse at the hands of her mother Lucille and her boyfriend Leonard; Lipsha and Lyman's rivalry over Shawnee Ray Toose; the aimlessness of Lipsha's early adulthood; the individualistic

materialism of Lyman, even more pronounced than in *Love Medicine*.
Furthermore, the greater spiritual outcome of Lyman's vision quest
over the more spiritual Lipsha, and the ambivalence of internalised
prejudice exemplified by Jack Mauser's 'passing' narrative in *Tales*, all
reinforce Erdrich's refusal to neatly resolve the essential ambiguities
and conflicts of her characters' lives. It is not that they exist in an
historical vacuum but that they endure against the odds.

Culture, Catholicism, syncretism

The above discussion hardly conforms to Cook-Lynn's conception
of Silko's 'effort to examine forms of narrative which do or do not
express the ideology of the modern nation' (1996a: 90) but it is in that
intersection and the interactions between her ancestries and their
culturally informed worldviews that criticism most consistently
dwells. The conventional readings of the dialectic at play in *Tracks* in
particular suggest that Erdrich stages a contest between Christianity
(Pauline/Leopolda) and 'old time' Ojibwe spiritual practice (Nanapush
and Fleur). While there is an essential truth to the dichotomy, and
certainly Nanapush's status as Ojibwe patriarch, while nuanced, is
never in doubt, it is the true power of Erdrich's work that nothing is
quite so simple as the binary model of Ojibwe–Catholic opposition or
even syncretism might suggest, even while Erdrich herself describes
the experience of being versed in both traditions as being ' "Torn . . .
honestly torn" ' (Chavkin and Chavkin 1994: 230).

Images of Catholicism abound, from the 'face of Christ' in the ice
in *The Beet Queen*, to Marie's attempts to achieve 'Saintly' virtue in her
epic battle with Sister Leopolda at the convent (*Love Medicine*). These
scenes, though often grisly, are again invariably comic and serve up a
deep satire of piety. Marie's hubris is repeatedly undermined through
the nature of her struggle with the equally hubristic Sister Leopolda.
The face in the ice is drawn out to comic effect by the fact that it is
actually the imprint of Mary Adare's visage, who smashed her face into
the ground at the bottom of an icy slide; that she sees her brother Karl's
face in its place; and that the community is so desperate for witness
that it invests in the 'miraculous' explanation. A similar striving for
miraculous explanation enfolds the climax of Sister Leopolda's life in
Tales. Worshipping at the feet of the statue of Mary, the elderly myopic
nun fails to remember that it has been removed in lieu of the new

statue, or to see that it is actually Jack Mauser on the plinth. There is
an oblique irony in that she now experiences the only true personal
epiphany of her life and then immediately dies:

> it seemed to her that the Virgin leaned down off her pedestal, and . . .
> transferred the carved bundle she carried into the cradle of the nun's
> arms.
>   Leopolda's head snapped back to her chest . . . her heart cracked, she
> pitched straight over, and was granted her request [to 'end this torment'].
> (*TBL* 53)

The mixture of piety (abject though it may be) and comedy in this now
parodic figure ironically lends Leopolda a sense of pathos in those final
moments.

Leopolda's sense of martyred forsakenness summarises *both* her
devotion and her cynicism, apparently reinforcing her role as a motif
of cross-cultural destruction. The point is emphasised when she refers
to Christ's crucifixion and subsequent resurrection as a 'trick': 'And,
too, you understand the love a child bears its mother, its father, a
parent bears its child. It is a love that is no other thing but pure
salvation, and by it, Christ's balancing trick was inspired and foretold
. . . We are held upon the cross by our own desires' (*TBL* 370–372).
Given that physical desire has been the very thing she has most forcibly
suppressed, her observation is profound and pathetic, emphasising
a more basic desire to belong. ' "Hear my prayer!" ' she implores, ' "Day
wi kway ikway!" ', exemplifying in one sentiment the pull of her life's
struggle between two apparently opposing ways of life.

Leopolda's lifelong struggle is taken account of by higher forces, of
course. Eleanor's assertion that 'Leopolda wouldn't mind lying in
the grass until she was naturally discovered' leads to the old nun's
cremation by lightning, the depositing of her ash in cruciform,
and the subsequent ecstatic response of her followers and believers
(*TBL* 56). The constant interplay of sacred and profane here provides
effective comedy – from rumours of assumption which cause Father
Jude to produce evidence that cases of human combustion and
conflagration had been documented before by the North Dakota state
weather bureau (63), to the gust of wind that carries off the ashes
just as the decision to fix the remaining ash in place and put the
whole site under glass, to consecrate it as a holy shrine, has been taken
(63). It is a fitting tribute for Leopolda, who in *Tracks* renounces all
worldly things for mostly ambiguous and questionable reasons, that

she wholly returns to nature, *con*sumed at least if not inhumed. Her lifecycle is thus completed, her devotion rewarded, the death that destroys her childhood in *Tracks* finally manifested in something beautiful:

> Perhaps because Eleanor had torn off boughs of honeysuckle and mock orange for Mauser and now remembered that their bloom was over, their season finished, she was the only one who paid attention to the actual source of the flowers. . . . for three weeks after the incident the blossoms on the old nun's favorite bushes renewed in such dense profusion and number that the fragrance wafted halfway around the building at night. (*TBL* 63–64)

The nun's transcendental fate brings her to a similar spiritual plane to that inhabited by June. She becomes more than ever a haunting influence for Eleanor, and a lasting symbol – paradoxically – of love and devotion, a re-visioning that is to ensure a similar instability to fixed ideas of Pauline/Leopolda's role in *Last Report*.

Her life begins of course in corporeal, macabre – if no less darkly comical – despair. In *Tracks* the contest between Pauline and Nanapush/Fleur is, on the surface, a starkly drawn battle between traditionalism and what Horne describes as colonial mimicry (2004). Nanapush is named after the Ojibwe creator-trickster Nanabo'zho (Nanabush, Wenabajo).[20] Fleur Pillager, whose family is well known for their 'magical' affinities, is linked to the water monster Misshepeshu (Micipijiu, Michibizhii, a clawed creature noted not for evil but for the ambivalence of nature itself) in Matchimanito Lake, since those saved from drowning were often said to have made an agreement of union with the water spirits. The real Pillagers after whom she is named were a strong traditionalist unit, tribal guards, who eventually settled on the edge of White Earth Reservation. A member of the bear clan like them, she echoes their role as camp guards, resistors of change, and traditionally dwelling at the extremities of their community, while her mystical heritage is emphasised by her apparent transmogrification into a bear at the end of *The Bingo Palace*.

In *Tracks*, Pauline is orphaned by the devastating consumption that decimates the reservation population: 'We heard that wood could not be sawed fast enough to build the houses for their graves . . . by the time they got around to it the brush had grown, obscuring . . . the marks of burials. The priests tried to discourage the habit of burying the dead in trees, but the ones they dragged down had no names to them' (*T* 15). It is only in her dreams that Pauline 'saw [her] sisters and [her] mother swaying in the branches, buried too high to reach, wrapped in lace [she] never hooked' (*T* 15). There is a clear significance to the further dislocation of Pauline's being prevented from participating in the grieving process – a symptom, perhaps, of her dispossession. She attaches herself to Fleur, who refuses to yield to the young girl's curiosity and needs, and it is this further alienation that leads her, gradually, into her ascetic life. Amidst large-scale loss, 'Catholicism at least allowed one to face [death] with resignation' (McKinney 1998: 156). Pauline takes this one step further, embracing death as a vocation:

> I handled the dead until the cold feel of their skin was a comfort, until I no longer bothered to bathe once I left the cabin but touched others with the same hands, passed death on.
> We set them praying into the ground if they were Christians, or if unconverted, along the death road of the Old Ones, with an extra pair of shoes. It was no matter to me what happened after life. I didn't care. (*T* 69)

The death of others becomes a comfort for Pauline, a territory. When Pauline joins the nuns at the convent, Erdrich advances this imagery, turning her into a harbinger figure, quite literally an angel of death. As Rainwater accuses the colonial powers of cannibalising indigenous cultures, so Pauline here embodies that image. Her position, as 'death's bony whore' for Sophie Morrissey (*T* 86), is spiritualised as she takes her vows of celibacy. She connects death with love/sex when she says of herself, '[d]eath would pass me over just as men did, and I would live a long, strict life' (*T* 75). Inverting the process of procreation, she undertakes to 'steal' souls for Christ – a vampiric image of cultural necrosis.

The role Pauline performs is easily subsumed beneath symbolic readings of her role in a Manichean allegory. The source of that subsumption is her greed, generally taken as a marker of western individualism. Foremost is the sense of desire to see herself as an immortal being, someone other than the vulnerable mixed-blood orphan that she really is. She is reborn and reinvigorated – although of course further abnegated – when she takes on her new name, Sister Leopolda:[21]

> I am now sanctified, recovered, and about to be married here at the church in our diocese and by our Bishop. I will be the bride and Christ

> will take me as wife, without death . . . I asked for the grace to accept, to
> leave Pauline behind, to remember that my name, any name, was no
> more than a crumbling skin. (*T* 204–205)

In this sense, Pauline becomes a visionary, aware of, and contributing
to, the expected fall of the old life, grasping the new. Others, such
as Friedman (1994), have read this dualism through 'hybrid' frameworks. Others still, in a useful development of the conflictual reading,
have stressed the ways in which such struggles between opposing
forces are emic aspects of Anishinaabe cosmology, not external
impositions.

Pauline's burnt arms (self-inflicted wounds) give her hands the
aspect of claws, contributing to the imagery above. Simultaneously,
however, she is described in birdlike terms as an old lady, likened by
herself and Nanapush to the scavenger bird, blue jay, Windigobineshi
(O'Hagan 1995: 61). Given her position as a Native American turning
on her people, it is tempting to draw allusions to various trickster
figures, such as Raven, frequently cited in pan-Indian terms, or to
other deistic figures, such as Thunderbird, a traditional enemy of the
water monster who, as noted, is allied with Fleur.[22] Other apposite
analogies include *Ko-ko-ko*, the owl, omen of death and guardian of
the Wa'bano, witches whom McCafferty describes as the frequent
subject of a struggle with 'a culture hero, such as White Rabbit or
Nanabush' in Ojibwe and Menominee traditional literature. 'The battle
of wit, strength, and stamina, in which players develop, test, and prove
their powers', McCafferty continues, 'demonstrates a shifting and
often adversarial nature to universal power alignments' (1997: 737).
Alternatively, Pauline's greed is central to another Ojibwe figure, the
cannibalistic Windigo. So, the ravages of the missionary – and by
extension colonial – endeavour aside and following O'Hagan's
reading, she also presents an intra-tribal threat:

> By Western tradition, Pauline is a prototypical mixed-blood who is
> torn between two cultures . . . However, traditional Ojibway will not
> necessarily read Pauline as simply an aspiring European-American.
> There is a figure within the Ojibway tradition and cosmology whom
> Pauline embraces in many respects . . . the Windigo, at once a mytho-
> logical construction and a state of psychosis, which is the most terrifying
> of all figures in the Ojibway worldview. (1995: ii)

Most significantly, highlighting Pauline's increasing distance from
the people, O'Hagan notes, 'the Windigo did not have proper respect

for the traditions of the people, indicative of what we later find as cultural alienation, due in large part to the encroachment of the whites and Christianity' (1995: 24). But whereas she should be feared, O'Hagan notes she is treated like a fool, a clown, or *Windigokan*.[23] The *Windigokanek* were a society of masked dancers also considered unapproachably brave warriors; more like Pauline, however, they were also allied with the Thunderers and were believed to hold strong medicine against winter disease. Their contrary function is lived out by Pauline's refusal to follow ritual process, her stark asceticism, including her refusal to urinate, which is a form of self-denial completely at odds with natural logic, along with her zealous insistence on going against the grain, such as her embracing of death as a means to sustain her own life.

Pauline's zeal is also pragmatic, depending not so much on her faith as on her desire to belong and, at all costs, to avoid the fate of the 'Indians'. Through disinheriting herself, becoming a voluntary scapegoat, choosing a new name and a new life, Pauline becomes the image of desperate survival. Asserting her Christian conversion as a form of cultural camouflage, McCafferty suggests:

> Moving Pauline to the institutionalized core of the culture that allegedly devoured Chippewa reality, inverts and interrogates historical assumptions. At the same time that the church – the 'civilizing' agent – attempts to assimilate Chippewa traditions, it is unwittingly and skillfully incorporated into a drama that has for ages motivated people to form human and supernatural alliances according to their deepest values. (1997: 749)

However we read it, in absorbing imagery from both Ojibwe history and cosmology and Christian theology and missionary history, Pauline also enacts *within herself* those dual modes of antagonism and complementarity. Her interactions with Nanapush and Fleur not only vitally emphasise that contest but demonstrate further nuances to what is already a highly complex discursive pattern. Such *cultural* readings, of course, lead in two directions. To what degree are they informed (by either writer or reader) by culturally inscribed expectation (Treuer's 'cultural longing')? And alternatively, ironically, do such readings threaten to dilute their force; to excuse, by obscuring, colonial culpability?

If we return to those Native–European contest narratives and see, in Pauline, the threat embodied by embracing western culture, in Fleur we see another set of dangers in resisting and dismissing it. In her version of the cultural contest reading McKinney privileges the fact that where Pauline acts in vengeance, betraying herself and her people, Fleur acts in defence of family allotment, of tribal land. But, as Gross suggests, her actions do not free her from culpability and her sense of vengeance threatens her family group: how easily we forget that Lulu hates Fleur because Fleur sends her away.[24] As Justice notes, community is an 'ever adaptive state of being', for the survival of which, 'the People are responsible . . . through attention to their kinship rights and responsibilities' (2008: 152). Conflictual readings of Pauline/Fleur ironically blind us to the key flaws that Gross insists are visible in Fleur's actions. Both characters embody conflicting codes, as Rainwater has it, but Pauline's 'assimilation' is deeply inflected by Ojibwe cosmology (furthered in *Last Report*), suggesting that we might read her use of Christianity within an indigenous framework, while Fleur's spirituality is, in Gross's view at least, compromised by what we might reductively identify as western individualism, an ironic failure of the decolonisation imperative.[25] In other words, Pauline takes up Christianity as a tool in her pursuit of other forces, rather than being subsumed by it, while Fleur *is* adversely altered by contact. Although the contrast between the community-damaging and the community-enhancing roles is palpable in these two women, and although Fleur comes out of the tetralogy as the more sympathetic of the two, they are both ultimately engaged in the same battle – a battle that is all too easily characterised in simpler terms as Christian against Ojibwe, full-blood against mixed-blood, progressive against traditional. Notwithstanding the often devastating impact of colonial imposition, these inflections begin to move towards a relational rather than an oppositional understanding of the nature of contact in Erdrich's fiction, stressing survival over loss, and agency over victimhood, and, perhaps most importantly, narrative attempts to represent the complexity of the human condition over polemical or ideological reductivism.

Narrativity and flux

The critical determinism that Sarris and Hafen notably reject speaks in no small way to the fluidity of Erdrich's lyrical prose. While for some, *Love Medicine* is a vehicle for orality (Sands 2000; Wong 2000), for others the nature of its postmodern fragmentation is indicative of a more general alienation and loss, rather than depth, of meaning (see Silko 1986; Cook-Lynn 1993). While Vizenor asserts a Native American claim to the very idea of postmodernism, prioritising the 'semiotic sign in a language game' of trickster discourse (1989a: 204),[26] and the accretive 'web-like' structures of Native storytelling and writing as described by Gunn Allen and Silko in themselves echo postmodern form, it is Owens who makes the clearest claim for direct connection between the fragmentary nature of the text and 'culture': 'For the traditional culture hero, the necessary annihilation of the self that prefigures healing and wholeness and a return to the tribal community often takes the form of physical fragmentation, bodily as well as psychic deconstruction, (2000: 56). Declaring June's dissolution at the opening of Love Medicine to echo this 'necessary annihilation', Owens bids for an understanding of the text as a quest for a return to centres. Reading it in this fashion might, for the wary postmodern reader, also serve to emphasise the novel's essential *modernism*; a core against which, Eliot-like, to shore the fragments. Under this reading, June's death becomes a mutually invertible metaphor for community reconstruction, as she is 'brought home' by Lipsha on the final page of Love Medicine.

Yet Owens himself is not entirely persuaded of this:

> Formally, the novel's fragmented narrative underscores the fragmentation of the Indian community and of the identity that begins with community and place; and the fragmentation of this community, the rootlessness that results in an accumulation of often mundane tragedies among the assorted characters, subtly underscores the enormity of what has been lost. (2000: 64)

That sense of Owens's own oscillation between two polarised, yet equally romantic, views – the Indian as holistically bound by community, which threatens to gloss over political history; and the Indian community as atomised and vanishing, which threatens to deny sovereignty – once more demonstrates the fiction's resistance to monoliths, while the fragmentary form itself (again, of the series combined) suggests the cracked shell that barely contains, while revealing, the vital substance within.

Through various means – the repetition of cyclical and homecoming motifs, for instance – the most important of which *is* the narrative construction itself, the tetralogy *begins* a process of the accommodation and even integration of diverse and disparate elements. Ruppert's statement that *Love Medicine* engenders a process of *becoming* is pertinent to the tetralogy as a single connected work: 'As the text opens its mysteries, perception expands beyond the boundaries of the text, overcoming otherness, and the universe reveals itself as timeless and mythic' (1995a: 81). The implicit mysticism of that assertion is perhaps unhelpful, but his sense is that the novel moves towards a revital- isation of understanding of Native epistemological traditions for Native readers, and an appreciation of the same for non-Natives, at least acknowledging its plurality, commensurate with the 'coherent multi- plicity of community' (Wong 2000: 89).

Early on in her career, Erdrich said of *Love Medicine*'s structure that alongside the experimentation of her key influences – Faulkner, William Gass, Toni Morrison, and certain Latin American writers – it also reflects a traditional Chippewa storytelling motif. That motif, 'a cycle of stories having to do with a central mythological figure, a culture here [*sic*]' (Jones 1985: 4), is directly refuted by David Treuer, who has 'looked through the stacks of memory and piles of books for something that resembles a "Chippewa cycle of stories" without success' (2006: 49). He makes another, more literary, objection to the idea of multivocality, finding simply that a number of stories about Wenabozho, told 'to entertain or teach', have, historically, been told and retold (2006: 50). There is no doubt that it is trickster stories that Erdrich is thinking of. These are the most commonly retold 'cycles', made most famous to a western audience through Paul Radin's transcriptions of the Winnebago trickster cycles. It is certainly to these types of tales Erdrich turns when, in *Baptism of Desire* and *Original Fire*, she develops the stories of 'Old Man Potchikoo'. Treuer declares the aspiration (among author and critics alike) an instance of cultural longing, and finds that the similarities basically end here.

Nevertheless, dealing with peripheries, boundaries, and borders, *Love Medicine* enlivens its own space with the interplay of its multiple narrators, none of whom offers an omniscient perspective but rather a fragment that in turn, as Wong and Rainwater suggest, places the reader in an equally marginal (thus 'involved') position. We know the whole story only through the collective pieces these narrators, albeit through 'almost identical rhythms', provide (Treuer 2006: 46). Thus, *Love Medicine* and by extension the tetralogy invigorate 'new visions' (Wong 2000: 100) by forcing the reader out of the comfort zones of conventional narrative. The claim that this marginalisation places the reader in the same position as an oral audience, is a curious one, for as Treuer notes in his analysis of another storyteller, 'I get the sense that Oakgrove is aware that his audience knows the story already' (2006: 53). While Wong, however, denies the orality of what she describes as a short story *sequence*, Sands identifies *Love Medicine*'s quotidian register:

> Not the enduring sacred tradition of ritual and myth that we have come to know in contemporary Indian literature, but a secular tradition that is so ordinary, so everyday, so unconscious that it takes an inquirer, an investigator, an artist to recognize its value and adapt its anecdotal structure to the novel. (2000: 42)

Continuing this line of argument, she asserts that the novel's narratives and narrators 'coerce us into participating in their events and emotions and in the exhilarating process of making the story come out right' (2000: 42).

We must of course remain alert to the potential cultural imposition of such readings. As a story cycle, if we take *Love Medicine*, or even the entire oeuvre, Erdrich's work carries what James Nagel refers to as an 'ethnic resonance of genre' in American writing, where we might also think of Amy Tan's *The Joy Luck Club* (1989) or Sandra Cisneros's *Woman Hollering Creek* (1991). It also of course echoes 'mainstream' texts such as William Faulkner's *Go Down, Moses* (1942) or even *The Sound and the Fury* (1929); not to mention Sherwood Anderson's *Winesburg, Ohio* (1919), Ernest Hemingway's *In Our Time* (1925), or Eudora Welty's *The Golden Apples* (1949) in method if not in spirit. All this, of course, before we even begin to reflect on the relationship between the narrative strategy of *Tales* and Chaucer's *Canterbury Tales* (fourteenth century) or Boccaccio's *The Decameron* (c. 1353; see Rosenberg 2002). While we are considering the intertexts, it is also notable that Matchie calls *Love Medicine* Erdrich's *The Scarlet Letter*, McCay reflects on Erdrich's 'response' to Fenimore Cooper, Jason Mitchell allies Erdrich's 'revisionist West' with the writing of Cormac McCarthy, and Karen Smith analyses Erdrich alongside James Joyce. All more or less deterministic – an inevitable consequence, perhaps, of the critical act – the many and varied readings Erdrich's work has produced beyond those of 'cultural' form or information testify to the ways in which the writing shrugs off monolithic shrouds.

The one incontrovertible 'fact' of the early work is that Erdrich's style, despite many features that seem unrealistic, even at times surreal, evokes the day-to-dayness of community life *in medias res*.

Elsewhere Sands notes of *Love Medicine*: 'The source of [Erdrich's] storytelling technique is the secular anecdotal narrative process of community gossip, the storytelling sanction toward proper behavior that works so effectively in Indian communities to identify membership in the group and insure survival of group values and its valued individuals, (1986: 269). The stories evolve as characters shift vantage points, as the reader gains insight through prior knowledge, and most significantly in the organic development of the tetralogy from tale, to novel, to series. Erdrich therefore emphasises the living story. In this sense, although the narrative itself is multifocal and depicts a time-ravaged community, the story cycle as a whole is brought together in the act of reading. Reading *Love Medicine*, as Pittman does, as an example of Vizenor's 'trickster discourse', is to 'participate in the "trickster sign"' in which '"author, narrator, characters and audience" ... perform an act of (trickster) transformation in the text – they create community' (1995: 782).

The multivocality of the texts, egalitarian in their individual insights and ignorance, in the absence of 'heroes' or even protagonists, implicitly prioritises the communal:

> Erdrich's story cycles chronicle the centrality of one's own relationships, tenuous though they may be, with one's land, community, and family, and the power of these relationships, enlivened by memory and imagination and shaped into narrative, to resist colonial domination and cultural loss and to (re)construct personal identity and communal history on one's own terms. (Wong 2000: 88)

Each novel in turn refuses to be an 'endpoint'. Instead, it is part of a cycle of generation and regeneration that is itself thematised. For Nanapush, for instance, the process of generation in which he participates as a narrator in *Tracks* is key to his role as 'father' to Lulu. The story he tells her is, in a sense, a rescue narrative. We are reminded of the notion that 'Perhaps we owe some of our most moving literature to men who didn't understand that they wanted to be women nursing babies' (*BJD* 148), highlighting the deep implicit connection between the maternal act and storytelling for Erdrich. Bruchac describes Erdrich's grandfather, Patrick Gourneau, who 'had a real mixture of old time and church religion' as having a 'storytelling voice, a voice connected to the past' (Chavkin and Chavkin 1994: 99, 97). That 'voice', while clearly not an immediate representation of her grandfather, is most obviously present in Nanapush, storyteller extraordinaire, 'incorporator' of Catholic ways into his Ojibwe practices and, most importantly, provider of some of the most humorous moments in the novels.

The comedy, particularly the sexual comedy, of Nanapush's relationship with Margaret Rushes Bear develops more in later novels but even early on, in his irreverent teasing of Father Damien for instance, is an important reminder of what Gross calls the 'healing power' of humour at the heart of Anishinaabe culture. 'While *Tracks* recognizes the severity of the collapse of our society', writes Gross, 'it also points the way toward survival, relying on the comic vision and use of one's wits to survive as embodied by *Nanapush* to meet the forces of colonialism and oppression' (2002: 458). Secondarily, that juxtaposition between the 'comic vision' of old timers like Nanapush, or the bathetic misadventures of Lipsha's love medicine (see Gleason 1987), and the eviscerating impact of consumption, deepens the rawness of the latter while emphasising the power of the former. As mentioned already, however, Nanapush's paternal role, the generative nature of his storytelling, is equally important to his role in *Tracks*:

> Many times in my life, as my children were born, I wondered what it was like to be a woman, able to invent a human from the extra materials of her own body. In the terrible times, the evils I do not speak of, when the earth swallowed back all it had given me to love, I gave birth in loss. I was like a woman in my suffering, but my children were all delivered into death. It was contrary, backward, but now I had a chance to put things into a proper order. (167)

Part of that ordering involves his mentoring of Fleur and his 'adoption' of Lulu (and her eventual rescue from residential school). That care is echoed in Marie's attempted and Eli's eventual adoption of June, and Marie's fostering of Lipsha.

The question of adoption speaks intimately to what several critics have identified as the centrality of mother–child relations in these novels. Tanrisal declares Marie Kashpaw a 'super mother', responding to her own losses by taking in children, being 'rebuilt' as she invests in them: 'The Native American notion of "family" joins the individuals living together in one house because it includes spiritual kinship as well as clan membership' (1997). This inclusive sense of family, adjoined to the idea of mother 'recovery' inherent in Lipsha's search and central to the representation of community and to the depiction of strong, empowered women in Erdrich's writing, is of course beset by deep conflicts. The conflict between the 'anti-mother' Pauline and the 'mythic mother' Fleur (both maternal 'failures' in Tanrisal's taxonomy) is echoed in the rivalry between Marie and Lulu for Nector's affection, the former existing in strange balance while the latter join forces in opposing Lyman's plans. While they feed the many and nuanced examinations of female power and feminism in Erdrich's work, they also provide resistance against too reductive or limiting a reading.

Similar connections are explored by Eleanor Schlick in *Tales*. As Jack Mauser's four living ex-wives and the disguised Gerry Nanapush spend a freezing night in Jack's car, the women develop strategies for survival. They forge a communal bonding for and of the moment, in which all members are equal and work to the same ends, telling stories of their time with Jack in order, quite literally, to survive. The women also develop personal strategies of survival, of which Eleanor's is the most pronounced. It is developed throughout the novel, appearing as a character trait right from the very first few pages set in the convent. Eleanor writes. Words keep her alive:

> They were, all of them, enclosed in the spoken words, both saved and cut off by the narrative trailing into the dark and shaping itself into the larger, flatter, patterns of crystals collecting on the glass windows of Jack's Explorer.
> *Must remember this*, she wrote. The ink in her pen was frozen and left no visible mark, but in the dark she couldn't tell and so she wrote across the ruled lines, jaggedly, in a fit of intensity. *If so, to breathe upon that window, opening a black space, is to erase, to forget some portion of the past. Perhaps when all is said and done and we are rescued, this cathartic account will help to lay undone feelings for Jack to rest.* (*TBL* 228–229, original italics)

There is, of course, no single cathartic account within the novel; Eleanor's hope alludes to the novel itself, Erdrich's account.

It is tempting to read this as an echo of Erdrich's position as a Native American writer attempting to 'write into' a dual cultural heritage and against hegemonic representation, where the impermanence of writing in the window-ice stands in creative tension with Eleanor's notebook.[27] Yet Eleanor herself is a white Euroamerican. Instead, her attempts to write are acts of recovery and survival, on the literal level, so that she *does not die*, and on the socio-political level as a single-minded woman struggling against her overwhelming feelings for the man she hates to love. This is further complicated by the fact that Eleanor's writing is lost. Is Erdrich suggesting that the *act* of writing is recovery enough? The ink is frozen, the marks on the page will never be seen, but in the very act of attempting it, Eleanor is ordering her life, taking control of both her past and, resolutely, her destiny. The point here is, as ever, twofold. First, the act of writing as recovery and survival speaks to those ideas of endurance germane to Native literature on the one hand (Quehenberger-Dobbs 1996; Sergi 1992), whether or not we prioritise the oral tale implicit in both the wives' stories and the impermanent marks; and to feminist literature on the other. These told tales are the binding agent of the newly created *communitas* – a reforged community. But secondly, there is a broader claim here for the fluidity of text itself; for the understanding of written narrative not as fixed but as equally part and parcel of the mutable nature of communication. This moment in *Tales* essentially grounds the nuances of the tetralogy in a clear sense of the boundariless nature of writing, as another mode of interchange, and declares the possibility of that fluidity and its attendant revisions in future work.

Elemental threads and the substance of story

The fundamental themes of Erdrich's early work serve to establish and sustain that sense of embattled community, with all the vagaries and vicissitudes of life writ large. The first and last books of the series begin with scenes of pain (both physical and emotional), sex, winter, death, the desperate search for union, and, uncannily, hope. For Albertine, June becomes a part of the earth, like the 'dry ditches, the dying crops … dried sloughs, ditches of cattails, potholes' (*LM* 11). Although dead, June is embodied, resurrected even, in the landscape. That June's presence is replaced for Albertine, symbolically at least, in other things might suggest coping by avoidance, although in spiritual terms – terms Albertine does not otherwise manifest – it also reflects a belief in perpetuity of the spirit. That belief is echoed on numerous occasions, from the transformation of the deer in the back of Gordie's truck, through to the 'presence' of June's ghost for Lipsha, her spirit car too making an appearance in *Tales*. June is an ever-present *sine qua non* for the narrative, an ephemeral thread from *Love Medicine* to *Tales*, whose 'loss will underscore each character's sense of identity within the tribal community and, concomitantly, each character's potential for survival' (Owens 1992: 196). If these are the major motifs, the ground for emplotment, it is fair to say that the novels are replete with a myriad other themes, motifs, and sub-plots, which not only magnify the effects of Erdrich's prose but invite a number of different contextual readings from the feminist, through the multicultural, to the problematic question of the Midwest.

In relation to the latter, Silko's earlier criticism of apoliticism perhaps invites another kind of regional understanding: if this is not the political geography of North Dakota in the mid-1980s, it does speak much more closely to a Midwestern, or at least Great Plains landscape and environment *per se*. In *Tales*, for instance, that Midwest becomes positively multicultural, even acknowledging the westward-spreading 'pierogi belt', where village after village was settled by eastern Europeans after earlier German and Scandinavian settlement. In all five novels, the terrain becomes, in itself, a catalyser and director of the action, often imbued with the same stark familiarity of June's demise. From the winter deaths at the opening of *Tracks* through the scorched prairie grasses of summer, to the snowdrifts that at once cover the manmade fences while creating a far more impenetrable boundary to movement, it is impossible to get away from the impact of the landscape and its seasonal shifts on the shape and even tone of the characters' lives.

Although scenes of heat, of arid summers, are frequent, there is an almost oppressive whiteness throughout the tetralogy. Lissa Schneider points out that white is the colour of death in Ojibwe culture (1992: 4), lending weight to the symbolism of an elemental scene that smothers the landscape literally, the tribe and tradition metaphorically. Who can forget the haunting opening of *Tracks*: 'We started dying before the snow, and like the snow, we continued to fall' (1). But who, too, can forget the moment of Jack Mauser's faked death, a symbolic rebirth as he digs his way out of his burning house through a drift of snow (*T* 114). It is easy to be caught up in that oppressive atmosphere and to forget the generative nature of these scenes, against which Erdrich repeatedly tells stories of survival. The time of *atisokan* in Ojibwe tradition, winter is generative of many of the stories Erdrich tells, imbued as they are with the *geni loci* of Ojibwe cosmology and also with the marks and scars of recent history. Storytelling also performs a strong *Völkisch* function in the lives of German rural classes as well as in the settling in of immigrant communities and in this sense winter is the basic canvas, across the Midwest, for tales of survival. If the characters of *The Beet Queen* float free because they appear to have no history, no ties, then the narrative itself is a storying of their belonging: 'Erdrich's region . . . pulses with tales that must be told, and times that must not be forgotten' (Clute 1995: 127). The broad strokes and minute details (the meadowlarks and beet fields) that both depict and suggest place (the reservation, the plains, the Midwest) inform Erdrich's writing every bit as much as cultural detail and narrative technique – are essential, in other words, to her aesthetic. 'Writing place' Blaeser notes, 'is not merely a mechanical kind of physical description . . . but rather an attempt to render a sense of relationship with the life and motion of place in our spirit' (1999a: 97).

In another corner of the socio-political scene Lyman Lamartine's plans to build a gaming complex on the shores of Lake Matchimanito, conceived in *Love Medicine*, developed in *The Bingo Palace*, and fully operational come *Tales*, carry with them another apparent duality – the entrepreneurial ambition of an individual man, and the impact of his entrepreneurship, for good and ill, on the community in which he lives. 'The furor that this issue generates', writes Purdy, 'is at once understandable and ominous. For Native nations, the potential for the generation of large sums of capital carries with it the potential for self-sufficiency and therefore self-determination, but with this potential also comes the threat of reprisal and loss' (1997: 9). The 'games of chance' that Erdrich invokes, however, clearly do not begin and end with the exploitation of federal loopholes permitting gaming on Indian lands. As Ron Charles suggests, they provide a somewhat ironic point of contact between Native and non-Native communities. The question of chance more broadly, from Lyman's pursuit of Shawnee Ray in *The Bingo Palace*, to Fleur's engagement in a card game with spirits on the road of death in *Tracks*, is a motif on the one hand of cultural ground – the stick and bone games in Ojibwe and other societies – and on the other of empowerment. Resonating too with the theme of gambling, chance, 'luck' in other Native writing, there is, in the tetralogy, a clear sense of what Purdy calls 'Narrative Chance', after Vizenor's collection of essays, in the novels themselves. '[E]vents reveal', Purdy notes, 'that probability is . . . in the eye of the beholder, and power is in the future of the gambler with a good heart' (1997: 10). This is reflected in strategies of manipulation such as Pauline's over Sophie and Eli (*T*), Sister Leopolda's over Marie (*LM*), or Sita's over Celestine and Mary (*BQ*); in leaps of faith such as Lipsha's love medicine or Shawnee's trust in Lipsha (*BP*) or even the reader's suspension of disbelief in relation to the many improbabilities of the novels' plots; and in calculated, deeply distressing games of risk such as the attempts in *Love Medicine* and *Tracks* to gain and retain land (see Sarvé-Gorham 1995). The throw of the dice, the anticipation of the outcome, and the will to influence events are fundamental to the orientations of characters' lives.

In Gish's terms, the hunt becomes a prevailing signifier of the negotiation between both real and metaphorical life and death – in other words also of the fluctuating relationship between old and new ways. It carries, like gambling before it, the same gestures of chance and balance, the risk inherent in the activity balanced by skill and wit, generator of stories, and frame for individual and collective identity. Of the men's talk in the opening chapter of *Love Medicine* (aptly entitled 'The World's Greatest Fishermen'), Gish notes: 'No longer a clan of true hunters, the men nevertheless still rely on hunting stories, remnants of more purposeful accounts and more authentic deeds, to bring perspective on June's death, on the death in life and life in death known to the hunter' (1999: 79). There is an irony inherent in this; the emasculated scene mirrors the male-dominated world that is essentially the death of June. If we turn to *Tracks*, however, we witness the true strength of the metaphor in a real hunt. When Eli kills his moose and straps the flesh to his body, he literally covers himself in death in order to save his, and Nanapush's, life. Albeit diminished, he enacts an exemplary community-serving function and risks his own life to save another. This motif is most explicit in the Easter imagery with which this chapter began, the repetition of eggs, emblematic of birth, spiritual rebirth, and the predominance of man's use of animals and nature: 'animals became metaphors for the relationships that the Anishnabeg draw for themselves in balancing human needs against the unforeseeable forces of the natural world' (Brehm 1996: 678).

In returning to the Easter imagery, the 'salfivic' motif of spiritual homecoming, we come full circle. Bevis's notion of 'homing in', a primary paradigm of Native literatures, if another blind alley for Treuer, is wholly apposite to the tetralogy. Even *Tales* opens with a double, false, homecoming: June's failed return across the snow; and the return of her short-term lover 'Andy' to his roots – the reservation – and, by turns, to his 'people'. In the introduction to her brilliantly variegated edited collection of Ojibwe prose, *Stories Migrating Home*, Blaeser writes, 'Repeating motions of memory, dream, liberation, or transformation. Repeating voices of family, vision, history, or humor. Repeating stories of search, survival, departure, and return. Repeating the names assigned loss, healing, origin, and ritual. The stories [in the collection] construct intricate patterns of home' (1999b: 4).

The patterns of home, patterns of belonging, the flesh beneath the shell of contemporary experience, however we choose to designate that experience – American, Native American, Ojibwe, Métis, female, male, the experience of the young and the old, the individual and the collective – form the substance of Erdrich's early novels. Despite the secondary, synoptic purpose this chapter has served, it has also attempted to show that taking the praxis and theory of symbolism as a starting point does not, by necessity, obscure or obviate the political or the social. If June's death, or alternatively the consumption at the beginning of *Tracks*, is the rupture, the substance it reveals is community in all its inchoate dissipation. Not necessarily com- munitistic in Weaver's terms, nor politically directive as Cook-Lynn demands, nevertheless, this early series constructs a network of relations that repeatedly return us to the negotiation of specific histories, and to the nature, and even shape, of community within those contexts.

Notes

1   June is the 'adopted' daughter of Nector Kashpaw and Marie Lazarre and the estranged wife of Gordie Kashpaw. She is first referred to as June Kashpaw but later designated a Morrissey originally and it is by this name that she is most commonly referred to in the criticism. Despite this, in *The Bingo Palace* she is acknowledged as the daughter of Lucille Lazarre, adding to her mystique.

2   'One of the characteristics of being a mixed-blood is searching. You look back and say, "Who am I from?"' (qtd in Smith 1991: 13).

3   From a short piece by J.H. Tompkins, qtd by Owens 1992: 193. The original was published in *Calendar Magazine* as 'Louise Erdrich: Looking for the Ties that Bind' (Oct. 1986).

4   Never an intended part of the series, *Tales* is often included as part of what Jacobs calls the 'North Dakota Novels' (2001: *passim*). This now includes *Last Report* and *Four Souls*, both of which stem directly from the early novels. These connections are clarified in Chapter 4.

5   Intermarriage is widespread, the connections complicated; the most comprehensive overview of plot and family trees is Beidler and Barton 2006.

6   In anthropology 'liminality' denotes a potentially transformative condition, but it has often been used pejoratively by literary critics. There is no doubt in Erdrich's work, however, that the 'liminal' space is a space of possibility.

7   Not simply an easy harmony, symbiosis includes the full range of relationships from parasitism to complementary survival.

8 Mathews (Osage) published his first and only novel in 1934. He earned degrees from the universities of Oklahoma, Oxford, and Geneva, was a pilot in World War I, and travelled extensively in Europe and North Africa, before returning to his roots on the Osage lands in Oklahoma where he was elected to tribal council in 1934. An almost archetypal mixed-blood homecoming narrative, *Sundown* ends in uncertainty, stressing alienation and the overwhelming of the Osage during their oil boom (Owens 1992: 49–89).

9 Nector's actions are cast explicitly as an act of revenge on behalf of his family. As with Fleur's later revenge, this can be seen dualistically, as a moment of personal empowerment and a misuse of power (see Chapter 4).

10 McCafferty notes that individuals possessing significant Manitou power *would* estrange 'him/herself from the human collective in many ways' (1997: 732).

11 This fact is revealed in *The Bingo Palace*, a fine example of the revisionist work of Erdrich's project.

12 Powerful and impassioned arguments both, which are still very much at the vanguard of ethically oriented criticism.

13 It is not the purpose of this text to affirm the greater validity of any of these approaches but to explore the ways in which critics have approached Erdrich's work. It does not seem unreasonable, however, to suggest, as these readings do, that while indigenism ought to be central to any use of postcolonial theory in this field, elements of that theory are themselves useful to indigenist and tribal nationalist approaches.

14 Barnouw compared the 'cohesive organization' of plains tribes with the 'intense individualism' of the Chippewa.

15 The slightly strange chronology to this suggests that the edition was printed late.

16 When asked what she thought prompted parts of Silko's review, Erdrich jokingly responded with 'Drugs' before saying 'Leslie Silko didn't read the book carefully. It happens, I've done it myself. She thought the main characters were Chippewa when they were actually depression-era Poles and Germans . . . They must have seemed shockingly assimilated' (Chavkin and Chavkin 1994: 237). It is clear that Silko *is* aware of, if confused about, the mixed 'cast' of the novel, suggesting that neither author has read the other's text carefully.

17 Owens's *Other Destinies* and *Mixedblood Messages* both contain slightly differing reflections on the issue; Cook-Lynn's reinforcement of Silko's argument is partly a criticism of Owens.

18 The *Argus* (est. 1879) had daily, Sunday, and weekly editions. The name lived on into the early twentieth century when it merged with another paper to become the *Morning Call and Fargo Daily Argus*.

19 As I very briefly suggest in Chapter 5, such a revisionist regionalism might alter the boundaries from the 'Midwest' as we know it to 'Ojibwe Country',

which stretches from Wisconsin to Montana and up into Ontario and Saskatchewan.

20 Basil Johnston notes that when disease hit and decimated the Anishina-abeg, Kitche Manitou sent Nanabush, his emissary, to teach them all they need to know to survive. Nanabush was of earth mother, spirit father. By the time he was born all his brothers had left, his father was not there and his mother died soon after, and he was raised by his grandmother (1990: 17).

21 Morace connects this choice of name to Leopold von Sacher-Masoch, encapsulating Pauline's (self-destructive) tendencies. I propose more complex interpretations. The Viennese 'Leopoldine Society', instigated by Archbishop Leopold of Vienna and named after the Empress Leopoldina of Brazil, funded missionary posts from the 1830s to the early twentieth century. This and references to the pious and virtuous Prince (later Saint) Leopold of Austria (1073–1136) are significant (Attwater 1983: 212). Equally important is the somewhat cut-throat colonial figure of King Leopold of Belgium, whose legacy in the Congo is almost an object lesson in the brutal exploitation of empire.

22 'Water monsters are the perpetual and repeatedly defeated enemies of Sky Supernaturals' (Landes 1968: 23).

23 O'Hagan describes the Windigokan as a contrary figure adopted by the Plains Bungi around the same time as they adopted the sun dance, 'sometime in the late eighteenth or early nineteenth century' (1995: 91).

24 Gross inflects the conventional reading of Fleur's strength where he notes: 'she cannot be blamed for being angry, as she initially isolates herself in the woods and uses her powers to make others fear her. Yet for all her strength, by the end of *Tracks* she is divested of what matters the most in Anishinaabe life: community, children, and land. Her ultimate failure speaks to the shortcomings of using great blessings to do great harm' (2005: 51).

25 In her study of the Ojibwe woman Landes notes that women who behave exceptionally are judged in individualistic terms according to their fortunes. Under this gauge Fleur comes out poorly since she loses everything by the end; by the same token, commending individualism is not as anathema to traditional Ojibwe culture as the popular stereotype holds it to be.

26 Vizenor privileges the ironic, what he calls comic discourse, as a means of destabilising the monolithic confines of social science 'monologues' and modernist individualism. Pittman relates this to the Bakhtinian picaresque (1995: 782–783).

27 Theories of 'cultural recovery' through writing are prevalent both implicitly and explicitly in postcolonial and indigenous studies, for instance in Owens's *Other Destinies* and Weaver's *That the People Might Live*.

4

From the cities to the plains:
recent fiction

The continuous 'North Dakota series' was completed in 1996 and Erdrich has written seven further novels to date (including *The Crown of Columbus* (1991), co-published with Dorris), not to mention volumes of poetry, memoirs, children's books, and other collaborative projects. This is an impressive oeuvre, and it is perhaps Erdrich's prolificacy that has prevented scholarship from keeping pace with her production. This chapter represents an attempt to bring consideration of her adult fiction up to date with a series of 'mini-essays' on selected aspects of each of these later novels: *The Antelope Wife* (1998), *The Last Report on the Miracles at Little No Horse* (2001), *The Master Butcher's Singing Club* (2003), *Four Souls* (2004), *The Painted Drum* (2005), *The Plague of Doves* (2008), and *Shadow Tag* (2010), which arrives too late for inclusion here. Scholarly attention is beginning to turn to these works, but it is, as yet, fairly limited. This chapter begins with the firm conviction that these novels, albeit to differing degrees, are worthy of, and repay, the same level of attention that the earlier work has received.

Although *The Antelope Wife* makes a decisive move away from the reservation, introducing a host of new characters and an ostensibly urban setting, much of this work extends the interconnections of the early novels. The undermining of perceived 'reality' as fixed, empirical knowledge is just one of many narrative strategies Erdrich employs. It draws and reflects as much on the nature and inheritance of western post-enlightenment epistemology in relation to other, in this case 'hyphenated' Ojibwe ways of perceiving the world, as it does the postmodernist (anti-)convention in which Erdrich is frequently placed. All of these novels continue that negotiation, in their own very different ways, between events and attitudes explicable according to the postures of modernity *and* in relation to indigenous ways of knowing – Ojibwe/Cree/Métis and other value systems – and in balancing acts between the two, unsettling authoritative truth claims. Thus, the fragmented, achronological structure of *The Antelope Wife*, common to the earlier books, may be implicitly understood as exploring the relation between a 'postmodern condition' and the cyclical, accretive processes of the oral tradition, for instance. Most importantly, though, this novel provides a set of keys to its own interpretation through the repetition of core motifs: namely, beading, twinning, and repetition itself; it is both story and theory. By no means the only leitmotifs that unify the several-stranded plotlines of the novel, these are at least the most clearly 'instructive', dialogically informing a sensibility of the word in relation to material culture with very specific – and yet somehow generic – cultural forms. They also define a standing metaphor – of balance and interweaving – throughout the later work that means *The Antelope Wife* may, in certain respects, be seen as the foundational text for Erdrich's later career.

The novel opens with a classic encounter, a cavalry raid on an Ojibwe village 'mistaken for hostile' (3). Having first shot two children, angered irrationally by their 'feral quiet', Quaker-born cavalry man Scranton Roy turns his bayonet on an old woman who attacks him with a stone:

> her body closed fast around the instrument. He braced himself against her to pull free, set his boot between her legs to tug the blade from her stomach, and as he did so tried to avoid her eyes but did not manage. His gaze was drawn into hers and he sank with it into the dark unaccompanied moment before his birth. There was a word she uttered in her language. Daashkikaa. Daashkikaa. A groan of heat and blood. He saw his mother, yanked the bayonet out with a huge cry, and began to run. (4)

In that moment of connection between Scranton and the old woman, between aggressor and victim, man and woman, the novel establishes several key themes against a momentous historical backdrop. Following a decade of unrest, the Dakota War of 1862 entailed 'the largest mass execution in American history' (Waldman 2000: 178).[1] From this moment the novel opens out the connections and aftershocks between three Minnesotan families. The reverberations of colonisation in this opening scene inform the core narrative of the novel, itself informed by the revisioning of traditional plains narratives of the antelope people.

The Last Report on the Miracles at Little No Horse, meanwhile, literally uncovers the truths behind Catholic presence on the reservation, revealing the priest, Father Damien, to be at one level a fraud and at another a border crosser. Understood as a 'Two-Spirited' individual as it is interpreted in the novel, he is shown to be not at all transgressive, while even without that kind of cultural inflection, his conduct, not least the relationship he forms with Nanapush, critiques the patriarchal, empire-consolidating power of the institution he serves. This direct brush with gender transformation is timely, fashionable even, enabling exploration of the balancing of needs and wants, of male and female, and of self and other amidst that broader narrative of cultural imposition and survival.

Turning again to a kind of borderland, *The Master Butchers Singing Club* is the most direct of Erdrich's books in dealing with her German heritage. Describing the immigration of a German butcher – Fidelis Waldvogel – and his wife (the sweetheart of his deceased best friend) after the First World War, the novel goes on to chart the establishing of a family and the growth of a community of émigrés and misfits on the North Dakotan plains. 'Indian' presence is limited in this novel, much as it was in *The Beet Queen*. However, the presence of the mixed-blood Lazarres, and particularly Cyprian Lazarre's reminiscence of the failed Riel rebellion,[2] the occasional mention of local Sioux residents, and a glance at the Wounded Knee massacre, culminating in the revelation that Step-and-a-Half is an Ojibwe/Cree survivor of that event, ensure that the territory the Waldvogels and their counterparts sink into remains enlivened by the shadow of its original inhabitants. Native America becomes almost literally a haunting – but enduring – presence. As with *The Beet Queen* this marginalisation of Native peoples (acrobats, shadowy figures, footnotes to history) reflects the German/European community from whose perspective the narrative is constructed, as they go about the business of coming-to-being on the plains.

In doing so, however, it emphasises presence in absence both directly through the transient incursions of Step-and-a-Half, and by analogy, as we witness the pain of the naturalised Fidelis (ironically a former German sniper). As his youngest twin children, Emil and Erich, move back to Germany and fight on behalf of the Third Reich, so too are we put in mind of the deeply wrought tensions in these mixed communities. The narrative, though more politically self-conscious than the earlier novel, explicitly picks up the carnivalesque

– the grotesque and absurd – as a running motif that both reflects and colours the complex intersections and balancing acts of the cultural/ ethnic borderlands. Delphine Watzka and Cyprian Lazarre perform a Vaudeville act together, Fidelis performs an impromptu strong-man act, while Eva Waldvogel, under her son Franz's care, fulfils her dying wish to take a plane ride, achieving temporary liberation from her mortal state. The plot turns to Delphine's marriage to the now widowed Fidelis and her efforts not only to survive in the harsh North Dakotan environment but to balance her own needs with those of her demanding alcoholic father, her gay friend/ex-lover Cyprian, her sick friend Eva, the jealous and domineering Tante (Maria Theresa), and her adoptive family. The playing out of these plotlines against the sobering backdrop of the Second World War speaks again to that motif of balancing and the interweaving of multiple threads that charac-terises *The Antelope Wife*.

If *Master Butcher* returns us in part to *The Beet Queen*, then *Four Souls* places us back in the purview of *Tracks*, picking up the revenge sought by Fleur over the dispossession and deforestation of her clan's lands. Like *Tracks* it is co-narrated by Nanapush and a new character, Polly Elizabeth Gheen, the sister-in-law of John James Mauser. Just as self-regarding as Pauline, she is at least more self-aware. The novel documents the mutually constitutive – and mutually degrading – nature of the 'colonial' relationship while exploring Fleur's drive to avenge herself and her family for the exploitation of their land. The tale's moral is of the responsibility Fleur has, but neglects, for the wellbeing of her family; a condemnation, of sorts, of the nature of revenge in what Kakutani sees as a double parable of Fleur's avenging her loss, and Nanapush his jealousy (2004: 7). While Fleur's story navigates the complex choices she is forced to make; and while in Polly Erdrich provides a satire of early twentieth-century urban 'society', it is that examination of the betrayal of Fleur's family by her own obsession, and the suggestion through Margaret Rushes Bear of a wholly different, community-focused ethic to the adversarial thrust of Fleur's retribution that makes its deepest impact at the close of this book. If we take from this merely the moral message that revenge is a limited and limiting emotion, or that it describes little more than a colonial relationship reduced to absurdity, the book becomes, as Kakutani proclaims, trite and limited itself – a virtual self-parody. But as it explores the attenuated ravages of *human* response, so its political force examines the nature of resistance and antagonism.

As Ruppert notes, 'Elaine Jahner argues that for the traditional story-tellers, narratives were valued more as explorations of particular ways of knowing and learning than as static constructs of knowing' (1995b: 15). Perhaps we can see the relativist morality of *Four Souls* in this light?

The Painted Drum shares a conceit with a book by another Mid-westerner, E. Annie Proulx's *Accordian Crimes* (1997), which makes use of the eponymous accordion as a substitute picaro. In this case it is obviously the drum itself which, discovered in a house clearance by New Hampshire antique dealer Faye Travers, makes its way back to the Midwestern reservation. We become party to a number of narratives through various stages of the late nineteenth and early twentieth centuries that negotiate matters both personal and political: from displacement and despoliation (the drum is found in the house left by John Jewett Tatro, grandson of Indian Agent Jewett Parker) through lost love, jealousy, alcoholism, premature death, and more. Framed by the personal narrative of Faye, estranged from her maternal Ojibwe background by more than two thousand kilometres and years of separation, the novel is ultimately a story of the vital power of the drum; of repatriation; and of the relationship between people, objects, and the stories that enmesh them.

And finally, for this book at least, *The Plague of Doves* explores in perhaps the most insightful terms yet, the deeply complex interrela-tionships between the plains communities Erdrich depicts: the fraught histories of settlement, of displacement and violently racist power struggle between the indigenous inhabitants and their émigré counter-parts. Most poignantly the novel reveals, with occasionally brutal force, the historical paradox as diverse groups settle into one another's company, and as contemporary Métis characters come to learn of the manner in which one side of their ancestry once fought against the other. Assimilation of those stories, the very uneasy reconciliation of past and present, and the ongoing permutations of historical and 'present-day' encounters come together in an intimate but vividly fresh portrait of the upper Midwest.

The sense that Native writers might be writing into region is, in itself, an awkward one, particularly where it threatens to elide critical claims for Native sovereignty. And yet at the same time it is broadly acknowledged – though seen as syllogistic by some – that Erdrich sits, if not outside, then at least on the edge of tribal community and that her position is highly nuanced: 'Her landscape is American, her viewpoint is Native, and her English prose, laced in this novel with Michif and Ojibwe, is the product of a world where cultural collision and colonialism have shaped entire centuries', writes Noori in a recent review (2008: 12). Being Ojibwe first, in other words, does not preclude those other possibilities for her writing. Perhaps more importantly than this, however, and most aptly demonstrated in *The Plague of Doves*, Erdrich complicates *and* complements the regional canon, evoking the immensity and particularlity of the upper Midwest, extending its scope northwards while forcefully reasserting the presence of Native people as actors and agents, collaborators and adversaries in the negotiated fictions of the nation state. Erdrich lifts away the occluding lenses of pioneer settlement narratives to focus light not only on the very real presence of Native and settler people on the plains and in the cities, but the ways and means in which these populations have both shaped and been shaped by those processes, by their relationships to place, and by their generational connections to kin and clan.

'Who is beading us?': power and culture in *The Antelope Wife*

In *The Blue Jay's Dance* Erdrich writes that '[p]erhaps we owe some of our most moving literature to men who didn't understand that they wanted to be women nursing babies' (148). In *The Antelope Wife* the idea of men nursing babies becomes both image and departure point as Erdrich explores two key qualities: the depths of human longing and instinct for survival and atonement; and how the moment of physical connection between the white officer, Scranton Roy, and the Ojibwe baby he nurses after murdering her grandmother has material and psychological consequences through subsequent generations.

   In the contemporary urban world of the novel the consequences of Scranton Roy's actions reverberate. The novel's focus on these three families presents a microcosmic range – static and artificial in one sense but nuanced through the intersections and interactions between the three – of urban Native life. Those families are the Roys, who are direct descendants of Scranton; the Shawanos, who represent the most 'traditional' family of the three, descending from Asinigwesance, whose lineage is 'interrupted' on two fronts – by Augustus Roy (who 'marries' the twins Zosie and Mary) and by the Antelope Wife herself; and finally, the Whitcheart Beads, whose lineage is less clear, but who seem most deeply implicated in the process of colonial exchange.³ The complexity of interconnections among these three families through intermarriages, adoptions, and so on is so great as to make attempts at their delineation deeply confusing. As Cally, daughter of Rozina Roy and Richard Whiteheart Beads, and principal narrator, explains: 'Everything is all knotted up in a tangle. Pull one string of this family and the whole web will tremble' (237). This setting both carries *and* transcends a palpable colonial legacy, from the spectre of the land that persists beneath and despite the city, *gakahbekong*, to the Hmong grandmothers who work the markets, to the ambivalent trade relationships that figure the book's central motif of beading, to the spectrum of 'hyphenated' Ojibwe characters. It depicts, above all, the legacy of endurance.

At the novel's very heart is a paradox first invoked by Lipsha Morrissey in *The Bingo Palace*. Speaking of his relationship with Lyman, Lipsha declares, 'Our history is a twisted rope and I hold on to it even as I saw against the knots' (*BP* 99). The rope binds in both senses; it strangles and secures. That twisted rope is replaced in *The Antelope Wife* with the metaphor of beading, established in the metanarrative of twin sisters beading the world. Described by Little as dramatising 'a vast web of interdependence brought about by the intersection of many cultures, pasts, and heritages' (2000: 500) beading becomes the primary symbol not only of the forming and intersecting of said histories but also of their reading. In other words we are given to understand the beading not merely as a metaphor for temporal, cultural, and social cross-fertilisation, but also as a metaphor for the reading and writing of intercultural exchange.

As such, we can see the book doing two things in particular. On the one hand, it seeks to comprehend the massive ruptures and changes in Ojibwe culture and cultural understanding from the point of its opening (the late nineteenth century and the plains 'wars' that saw the end of complete tribal autonomy) to its present moment (a mid-1990s world of urban multiculturalism and globalisation) while teasing out notions of continuity and cultural survival. In Weaver's terms, it helps the modern Indian to imagine herself as Indian (1997b). On the other hand, *The Antelope Wife* seeks to blur the various codified boundaries of western epistemes concerned with power: namely, gender and gendered roles; self and other; 'culture' and nature; presence and absence, and so on. In other words, it complicates and perhaps even transcends the binary structures by which social hierarchies in western societies are commonly simplified (see Ahokas 2004).[4] As these two threads combine, we begin to see how the conventional 'split' by which the mixed-blood is often defined in literature – here we have Irish-Ojibwe, German-Ojibwe, even Hmong-Ojibwe – comes to be a source of both radical differentiation from root culture *and* enrichment. Both 'halves' may be respected and celebrated, not as fragmentated or distilled but as a kind of creative heterogeneity that enables Cally, by the end of the novel, to both live in the modern world *and* understand her relationship to her past and her genealogy as 'well-mixed' and 'all one person'. As Magoulick points out, the 'blend of cultures and patterns inspires rather than worries her' (2000: n.p.).

Deeply implicated in trade – and particularly in instances of greed – within the novel, the beading nevertheless also represents an example of individual and 'cultural' expression and independence. The beader is free to make or break the pattern, although as with the patterns of continuity and rupture in naming in the novel, they do so at a risk to the continuity of tradition. Beading enacts a double metaphor in this sense, in that the characters and families quite literally echo the structure of the beadwork – strings of objects, relationships, ideas, individuals, in which components, despite making or suggesting a whole, remain distinct, separate. Beyond the beads, we see a similar set of motifs in the repetition of twins – separate but complementary/balancing forces in traditional Ojibwe stories – or the split hoof of the antelope and deer, for instance. It is, then, in those instances where the balance of power is affected, or disrespected, through greed, obsession, or ignorance, that the pattern breaks.

As already suggested, the role the animate world plays in these relations is key and will briefly close this section out. Van Dyke notes:

> Traditionally, [Lakota] Deer Woman narratives were used to help community members to understand the behavior expected of them, particularly through the difficult period of courtship and marriage. Both men and women were not to give way to individual passion, but were to establish relationships that would add to the stability of the tribe. (2003–4: 168)

This incorporation of plains mythology into a narrative of urban existence is, in itself, reflective of the historical processes described above. 'The antelope people', writes Connie Jacobs, 'are transformational beings who become a part of Chippewa mythology once the

Ojibwa establish themselves on the plains' (2001: 169). The stories, reflective of natural reciprocity, and instructive as to the reciprocity integral to community, are drawn upon by the author 'to weave cautionary tales about the kinds of relationships between men and women which are needed to sustain the community while delineating those which destroy group cohesiveness' (Van Dyke 2003–4: 168). The reciprocity of these relations is indicated most vividly by the forcefulness with which Jimmy Badger warns Klaus against pursuing the antelope woman, and the respect with which he suggests 'The antelope are a curious kind of people' (*AW* 27).

As important as these parameters are, the stories about – and narrated by – animals within the novel serve another purpose, emphasising the ways in which the novel intervenes in and disrupts those initial contact narratives. More importantly, these stories feed into literary assertions of sovereignty found elsewhere in Native literature. According to Little:

> In *The Antelope Wife*, Erdrich implicitly suggests that Native American survival depends in part on extending traditional epistemologies that stress reciprocity, interdependence, and revision to the idea and practice of multiculturalism . . . Through the application of the Ojibwa sacred metaphysic to the contemporary multicultural world, Erdrich outlines ways of improving the broader collective society while also providing a sense of an empowered Ojibwa identity. (2000: 523)

This notion of reciprocity and interdependence both reflects and asserts Native identities above and beyond the so-called 'multi-cultural' milieu of the novel's urban centre. Indeed, it cannot be lost on readers that, but for the brief intercession of a German soldier and the Hmong grandmothers, all of the novel's characters are, in fact, Ojibwe, although also all 'hyphenated'. The symbolic framework of the novel surely diverts our attention from whatever 'hybrid' nexus that hyphenated identity might invoke, to emphasising the importance of tribal-specific frameworks. It vividly reflects what Blaeser describes when she writes: 'Spatial, temporal, and spiritual realities of Native people reflect a fluidity that disallows complete segregation between experiences of life and death, physical and spiritual, past and present, human and nonhuman. Thus they are reflected in cycles that involve return, reconnection, and relationship' (1997: 556). Disrupting narratives of power and coercion, deconstructing the codices of global capitalism, these stories turn on, and return to, the examination of moral and ethical coda.

The role that dogs play in this return is a powerful, playful, indicator of all of the above themes. While Castor notes that 'In *The Antelope Wife* dogs are important agents of change, and they serve as doubles for absent humans' (2004: 127), we might simply point out that their role includes narration. They intervene directly in the human narrative, not only disrupting literary conventions but literally altering the course of lives either through their flesh (the dog Sorrow, whose meat saves Matilda's life having previously been suckled by Blue Prairie Woman) or their instructive presence (Windigo Dog, who speaks to Klaus and helps him gain clarity before releasing his 'wife'). This use of animals, particularly of animals as narrators, very clearly echoes a Vizenorian 'native aesthetic':

> Consider, for instance, the ancestral storiers who created animal characters with a tricky sense of consciousness, the natural reason of a native aesthetic. Many contemporary native novelists present the imagic consciousness of animals in dialogue and descriptive narratives, and overturn the monotheistic separation of humans and animals. . . . [N]ative authors have created memorable animals and a native aesthetic in their stories and novels. . . . These practices and sentiments are a native literary aesthetic. (2006)

Windigo Dog/Almost Soup is a 'reservation mongrel' very much in the spirit of Vizenor's 'memorable animals':

> You will end up puppy soup if you're born a pure white dog on the reservation, unless you're one who is extra clever, like me. I survived into my old age through dog magic. That's right. You see, you see the result of dog wit. Dog skill. Medicine ways I learned from my elders, and want to pass on now to my relatives. You. So listen up, animoshug. You're only going to get this knowledge from the real dog's mouth once. (*AW* 75)

Almost Soup goes on to recount a story that echoes the historical and political realities of the Ojibwe, simultaneously confronting the conventions of literary realism. It combines magical properties ('dog magic') with an otherwise realistic and wholly plausible narrative, indicating dogs' reliance on, *and importance to*, the human community in which they live. Stressing companionship and interdependence, this weaving of human with animal narration opens up the novel's major narratives within that broader aesthetic, not least for the way this inclusion of *shared* stories incorporates, assimilates even, the earlier colonial narrative of dispossession *into* that larger story of Native survivance, redirecting its power through subversion.

The single dying word of Scranton Roy's elderly victim, *Daashkikaa*, is later translated by a descendant, Zosie Shawano Roy, as 'cracked apart' (*AW* 213). We might read it as referring generally to the single moment of choice or imposition that leads to divergence from a given pattern; it fuels the recurrent dialogue between chaos and order, free will and predetermination, chance and design that runs throughout Erdrich's oeuvre. Cracking apart, while signifying a process of destruction, also anticipates the multiform regenerations, recastings, and patterns of healing that such historical processes have gradually manifested. It connects to a second theme, symbolised by the 'unaccompanied moment before his birth' into which the old lady's gaze draws Roy, that points to a psychological void latent particularly in the male characters: a longing for something lost that relates here to 'mother' and later to 'mother culture'. Both of these themes – cracking apart and mother-loss – are intimately related to a third. Dialogue between fragmentation and unity, individual and community, and tradition and modernity inherent in the recursive imagery of beads and beading becomes the ground for the exploration of many other apparent dualisms in the book. These themes meditate on the human condition in broad universal terms but they also speak to the novel's working out of intercultural matrices, family relations, and urban life in more local terms, relating that major historical moment to a whole pattern of personal ramifications for those who come after. Through one simply instated backdrop, Erdrich shows the mutually confining implications of both colonial processes and patriarchal modes for the lives of her Midwestern cast: and more importantly their resistance to, and survivance despite, said control.

Running from the slaughter site, Scranton Roy notices and pursues a baby who has been strapped to the back of a dog by her mother, Blue Prairie Woman. The dog flees and Roy, transfixed in the moment of seeing his mother in the dying woman's expression, takes off after it. He chases it down, allows it to become accustomed to his presence, and removes the child, thus initiating another rupture in the process he had been engaged in, taking the 'other' literally to his breast and nurturing her not only as his own, but as if he were her mother. Implicit in the grandmother's first warning, that rupture then reflects Blue Prairie Woman's desolation at her loss. Moreover, and catalysing another 'crack', it informs her decision to pursue her daughter to the 'Other Side of the Earth', the name she is given by 'the strongest of the namers . . . nameless and . . . neither a man nor a woman' who

'took power from the in-between' in order to save her bifurcated soul
from endless wandering (*AW* 14):[5]

> Blue Prairie Woman's name was covered with blood, burned with fire.
> Her name was old and exquisite and had belonged to many powerful
> mothers. Yet the woman who had fit inside of it had walked off. She
> couldn't stop following the child and the dog. Someone else had taken
> her place. (*AW* 13)

The repercussions of this are potentially great, in that her decision
leaves her twin daughters motherless, to be baptised Mary and
Josephette, and raised by their grandmother, Midass.

Little draws attention to the way Blue Prairie Woman, in becoming
Other Side of the Earth, illustrates the Anishinaabe belief in the
'structural intuition' of the Ojibwe self,[6] sending her shadow self out
into the spirit world to locate her lost child: 'The disembodied journey
she takes, which is made possible by the power of her name, prepares
her finally to take the embodied journey west to follow, "the endless
invisible trail of her daughter's flight"' (2000: 504). It is of course in
this literal 'cracking apart' that she is able to locate her daughter, to
track her down, and remove her from Scranton's care. Like Fleur
Pillager, another strong woman whose actions have ambivalent out-
comes, Blue Prairie Woman explicitly embodies a cross-species space.
Where Fleur, it is intimated and finally 'revealed' at the end of *The
Bingo Palace*, has the capacity to transform into a bear, Blue Prairie
Woman is automatically associated with the animal world: 'As an
antelope woman, Other Side of the Earth crosses the line between
human and nonhuman' (Little 2000: 504). This 'crossing' proves to be
the ultimate sacrifice, as Blue Prairie Woman succumbs to the white
sickness her daughter is carrying and dies.

Van Dyke sees the desire of Blue Prairie Woman to relocate her
daughter as the first act of recurrent obsessive behaviour:

> When Blue Prairie Woman loses her baby daughter on the cradleboard,
> she becomes obsessed with finding her. . . . She has obsessive sex with
> her husband 'until they become gaunt and hungry, pale windigos with
> aching eyes, tongues of flame'. From such obsessive sex, a long line of
> twins extend, and in these descendants . . . humans and antelope/deer
> people become intertwined, causing Cally Roy Whiteheart Beads' twin
> grandmothers to say that Cally and her sister are 'part deer' in the mid
> 1990's. (2003–4: 176)[7]

The passion and danger of this union persist to the present day along
a trail of fraught family relations and are made manifest in the motif

of insatiability, from hunger for sex, love, or food, to thirst, including spiritual thirst (see Brozzo 2001; Tharp 2003). Even before Blue Prairie Woman's death, the traditional Ojibwe kinship unit – a close-knit family model – is severely threatened, although 'overseen' by the spirit of Blue Prairie Woman's mother, by this opening event and the resulting obsessive behaviour. That very fine balance between Blue Prairie Woman's strength and sacrifice and the abandonment of her remaining children characterises the knife-edge equilibrium of the novel's contemporary world.

In this sense, the old woman accurately predicts the end of a particular way of life, illustrated when Scranton and his grandson, Augustus, track down the original community from which Matilda came:

> Into that perfectly made land they wandered, searching out the people now confined to treaty areas, reservations, or as they called them ishkonigan, the leftovers. Seeking town to town, following the lumber crews and then the miners, the Indian agents and at last the mission-aries, *Scranton and his grandson came to the remnants of the village and the unmended families, the sick, the bitter, the restored.* (AW 239, emphasis added)

This scenario, not only of geographical displacement but of social fragmentation, is ubiquitous in early anthropological documentation of the Anishinaabeg, and yet the great-grandmother's prophecy is far more complex than that narrative (of colonial victory, after all) tends to allow. On the one hand, this prophecy alerts us to the way this moment – and Scranton's decision to pursue the baby, taking her in and naming her Matilda – changes not only the oppressed but also the oppressor, disrupting the apparent paths of several lives and ways of life. It unsettles the core binary at the centre of conventional western notions of identity – male/father and female/mother. On the other hand, it acts as a formal gesture or forecast, insisting that in that moment of mingling Euroamerican force with Native blood, rending the Native body with the European sword (or bayonet) everything changes, from culture to its products, including writing. It shows the mutually constitutive (and potentially destructive) nature of contact, refusing to procure a simple correlative between power and progress, or a simple binary of enlightened European values mastering and overwriting a 'primitive' indigenous cosmology. Nowhere is this more clearly illustrated than in the influence the old woman continues to have on Roy's life. As Stookey notes:

It appears to readers, through most of the novel, that with his slaughter of [the old] woman, Scranton Roy has taken it upon himself to determine her fate, but, when the storyteller reintroduces the woman in the last chapter of the book, it becomes clear that she is in fact not simply dead to Scranton but rather is transformed into a woman who has the power to shape his own family's destiny through the person of his grandson Augustus. When she assumes the form of a ghost, and thus resists her obliteration, she defies the will of the man who imposed upon her the condition of death. (1999: 140–141)

This echoes the persistent nature of Blue Prairie Woman's own story which hints, through the passage of names conferred on her and, in turn, by her on her daughter, at the manifold presence of the past in characters' lives. It reminds us, also, of the impact of that earlier moment of choice or imposition on the present.

Post-enlightenment western epistemologies conventionally insist on the binary nature of power: the political and economic hierarchies of western capitalism depend on the assumption of dialectical relationships such as that between master and slave, bourgeoisie and proletariat, understanding them to be models of coercion rather than simple cooperation. Castor, having posited a string of hierarchical binaries to be at the root of tragedy, goes on to say: 'Although tragedy may be an outmoded form of aesthetic expression in our postmodern culture, the Manichean worldview on which it is based is alive and well in the rhetoric of economic and ideological globalization' (2004: 123).[8] Erdrich, as many critics argue, draws on more complementary conceptions of relationships between animate beings to highlight the reciprocity inherent in this scenario (a major theme in the novel). This is never clearer than in the moment that Scranton, having suckled the baby for her comfort, begins to lactate:[9] 'The baby kept nursing and refused to stop. His nipples toughened. Pity scorched him, she sucked so blindly, so forcefully, and with such immense faith. It occurred to him one slow dusk as he looked down at her, upon his breast, that she was teaching him something' (7). While Brozzo reads this sequence as a captivity narrative, Castor notes:

Ironically, what looks at first glance like a captivity narrative is trans-formed into a narrative that challenges not only the white/Indian polarity, but also assumptions about biological differences between men and women. This passage suggests that as soon as the child takes hold of Scranton Roy's nipples, she is the one who captures him. (2004: 126)

As a male soldier involved in the suppression of Native unrest, Roy is
emblematic of colonial and patriarchal control and yet in one sequence
of events – the matricide, the rescue of the girl, and his reconfiguration
as maternal, nurturing force – he exposes the inadequacy of those
conventional knowledge structures, including the one that places
parents and children in authority–subject positions rather than seeing
them as mutually informing and forming subjects. That reciprocal
relationship takes one step further: as the baby teaches the surrogate
father, she teaches him, with an ironic twist, to be a mother, to locate
and immerse himself in that 'oceanic oneness' that he identifies
as *'faith'*.[10] His mysterious epiphany ironically evokes medieval
iconographic depictions of the maternal Christ, his blood shed at the
Passion a form of spiritual nourishment.[11] It becomes, quite literally,
a 'cracking apart' of normative assumptions and a symbolic humbling
of the hegemony.

The net result, a dissolving rather than redefining of borders,
becomes one facet of the anti-colonial project of the book. Carter
explains:

> The production of political and epistemological borders was essential to
> the Western colonial project of constructing and signalling the European,
> and separating out the Other. Once established, borders worked as signs
> of modernity, encoding a stable system of coordinates, where unambigu-
> ous and guaranteed boundaries differentiated, separated and regulated
> between social spheres, between nature and culture, and between the
> scientific and unscientific. (2006: 682)

The breastfeeding sequence in *The Antelope Wife* serves to complicate
that set of binary assumptions of power and knowledge, but also to
transmute the constitutional boundaries of colonial authority. One
result is the 'queering' of the border site – to signal the intended
dismantling, in effect, of the 'Western colonial project' signified at the
novel's violent inception, and to prefigure recurrent transformations
and traversals throughout.

The intimate connection between obsession and 'cracking apart'
is perpetuated in other significant couplings in the novel and they are,
in turn, equally implicated in what Barak calls 'white' perspectives
(2001). So intricately connected are these matters that it is difficult,
even reductive, to separate them out, for as one logical methodological approach to analysing the novel avows, 'Ecofeminists identify
globalisation as an outgrowth of capitalism which, according to their

analysis, is the locus of social and environmental crises. They argue that the essential characteristic of capitalism is its patriarchal nature' (Beder and Sydee 2001: 281). For instance, Richard Whiteheart Beads and Klaus Shawano run a waste disposal company together, an operation that (literally and figuratively) feeds on the theme of waste and wastefulness that is key to Erdrich's portrayal of the urban space, globalisation, and the contrast with, as well as loss of, more sustainable attitudes towards ecology in the novel. Lauded as the 'first Native-owned waste disposal company in the whole U.S.' and proud of their 'old-fashioned ability to haul shit. Not mention stabilize it' (AW 44), the company is exposed as a vehicle for greed, a short cut to profit – as Rozina has already hinted when she says 'there's money to be made in garbage' (AW 40). Literally capitalising on capitalist excess, or even embracing the entropic disposability of the capitalist free market,[12] Klaus and Richard's enterprise is further beset by individualistic greed, exposed when Klaus is mistakenly arrested for Richard's illegal dumping practices – 'terrible poisons in endless old wells' (AW 50).

The affinity between these two men derives from their equally unsatisfactory relationships with women. Driven, in both cases, to obsessive lengths to 'ensnare' and keep the women they allegedly love, they represent both sides of the masculine coin – arrogant machismo on the one hand, and deep insecurity on the other. In first kidnapping and then refusing to release his 'antelope wife' Klaus becomes both emblematic of, and victim to, control as it is figured in patriarchy. As Barak explains, 'Klaus is tortured by his cruelty to his antelope wife, by what she turns into – a smoking, drinking, tight-skirted, high heel-wearing wanderer – by what she turns him into. She is that other inside that stretches out of recognition the shape of the self' (2001: 8). Richard's obsessive behaviour, which leads to the death of one of his daughters, driving a wedge between himself and his wife, Rozina, also leads to his own suicide. The process, suggests Barak, is self-explanatory.

> Klaus Shawano, urban Indian, is not only named after a German, he's got a cornucopia of bloods mixed up in him. One of his ancestors was a buffalo soldier; he's got some Irish ancestors and maybe some French, as well as his Ojibwa forebearers. He is, by ancestry, culturally split. His place is on the rez, in the city, east, west. He belongs everywhere and no where at all. He's also got a split profession, which is where he gets in trouble. During the week he's a sanitation engineer in the city, but on the weekend he sets himself up as a trader. (2001: 7–8)

This reading may be overly simplistic. It is not simply the 'split' that figures his downfall, so much as his selfish behaviour embodied, as ever, in the mechanisms implicit in these various images of globalisation, capitalism, and modernity. In the bondage by which Klaus captures and names his 'Sweetheart Calico' (a fabric itself derived from imperial sources) and in the location itself – Minneapolis as centre of Indian–white trade having begun its life as a trade post – we witness another instance of the way power corrupts and controls. However, this singular focus overlooks the irresistible, siren-like quality of the antelope people both mythically and literally, as they are embodied by *both* Auntie Klaus and Rozina, and the nature of their 'power' (though debilitating to them) over men. If I have prioritised that reading here, it is with the awareness that a fuller understanding of the nuances of power and relationships in the novel will only be achieved through close scrutiny of the far more complex processes of ensnaring and releasing, devotion and obsession, that the novel explores.

Vestments, investment, and the holy zeitgeist: *Last Report on the Miracles at Little No Horse*

An interview with Karen Olson reveals that Erdrich had been working on *Last Report* since 1988, 'intending it to explain how all the earlier novels came into being' (Olson 2001a). Envisaged as a marathon confession by Argus's Father Damien to a 'writer, who would turn out to be Erdrich herself',[13] the book holds to that central idea of disclosure. Paralleling this, however, are several acts of *profession*. Acts of faith, love, loyalty, and disavowal proceed from one initial all-encompassing conceit: Father Damien is in fact Agnes DeWitt, or one-time novitiate nun Sister Cecilia.

The various stories that the novel relays pertain to two overlapping contexts. The first, embodied in Johnson's terms by a 'turn to the local' (2007: 103), witnesses the broad implications of, and resistance to, the presence of the Catholic mission. The second is the life story of Father Damien Modeste and his transformation from woman to 'man-acting-woman'; from passionately sexual lover to (almost) self-denying priest; and from Catholic to heterodox quester. Krumholz, like Johnson, perceives in the novel a narrative of translation – from 'Christian Sainthood to a trickster tale' and from 'Euro-American secular, through Christian and Catholic, to Ojibwe stories, language

and forms of knowledge' (2007: 10). In both of these movements
the narrative refuses to embrace absolutes, resists easy syncretism,
and, like Damien, exists in balance and flux, the paradox of unified
oppositions: 'For Damien, to be Catholic and Ojibwe is like being both
woman and man – it is not entirely possible, and yet it is so' (Krumholz
2007: 5).

Damien's work in the mission reflects this balance/split too, his
primary foci in the fundraising newsletter he creates being the issues
of land loss and spiritual thirst. While the latter heralds the 'timely
response' of the colonising mission, the former draws our direct
attention to its historically catastrophic impact on local indigenous
communities. If this is the practical side of Damien's 'patronage' the
spiritual side of his time among the Ojibwe is equally, yet less simply,
caught between his white-Christian roots and the needs and values of
his new community. Never fully resolved within Damien's 'theatre' of
identity, there is a sexed identity at play that itself alters the perception
of the lexis 'priest' while simultaneously being modified *by* it. His
broad, blank cassock provides a blank canvas in many senses,
becoming the ground for Ojibwe beadwork and the veil for Agnes's
deceit; the testing ground for notions of embodied, socio-cultural, and
performative identities.

Recalling *Tracks*, *Last Report* returns us to the early twentieth-
century reservation setting. Nanapush and Fleur have sequestered
themselves in Nanapush's cabin to die, and their arch-nemesis Pauline
Puyat is beginning her transformation from orphan to nun. The
humorous interchange between the tricksterish Nanapush and his
'love' Margaret Rushes Bear is also re-emphasised in *Last Report*, as is
the fraught relationship between Fleur and her daughter Lulu, who
is sent to boarding school by her mother while she seeks to retain
her land and gain revenge over the men who take it from her. Yet all
of this occurs by way of a new set of intrigues and adventures – not
least the transvestism of Damien himself – introducing new questions
and explorations into the theme of transformation and mutable
identity, and engaging more directly with issues of Anishinaabe
cultural sovereignty. While Catholicism, particularly its emphasis
on revelation and devotion, is central to the plot of *Last Report*,
Damien's faith wavers. And of course as Pauline, like the saintly
archetype she ironically aspires to, insists on notions of perfection,
Damien, like Nanapush, more closely reflects the imperfections of the

Anishinaabe culture hero Nanabozho, by turns arrogant, self-centred, immodest, immature – so, human, vulnerable, but generally, if not always, community-minded. *Last Report* takes this further, investigating, through Damien, the influence of Anishinaabe culture in moderating the spiritual outlook of the priest himself.

As in *The Antelope Wife*, this establishes a nuanced subversion of the myths of patriarchy wherein the priest, as colonial agent, represents perfidy – 'because [missionaries] steal their traditional beliefs and their souls from the Ojibwe' (Chapman 2007: 162). It prioritises Anishinaabe contexts and presence over colonial primacy. Equally importantly, in displacing the signifier 'priest', both male and authoritarian, it establishes a conversive, transcultural relationship, 'a complex web of borrowings, reappropriations, and transformations' (Chapman 2007: 151) between Catholic and Anishinaabe traditions that complicates the reductive rhetoric of conflict and coercion. For Johnson, this shift in intellectual perspective transforms another dominant mode of colonial acquisition:

> In *The Last Report* . . . Nanapush contrasts two mapping traditions: 'White people usually name places for men – presidents and generals and entrepreneurs,' he tells Father Damien. 'Ojibwe[s] name places for what grows there or what is found' (359). For Erdrich only those who know 'what grows there and what is found' . . . can correctly map the place because of their relationship to and knowledge of the land. [The Anishinaabeg] are 'the keepers of the names of the earth'. Erdrich insists that mapping requires local, Indigenous knowledge. (2007: 103)

Such a move echoes the journeys of Erdrich's latest memoir (see Chapter 5). In *Last Report* this relationship is further explored in the degree to which Damien's character, his worldview, is shaped and reshaped by both dominant cultural (Christian) forces, and the local cultural forces that subtly challenge those prior strictures, through more diffuse senses of embodied identity, gendered roles, the status and authority of the religious hierarchy, and the rigidity of spiritual practice.

In a Christian context, the transgressive choice Agnes/Damien makes is one of dangerous indeterminacy.[14] Kashpaw, Nanapush, Margaret, and even Pauline, however, take Damien's duality at face value, though the latter understands his tenuous position. When Mary Kashpaw discovers Damien's artifice her response is to loyally, unquestioningly aid in its maintenance, even on his deathbed (*LR* 212, 355). Kashpaw, Damien's first 'Indian' encounter, muses on the 'girlishness' of the priest:

> He was a shrewd man, and he sensed something unusual about the priest from the first. Something wrong. The priest was clearly not right, too womanly. Perhaps, he thought, here was a man like the famous Wishkob, the Sweet, who had seduced many other men and finally joined the family of a great war chief as a wife . . . Kashpaw thought, *This priest is unusual, but then, who among the zhaagannashiwug is not strange?* (64)

Although the language – 'wrong', 'unusual', 'strange' – evinces un-certainty, the ambiguity of Damien's appearance does not seem threatening to Kashpaw, who had once 'addressed Wishkob as grandmother' (64).

That lack of threat is later seconded by Nanapush. While playing chess he challenges Damien as to 'what' he is. The anxious response '"A priest"' so clearly signifies masculinity that Damien hopes it is unnecessary to defend himself further, but Nanapush's persistence – '"A man priest or a woman priest?"' – won't be curtailed by deflection. He insists, '"Inside that robe, you are definitely a woman"', offering 'simple recognition' and 'level practical regard' that causes Damien to weep in relief (230–231). That Nanapush sees this as an uncom-mon but unthreatening situation is proved in his easy acceptance: '"So you're not a woman-acting-man, you're a man-acting-woman. We don't get so many of those lately . . . we couldn't think of more than a couple"' (232). This reflects his original motive: 'Something struck Agnes, then, and she realized that this moment, so shattering to her, wasn't of like importance to Nanapush. In fact, she began to suspect, as she surveyed the chessboard between them . . . that Nanapush had brought it up on purpose to unnerve and distract her' (232). Absolutist anxieties may be unsettled by the confirmation that 'Damien' is not really 'Damien'. For Nanapush, however, Damien *is* who he says he is, transcending surface by declaring, '"that is what your spirits instructed you to do, so you must do it. Your spirits must be powerful to require such a sacrifice"' (232). In fact Agnes/Damien is prone to visions throughout the novel, evoking what McKinney calls 'the intense revelation to the individual'. 'The Chippewa believed', she notes, 'that individuals, if their motives were pure, had the ability to find truth and spiritual solace within themselves' (1998: 154–155).

Indeed Nanapush only expresses consternation at all at the act, rather than the nature, of the deceit and then only in response to Damien's accusation of cheating: ' "You've been tricking everybody!" ' (232).

The term two-spirit, from the Anishinaabemowin *niizh manidoo-wag*, is used 'in academia to refer to a number of Native American identities,' which 'include but are not limited to Native American people who are lesbian or gay, who are transgender, or who follow some or all of the parameters of alternate gender roles – which may include specific social roles, spiritual roles, and same-sex relationships – specific to their tribe or pan-ethnicity' (Adams and Phillips 2006: 274).[15] One's sex does not limit one's behaviour to the prescribed roles 'man' or 'woman' but opens up alternative roles – 'man-acting-woman' or 'woman-acting-man' as Nanapush describes it – between the two. How one acts, in other words, is neither defined, nor perceived to be defined, by biology or physiology; it is, partly, a matter of choice, or *being chosen*.[16] The social models of male and female, then, while strictly delineated, are accompanied in many Native cultures by alternative gender constructions that accommodate those who do not conform to the standard two, defined as an incomplete shift, 'a movement toward a somewhat intermediate status that combined social attributes of males and females' (Callender and Kochems 1983: 443, qtd in Barak 1996: 51). In Erdrich's extrapolation of this inclusiveness, the boundaries between gendered behaviours become far more fluid than in dualistic paradigms, where behaviour outside the heteronormative categories, contingent on the simultaneity of sex and gender, has long been considered transgressive and unclassifiable. Humorously, the patriarchal institution of the church, symbolic of western society more generally, is doubly subverted by an imposter who turns out to be a woman passing as a man. But this also deals more generally with the mutable, prescribed nature of identities that are negotiated, acted out, and fought for within the various boundaries of embodied performance, emphasised through the fluid deconstruction of static binaries, at the heart of which is the colonial 'them' and 'us'.

Another equally political layer questions the logic of the church that, at this present moment in history, still debates female priesthood, making the church and its hierarchies emblematic of all other questions of power we might raise here. The seriousness of this debate is highlighted when Damien ponders the consequences of his potential defrocking. He does this first in Christian terms:

Were he exposed, were he known to have fooled, deceived, and hidden
his most fundamental nature, all would be lost. Married couples Father
Damien had joined would be sundered. Babies unbaptized and exposed
to the dark powers. Deaths unblessed and sins again weighing on the
poor sinners. (276)

Later he reflects on its effect on his place in the Ojibwe community:
'And, if in spite of her own fears, Sister Leopolda should expose
him and cause him to leave, there would surely be no one who would
listen to the sins of the Anishinaabeg and forgive them – at least not
as a mirthless trained puppet of the dogma, but in the spirit of the
ridiculous and wise Nanabozho' (both 276). An ironic gesture,
Damien becomes an antidote to the subjugating power of the Christian
patriarchy, his church, in a sense, its final frontier. Here, the world
confronted by contact is one in which Ojibwe mores and customs
radically alter colonial agency, nuancing personal identity *and* social
identifiers. In Agnes's case, the tragicomic nature of her liberation/
confinement through, and in alternative roles to, those prescribed by
American society reflects, or rather magnifies, the essential paradox of
the balance/split of inner and outer selves, neither of them absolutes,
none of them entirely reconciled, but all of them going to make up
who and what Agnes becomes.

This exploration of the instability of category is also invested in the
question of sainthood, the purpose of Father Jude's investigations of
Pauline/Leopolda, another 'creature of impossible contradictions'
(123). Her wilfully eccentric behaviour scares the horses during the
Feast of the Virgin Mary parade, leading to the deaths of Kashpaw and
Quill, yet she makes an attempt at compassionate reconciliation with
the dying Quill that belies the almost rabid desire to convert and
control that characterises her in *Tracks*. The murder of survivor Dutch
James's co-workers in defence of Fleur in *Tracks*, and the violent
murder of Napoleon Morrissey, are in themselves acts of (self-)
defence, the latter deeply complicated by her belief that he is the devil.
They defy easy condemnation even as they echo her violent treatment
of her daughter Marie.

Beginning a quest to authenticate Leopolda's 'miracles', Father Jude
develops a genuine interest in his source, Damien, whose actions,
however deceitful, are both more 'down to earth' and more humane;
saintliness becomes a question of perspective. But the narrative also
performs a second task, demonstrating just how the same conditions
responsible for cultural devastation provide the means for survival,

and even revival; the church as *pharmakon* to colonisation. One such reading might present Leopolda in the mould of such figures as the Virgin of Guadalupe or the Blessed Kateri Tekakwitha. As 'the Catholic Church has evolved', Alison Chapman informs us, 'more and more saints have come from the non-European peoples converted by Catholic missionaries, so that sainthood can be a vehicle for the disempowered to rise to a position of ultimate spiritual empowerment' (2007: 154). While missions are inevitably proselytising, and generally seek to eliminate traditional practices, Jesuit missions in particular often sought to integrate those aspects that they did not consider damaging to either Catholicism or the local community. In instances such as Guadalupe or the Lakota White Buffalo Calf Woman, sites and figures of importance in local cultures were adapted to Christian archetypes (see Enochs 1996: viii).

Such manipulation is, without doubt, indicative of what Tinker calls the 'covert lie of white self-righteousness' (1993: 4). Its significance is twofold. First, it demonstrates the acculturative (and potentially devastating) mode of the Catholic mission: 'Unwittingly no doubt, and always with the best of intentions, nevertheless the missionaries were guilty of complicity in the destruction of Indian cultures and tribal social structures – complicity in the devastating impoverishment and death of the people to whom they preached' (Tinker 1993: 4). Indeed Damien himself declares conversion a 'most loving form of destruction' (55). Ironically enough, those same circumstances lead, essentially, to the need for external support structures: people *need*, in the face of great loss, to *believe* (McKinney 1998). This is reinforced by Nanapush in *Four Souls*:

> Supposing the world went dead around you and all the animals were used up. The sky, too, of pigeons, doves, herons, and rain. Supposing one new sickness after another came and racked deep . . . Suppose this happened in your own life, what then, would you not think of surrendering to the cross, of leading yourself into the hands of new medicines? (*FS* 49)

But secondly, these symbols also speak to a sense of resistance, and to an earlier narrative of agency. As McCafferty notes, Jesuit priests were 'graciously received' by seventeenth-century Algonquian groups because overlapping practices, which included 'fasting, seeking of spiritual mediators, similarities between medicine bags/bundles and the paraphernalia of the mass . . . intense conflict between

powerful universal forces, and . . . chanting and song, seemed to imply
important similarities' to their own practices (1997: 745). This crucial
modification stresses indigenous agency over colonial guilt.

In *Last Report* the statue of the Madonna of the Serpents, created for
the mission by 'an old *mangeur de lard*' in Winnipeg, is an example
and embodiment of an *in*version narrative, in which something of
symbolic and spiritual value to the indigenous community modifies
the intended meaning of an archetypal church narrative – that symbol
is the serpent in this case, which can signify knowledge, healing,
or protection as well as more threatening elements of Anishinaabe
cosmology.[17] Classical representations depict the Madonna or infant
Jesus crushing a snake, representative of heresy or sin. Damien's
Madonna, however, explicitly subverts this expectation: 'The snake that
writhed beneath the Virgin's feet . . . did not look at all crushed down
by her weight' (226). This is doubled in the story of Damien attracting,
rather than repelling, serpents in 'The Sermon to the Snakes' (226–227).
Reinvesting the narrative offers a *r*eplacement of the storied experience of the oppressed group; Erdrich's Native characters, 'especially
those converted to Catholicism, become special sites of . . . miraculous
events' (Rowe 2004: 203). Beyond syncretism, this kind of trans-
culturative modification of the Christian story plays a part in that
resistance model while modifying, and thus alienating, the hegemonic
version. Its theme is played out through the catalogue of references to
specific saints and their histories, and the overt gestures towards
unnamed figures, particularly the transvestite saints (St. Marina,
St. Pelegia, St. Eugenia, St. Susanna, and St. Theodora) identified by
Alison Chapman (2007: 159). We could also include the apocryphal
ninth-century Pope Joan (John Anglicus/Pope John VIII), who allegedly gave birth to a child, thus revealing her true sex (Boureau 2000;
Durrell 1954). A likely hoax, her existence in Catholic lore nevertheless
reveals a curiosity for this kind of deception and places Damien's story
in a long and richly subversive tradition.

The implications in the novel of this 'witness' to the confining
structures of external authority are, however, far broader than any
issue of relevance to, or revision of, the arcana of the Church of Rome.
Chapman asserts:

> *Last Report* both alludes to and revises the stories of medieval and early
> modern figures such as St. Cecelia, St. Agnes, St. Damian, St. Patrick,
> St. Dismas, St. Stanislaus Kostka, and the women known as transvestite

saints. *Last Report* can be read as a revised hagiography in which Erdrich reworks centuries-old stories from the Catholic canon into a narrative about Ojibwe spirituality. (2007: 150)

We might of course read this audacious move as an allegory for historical revisionism, a counter-canonical claim that, like early colonial narratives, reinvents the subject – this time the Catholic – in its own terms. Most importantly, this argument illuminates the satirical possibility of such revisionism:

> More specifically and more pressingly, Erdrich uses the saints' lives in *Last Report* to challenge the question of imitation that both lies at the heart of Christian piety and that confronts American Indians trying to create and sustain a sense of identity against the hegemonic impulses of dominant society. (Chapman 2007: 150)

Addressing colonial mimicry at one level, it relates more broadly to the notion of the pious exemplar, and the Judaic Law that Paul grapples with in his letter to the Romans. Because the law requires certain behaviour, breaks with that behaviour are defined as sinful; Paul contends that Christ's sacrifice annuls that earlier covenant and it is also that prior logic that Erdrich's saintly parodies interrogate, in establishing Damien in particular as conforming to typology, only to undermine it with a diversion or counter-narrative.[18] In other words, in subtly demonstrating the ways in which saints have often acted independently of the church, Erdrich illuminates the controlling mechanisms of the institution and, by extension, the colonial powers it has served, while simultaneously demonstrating a much more playful and inclusive economy of relations.

Erdrich leaves us, according to Chapman, with a contest/contrast, not of Ojibwe-Christian traditions but between two versions of piety or spiritual behaviour. Leopolda, described by Damien as a 'spiritual arsonist', *acts out* the role of the holy woman, exploiting common signifiers – the stigmata, self-denial, pious distress – and representing an opportunism that intentionally manipulates her audience. The other, Damien, *despite* his opportunism, ironically embodies the Christian ambassador, truer still the more 'Ojibwe' he becomes. He makes genuine self-sacrifices, seeks to help the people he serves, is humble, acts on love, and follows a broad church, even incorporating Ojibwe values into his belief structure. 'Ultimately', Chapman writes, 'the Ojibwe-turned-Catholic, Sister Leopolda, is a travesty of a saint whereas the Catholic-turned-Ojibwe, Father Damien, epitomizes

saintliness in the highest degree. In turning from 'Leopolda's Passion'
to 'Father Damien's Passion', Erdrich sides with heroic virtue as the
defining characteristic of the saint' (2007: 152). The latter, despite
acting the role of a male priest, is true to himself, while the former,
living according to the tenets of her conversion, is the real actor.
Despite Damien's need to maintain his disguise he does not withdraw
from duty or act selfishly but goes out among the people.

Christianity aside, we sympathise with Agnes/Damien who, albeit
uneasily, welcomes her sexuality, in contrast to Pauline/Leopolda, who
represses hers or uses it as a weapon of ill purpose. Although both
characters betray through their deception, Damien's deception
becomes an act of deep devotion; Leopolda's, meanwhile, begins and
ends as an act of self-loathing and malignant revenge. As Nanapush is
to make clear, love – loving – is a core aspect of Ojibwe relations,
celibacy a form of self-denial that is anathema to the old trickster. The
irony of this inversion is further underscored in Damien's prior
incarnation as Sister Cecilia, orgasmic at the piano, passionate (as
Agnes) with Berndt Vogel; the material inversion of her namesake.
While Saint Cecilia, a brutally martyred virgin, denied the flesh entire,
Sister Cecilia (who once used the pseudonym Cecilia Fleisch (221))
fails utterly in that self-denial.

The paths of connection between Erdrich's novels are various and
range from the obvious to the encoded but *Last Report* develops one of
the more subtle aspects of *The Antelope Wife*. In the juxtaposition of
Pauline/Leopolda and Agnes/Damien, we are shown how the stock
narrative of colonial coercion must be complicated: Damien, like
Scranton Roy, is deeply transformed by his contact with the 'other',
while Pauline becomes as threatening to the order that 'creates' her as
to her own people. Nowhere is this mutual influence clearer than in
that characterisation of Damien as a figure of two powers 'warring' for
one soul:

> Not quite of the body, yet not entirely of the soul, pain closed in like a trap
> on Agnes and held her tight. Some nights it was a magnetic vest drawing
> blood to swell tightly just under her skin. Agnes wanted to burst from the
> cassock in a bloody shower! Other nights a shirt of razors slit and raked
> her and left no mark. Her womanness crouched dark within her –
> clawed, rebellious, sharp of tooth. (*LR* 209)

While conflictual, it is in the appreciation of what both aspects of the
duel bring to Damien's character that we understand the vital *power* of
that dialectic, a twinship dependent on 'complementarity . . . duality

that is not the same as opposition,' a concept of balance that perceives the holistic co-existence of two diversities (Sarvé-Gorham 1995: 167).

Where we see the motif of balance at work – in Pauline and Fleur's battle, in the balancing act of Cyprian and Delphine in *Master Butcher*, or in the ways Damien and Pauline balance, each seeing through the other's artifice – it often unfurls both within the dynamic between two or more people *and* within individual characters. Jude notices feminine features cross the face of the priest whom he believes to be a man, features that prompt him to ask if he has a twin (*LR* 139). While the motif of twinship pertains to Agnes/Damien's own being, she is also twinned with the real, dead, Damien and Pauline/Leopolda in the traditional conflictual-yet-complementary terms of Ojibwe twinship stories as described by Sarvé-Gorham. While the real Father Damien's dogma-driven, doctrine-led masculine assumptions of 'civilised' superiority identify evil in *les sauvages* whom he is bound to serve, Agnes/Damien has a vision of evil in a 'rumpled cassock' (35–37). By no means her only vision, this moment acts as a prophetic catalyst to her own decision first to go north and then to assume the mantle of priest, an only half-consciously considered corrective to missionary legacy. This emphasis on the instability of perspective must also force us to revisit the nature of Pauline/Leopolda's actions. Remembering McCafferty's arguments (see Chapter 3), Pauline's transition from Ojibwe/Métis to Christian, then, is only ever a partial shift, illustrating the codified resistance implicit in scenes that tend to be read as manifestations of cultural erasure and self-abnegation: a wholly alterNative possibility.

Place and displacement: the immigrant experience in *The Master Butchers Singing Club*

The master-narratives of Native American displacement emphasise geographical removal, cultural and spiritual dislocation, the ravages of war, disease, poverty, and the impacts of divisive federal Indian policies such as allotment. The latter literally divided tribes, communities, families, even individuals down lines predicated on abstruse notions of 'tradition' and 'progress'. The emphasis this master-narrative tends to place on issues of loss, dislocation, and devastation is itself an element of its own controlling function. As Benjamin explains:

> To articulate what is past does not mean to recognize 'how it really was.' It means to take control of a memory, as it flashes in a moment of danger

> ... it is a question of holding fast to a picture of the past, just as if it had
> unexpectedly thrust itself, in a moment of danger, on the historical
> subject. The danger threatens the stock of tradition as much as its
> recipients. For both it is one and the same: handing itself over as the tool
> of the ruling classes. (2001: 2)

The Master Butchers Singing Club opens with a quite different scene
of violent displacement, one that relies on – even intervenes in – that
story of 'Chippewa survival' in the tetralogy with a more universal (yet
paradoxically no less localised) story of survival on the North Dakota
plains. More importantly, it reflects directly on the process of historical
narrative – the privilege and prejudice of power. It retells that story of
endurance; of *becoming*; and of continuity in change. That the principal
focus of the novel is a German émigré family following Germany's
defeat in the First World War does not cancel out the ways in which
this novel's consideration of cultural adaptation, divided loyalty, pride
and perseverance, and above all the personal and collective question of
national allegiance, inflects the history and survival of another nation,
the Anishinaabe. That Natives are virtually absent from the novel,
physically persisting only in a Métis man and a Cree woman, is telling.
Yet their presence – 'latent' as Walsh and Braley suggest of Native
presence in *The Beet Queen* – attends to what Rowe sees as the key
political unconscious of the work.

In her representations of Euroamerican towns as 'either fiercely
repressing or blithely unaware of this native American presence',
Rowe notes that 'Erdrich works self-consciously to counter this
repression and overcome such ignorance, rendering native Americans
in her imaginary upper Midwest as ineluctable characters in this
landscape' (2004: 197). It returns to the material of *The Beet Queen*, yet
where that book is often seen as hermetic and ahistorical, *The Master
Butchers Singing Club* provocatively engages with the stark realities of
its historical context:[19]

> Fidelis walked home from the great war in twelve days and slept thirty-
> eight hours once he crawled into his childhood bed. When he woke in
> Germany in late November of the year 1918, he was only a few
> centimeters away from becoming French on Clemenceau and Wilson's
> redrawn map, a fact that mattered nothing compared to what there might
> be to eat. (*MB* 1)

True to Erdrich's method, the story evolves from the very personal
circumstances of its protagonists, the specific physical, spiritual, and

emotional needs they face. And yet this novel also engages directly with the global contexts and consequences of its starting point, evoking the 'punishment' meted out to defeated aggressor Germany at the Treaty of Versailles.[20] The conflict between the right-wing French prime minister Georges Clemenceau and 'pacifist' US president Woodrow Wilson is simultaneously acknowledged and deflated, the return of Alsace-Lorraine to France less important in the moment than Fidelis's stomach: 'He smelled food cooking – just a paltry steam but enough to inspire optimism. Potatoes maybe. A bit of soft cheese. An egg? He hoped for an egg' (*MB* 1).

This material history serves as both contextual backdrop and rejoinder to the 'official' historical narratives insofar as it juxtaposes quotidian experience with the documentary record of national and international history between the wars. Both Austenfeld and Cornelia have made similar arguments on slightly different terms, the former arguing that Erdrich 'necessarily confronts twentieth-century German history' (2006: 7) and the latter that 'Erdrich is willing to confront the truth – and shame – of both the butcher's art and the treacherous policies employed by the United States government against the original inhabitants of its continent' (2004). The novel does so as an intervention into the historiographical record, constructing an architecture of late nineteenth- and twentieth-century trauma, from Wounded Knee to the Indian Reorganisation Act; and from the First World War through the Great Depression, to the atrocities of the Second World War, within which the living histories of individuals operate. In doing so, they modify those official narratives with a sense of the local, the personal, the purely subjective, and the mutable; demonstrative, in the end, of the prismatic history of the United States.

But further, Erdrich places all of these events, as Rowe argues, into a single continuum that both exposes and diagnoses the colonial malaise, 'anachronistically constructing Wounded Knee as a sort of European original sin and the symbol of colonial violence' (2004: 203). Rowe identifies the novel's multiple scenes of both live burial and rescue as the symbolic means of illuminating and then dismantling the systems of codified authority through which imperial agency asserts control. He highlights these scenes as a means of representing the 'weight' of history (of authority) *and* as sites of Anishinaabe origin and emergence, demonstrating an entangled yet vital historiography that maps localised incidents on to the national and global events above. Far from reflecting the vanishing that these historical processes predict and even 'prove' through their own excoriations, these moments address the active presence of Native people in the material and spiritual balance of European survival on the plains.

Erdrich also constructs a self-reflexive critique of narrative process, subsuming those earlier accusations of apoliticism and ahistoricism into a self-conscious dialogue as Fidelis, Delphine, and Mazarine sit and read the paper:

> By that night they had the evening edition out of Fargo with the headline ATOM BOMB HITS NIPS. They spread the paper out on the kitchen table and pored over all the front-page stories. Terror Missile Has 2,000 Times More Blast Than Blockbuster. Sun Power Holds Key to Explosive. Churchill Says Germans Had Some Secrets. Kitchen Dream a Reality – Combined Clothes, Dishwasher, Potato Peeler Due in 1946. Quadruple Amputee PFC James Wilson Uses Artificial Limbs. Husband Shoots Wife, Kills Self While They Are Dancing. (MB 368–369)

Placing two stories alongside one another – namely the atomic blast and the imminence of the 'combination clothes washer, potato peeler and dishwasher' – serves the dual function of enacting and illustrating historical reportage *in its own moment*. History is relative; there is a disjuncture between the narratives presented as important and the contingencies of daily domestic life – will there be food on the table as the novel's opening suggests? Indeed there is a wide range of 'voices' in the historiographical sense here, references that encode the historical context ranging from the global (war, the Jewish purges in 1934), to the local (vaudeville, which was fading in popularity by the 1920s; the first transatlantic flight by Charles Lindbergh (1927); rationing – and the 'C' sticker Fidelis was entitled to carry on his truck that indicated supplemental fuel rations; the decline of the bonanza farms), to the personal, such as the emphasis on food, the nature of Eva's treatment for cancer with radiation 'bombs', Roy Watzka's funeral, or Cyprian's second Vaudeville act, satirising Hitler, which spans all three categories. This also all intersects in the booming business Fidelis and Delphine experience during rationing, partly due to burgeoning demand for kosher meat from Minneapolis Jews – an indicator of a growing displaced Jewish population.

The difference between the atmosphere of *The Beet Queen* and the greater historical awareness of this novel is to be found in Fidelis's arrival, which draws the global context into the frame. It lends a newfound sense of the external world to the Argus of the tetralogy, which unsettles a truism to be found in a regionalist sense of the Midwest. Reflecting on the universal shock in the wake of the Oklahoma City bombings, for instance, Dorman writes, '[h]ere was a traditional, small-town place of decent, conservative, hard-working people, disaster prone, to be sure, but otherwise safe from history' (2006: 179). In one sense, Erdrich's characters are refugees from history; in another, they *are* history itself.

The novel's opening carries many of the motifs that abound in Erdrich's work – such as the importance of food, whether to survival or physical/sensual gratification, or homecoming.[21] It speaks not merely to the local but also to universal ideas of constructed identity (Fidelis 'nearly' wakes up French and we are left wondering what that might have meant for him) and land loss, both of which carry different implications when Fidelis emigrates. The individual scenario, then, rapidly becomes microcosmic, without being subsumed by the symbolic. In other words, this *is* a story about Fidelis and his family, but it is also a much larger story about choice and coercion, migration, individual and collective responsibility, ethics, and chance.

In view of the major events the novel encounters, and the major issues it raises, from political dispossession to migration, and from surrogacy to sexual taboo, the book's principal leitmotif is, unsurprisingly, equilibrium. Balance, in the literal sense, begins with the vaudeville-style act of Delphine Watzka and Cyprian Lazarre and permeates virtually every area of the narrative's social and cultural fabric. This central metaphor casts balancing as an existential dilemma, simultaneously enacting a bathetic deflation of that 'high' agenda. Looking into Cyprian's eyes as he performs a handstand on Delphine's washboard stomach, a stack of chairs balanced on his upturned feet, the narrator asks: 'what do you really see in the eyes of a man doing a handstand with six chairs balanced on his feet?' The answer: 'You see that he is worried he will drop the chairs' (21). When Delphine later poses the 'how' question directly to Cyprian, two significant things have occurred: the two of them have had their first complete sexual union; and Delphine, while walking along the river in their host town of Gorefield, Manitoba, has witnessed a homosexual coupling. The reader of course beats Delphine to the understanding that one of these men is Cyprian. Lying in bed, desperate to know how and why he does such things with another man, Delphine uses the word 'balance' as a euphemism for all subsequent negotiations – be they physical, spiritual, sexual, historical, racial, or interpersonal:

She meant to say something cutting about his betrayal, to ask didn't he remember how they'd looked into each other's eyes? She meant to ask him why the hell he never told her he was *that way*, to shout in his face or just wail miserably. But in the second before her voice left her lips, other words formed.

'How do you balance?' (27, Erdrich's emphasis)

Speaking both to the physical act and to the social/psychological feat of being a gay man in a small Midwestern postwar town ('For sure there was no future in living with a man. In setting up a house. He'd never heard of that, except for in the cities' (149–150)),[22] Delphine's question, which is repeatedly (implicitly) asked throughout the book, provokes metaphysical and pseudo-philosophical responses. Cyprian's response – 'If you become too aware of knowing you are dreaming, you wake up. But if you are just enough aware, you can influence your dream' (28) – ensures that balancing becomes a metonym for questions of fate and free will, deeply implicated in the historical contingencies to which Rowe alludes. Like *The Antelope Wife*'s beading, the 'act' suggests that one is simultaneously responsible for one's own balancing and dependent on the will, and choices, of others.

In every sense, Cyprian provides the model by which balance is judged in the novel. As an acrobat he is suspended, neither grounded nor airborne; as a gay man he has to balance his existence both in a world that will not easily accept him, and in his relationships with women; and as a Métis man apparently alone in Argus, he must find his place between the European émigrés and his investment in Métis community as embodied by Riel's rebellion. His status as mixed-blood Ojibwe is introduced subtly, almost in passing, and yet it carries 'rhetorical' implications that form Cyprian's character as a travelling 'circus' performer, always on the edge of things, never at the heart of the Euroamerican community, transitional as he flees with Clarisse Stubb and returns in passing with a new act. Like the Cree woman Step-and-a-Half, his itinerancy marks his liminality, and yet, like Step-and-a-Half, whose story takes in a history of Indian affairs in the Midwest since Wounded Knee and the rescue of the abandoned Delphine Watzka, he is more deeply embedded in the community than even its members can know.

His career choices emphasise the double marginality of his status as both gay man and mixed-blood Indian, most explicitly illustrated by his political non-status following the war: 'He came home before it even occurred to him that, as an Ojibwe, he was not yet a U.S. citizen.

During his slow recuperation, he couldn't vote' (15). The Indian Citizenship Act of 1924 was passed in recognition of the disproportionate numbers of Native Americans who served in World War I.[23] Although the act granted suffrage to Native American peoples, the liminal status of other Native characters in the novel, from the 'family of Dakota Sioux who . . . traded wild meat or berries for flour and tea' to the elusive Step-and-a-Half, 'a rangy stray dog of a woman who was probably still young . . . and yet moved with an air of ancient bitterness' (82), testifies to their peripheral relationship to the townsfolk and carries an almost anachronistic air in this period of new immigration.

Later, when describing his background to Delphine, Cyprian makes clear his affiliations, declaring himself a descendant of Louis Riel, leader of Métis rebellions in Canada in 1867 and 1885:

> 'Have you ever heard of michifs or métis?' Cyprian peered at her, then shrugged and looked away. 'I guess not, but if you had, you'd have heard of my famous ancestor, Louis Riel, who died a martyr to the great vision of a mixed-blood nation – not a loose band or bunch of hunters. A place with boundaries and an actual government taking up a big chunk of Manitoba. There's lots of us who still do dream about it!' (77–78)

Dreaming of boundaries is an ironic pastime for Cyprian, who spends his time transcending physical boundaries – as a travelling performer and later as a bootlegger into Canada – and transgressing social ones, frequently traversing both sexual and legal 'borders'. The point, however, is once again reached by Delphine, who asks, ' "Was [Riel] a good balancer?" ' only to receive the ominous response, ' "He was an excellent balancer, but they hung him anyway" ' (78). The dichotomous sense of heroism and treachery this story carries reverberates throughout the novel's principal narrative of German-American immigration.

This deceptively central 'side' narrative of negotiated Indian identity coincides with the nationalist argument in a strand of Womack's important thesis on literary separatism, wherein the term 'queer' and the status of gay Indian men is tied intricately to the anti-assimilationist stance he takes there (2000 *passim*). Commenting on Womack's position in both *Red on Red* and an earlier essay, Bethany Schneider writes, 'I'm trying to articulate how queerness and Indianness form a sort of tag team in their very relationality within colonialist discourse, sometimes operating together in the service of Indian identity' (2007: 608). Long stratified into separated layers of advocacy against forms of oppression, assertions of identity begin to be rewoven through the enmeshing of alternative renderings of history. Importantly, in reminding us, via Riel's activities, of the longstanding and ongoing claim for sovereignty and autonomy of North America's indigenous groups, Cyprian's self-searching is displaced from the Eurocentric paradigm of the hybrid-as-fractured to Womack's return to centres: he may be walking a tightrope – a clear metaphor that offers a *trompe l'œil* to the theorisation of hybridity and even carnival – but equally that line to the nationalistic discourses of the late nineteenth century could be a bridge. Although this is peripheral to the main plots of the novel, Erdrich gestures to that alternative and, in the critical arena of her novel's publication two years after Womack's book, timely possibility for a radical, liberatory discourse-in-development.

Central to the status and experience of the Métis, Nation as imagined by Louis Riel is also important to the central ethnic dilemma faced by Fidelis and other new immigrants, who have left a home-land to forge a new life. Both originary homeland and this newfound home, *America*, are up for grabs, even though the USA had, by the First World War, become increasingly hostile to Germans. The German population, perhaps counter-intuitively, responded to disquiet by applying for citizenship: by the time of the 1920 census, three-quarters of Germans in America, the highest percentage among foreign-born white ethnic groups, had become American citizens (Rippley 1985: 223). Fidelis's 'Germanness' is manifest in his sausage-making of course (rather than the bakery of *The Antelope Wife*), in his singing, in his family – particularly Tante – and in the choice he has to make between holding on in the USA and returning to Germany for the sake of his children after their mother's death. If Cyprian maintains equilibrium, then Fidelis's condition is perpetual tension. Nowhere is this more evident – and more starkly at odds with that hard-edged image of Fidelis as sniper and butcher doling out death – than in his first wife's final days:

> In that moment of tremendous effort [as Fidelis picks up Sheriff Hock with his teeth], Delphine saw the true face of the butcher – the animal face, the ears flaming with heat, the neck cords popping, and finally the deranged eye straining out of its socket, rolled up to the window, to see if Eva was watching. . . . He was trying to distract her, and from that Delphine understood Fidelis loved her with a helpless and fierce canine devotion that made him do things that seemed foolish. Lift a grown man by the belt with his teeth. A stupid thing. Showing clearly that all his strength was nothing. Against her sickness, he was weak as a child. (125)

Through Fidelis we witness another balance: hardness alongside a certain helplessness; paternal sternness offset by the lullabies he sings to his children; his survival as both a feat accomplished in himself and a challenge faced on behalf of his family – the latter fact affirmed by his name.

Just as Fidelis negotiates those tensions, the émigré family's stories also come to represent the pressure to choose between ethnicity and nationality, revealing the pre-war necessity of giving up the home-land in order to make oneself at home.[24] In the early days of Fidelis and Eva's residence in Argus, there is a clear sense of resistance to assimilation in the way that specifically German characteristics are accorded value – most notably a strong, if destructive, work ethic[25] – and a particularly German 'cause' is defined in relation to Cyprian's career as a bootlegger:

> Avoiding the slap of sales tax was not only a very common thing to do, it was patriotic if you were German, or supplied the liquor to them. No one had hated Prohibition like the Germans, who were convinced it was a law passed as a direct comment on their tradition of Zechkunst, the art of friendly drinking. Since Prohibition was over, heavy taxes on liquor were the new source of resentment and no one took such pleasure as Germans in thwarting the government. (*MB* 93)

Both stereotype and truism, the German bierkellar tradition trans-ferred to America and it was German opposition that held back Prohibition to 1919, with the 'German' State of Wisconsin the last to give in and Wisconsin and Michigan first to repeal Prohibition laws in 1932 (Rippley 1985: 226–228).

Despite mounting suspicion of things German, exacerbated by the general anxiety fostered among German émigré communities by a forceful Americanisation programme in response to National socialism (recalling anti-German sentiment in the First World War), strong ties did often remain between Germany and German émigrés. Tante exploits these ties in her attempts to persuade Fidelis to let her take the children back to Germany. Evoking the fact that Germany had once been seen favourably by the US as an admirable intellectual and cultural centre, Fidelis's earlier hopes for American progress are thrown into sharp relief by Tante's 'discovery' of the superiority of German technology – particularly the sewing machine – on her return. The palpable dangers of language loss and cultural alienation split Fidelis's family in two, between Tante and the younger boys, and Fidelis/Delphine and the two older sons, both described as having become American despite their lingering accents. We witness, in no uncertain terms, the disintegration of the German family – leaving a landscape sparsely populated with literal, spiritual, and psychological orphans, as if history itself, and the environment of the North Dakota plains, conspire to break the immigrant units up.

The cultural material of the fatherland, then, plays a subtle but significant role in the novel, emphasising the contrast between strong ties to Germany and the drive to assimilate. 'Loyalty leagues' and loyalty resolutions among immigrant social organisations encouraged the latter, precipitating a proliferation of name changes from German-sounding to more Anglicised names, and renewed attempts to suppress German language and culture in the US (Kraus 1966: 186–187). These manoeuvres are reflected in two key ways in the novel. The first, integral to the singing club, involves an awkward conversation about the state of affairs:

> Chester Zumbrugge was concerned that the singing in German might be construed as treasonous activity.
>
> 'Not that it could be considered a real crime. Not that we'd be prosecuted! However, I think we've got town sentiment to consider.'
>
> 'Those Krauts beat the beans out of the damn Polacks,' said Newhall. 'I don't care what you say, they're a war machine.'
>
> 'They're a bunch of damn butchers,' said Fidelis, and the others laughed. (336)

The uneasy humour here, as Newhall's comment unconsciously evokes the early competition-turned-enmity between Fidelis and the Kozkas, and as Fidelis self-consciously alludes to his own activities as sniper and butcher, indicates a lack of assurance as to the men's own relations to events in Europe. That sense of diminishing confidence among the immigrants finds no clearer symbol than in Fidelis's inability to crack a walnut first time with his fingers, a party trick he has used on multiple occasions. As if to underline this uneasiness, their conversation is shortly followed by a gesture of patriotism in the singing of what Fidelis calls 'America songs', finally fusing into a 'métis waltzing tune called "The Bottle Song"' (337) taught to them by Cyprian. Clearly the ultimate *American* song, it fuses European (French) heritage with that of its indigenous inhabitants, the mixture that as we have seen is always-already at home and always-already displaced in the Midwestern landscape (ironically highlighted when Tante describes Cyprian as a 'foreign-looking fellow'). What once represented pluralism and anti-assimilation passes through a brief sense of the reverse – of the need to articulate one's Americanness – before finding that articulation in another site of resistance, thus playing out the ethical balance of advocacy and imposition in both experiential and historiographical terms.

A story of land acquisition in *Four Souls: A Novel*

Tracks climaxes in an act of apparent self-abnegation that is simultaneously an act of 'interpretation [of] and resistance' to the government treaty (Allen 2000: 76), as the trees on the Pillager parcel on Matchimanito Lake begin falling, sawn through at the base by Fleur. With a sense of historical inevitability, she defiantly leaves her land to the lumber barons and those mixed-blood members of the tribe who are willing and able to manipulate the changing times. While most critical writing on *Tracks* celebrates Fleur's refusal to let the lumber company have their triumph, Gross sees it as a failure, in stark contrast to the energetic, humour-filled response to adversity of characters like Nanapush (2005). As Cornell notes, Nanapush himself forecasts Fleur's resistance in *Tracks* as a kind of 'noble failure':

> At the end of the novel, Fleur achieves a psychological victory over the logging company, but it is a victory that Nanapush represents as a noble failure. Although Fleur manages to have the satisfaction of terrifying the loggers . . . her victory is pyrrhic: The trees still fall and she must move. Even as Fleur tries to hold on to Misshepeshu and her Chippewa identity, taking the 'weed-wrapped stones from the lake-bottom', Nanapush predicts her loss of power among Euroamerican institutions. (Cornell 1992: 62)

In *The Bingo Palace* she reappears, fourteen years later, dressed sharply in white, with her 'white' son in tow,[26] to avenge her loss through a card game against the former Indian agent Jewett Parker Tatro, who has bought her land from the lumber baron John James Mauser. *Four Souls* explores those intervening years, tracing Fleur's journey from the reservation to Mauser's marriage bed and back again, proving Nanapush's predictions overly simplistic if not entirely wrong.

Four Souls makes explicit, through the figure of the tree, the human toll of the project of building America. The intricate relationship between lumber, capitalism, and the Indian is highlighted in the narrative journey, a physical, psychological, and historical migration from reservation to metropolis and back again, becoming in its turn a metaphor for nineteenth-into-twentieth-century American

Indian history. The journey's starting point, several pages into the narrative, is a familiar location:

> And to the north, near yet another lake and to the edge of it, grew oak trees. On the whole continent and to each direction these were judged the finest that could be obtained. In addition, it proved easy and profitable to deal with the Indian agent Tatro, who won a personal commission for discovering that due to a recent government decision the land upon which those trees grew was tax forfeit from one Indian, just a woman – she could go elsewhere and, anyway, she was a troublemaker. (*FS* 6)

The description of Matchimanito, Pillager land, follows several pages of description of John James Mauser's Twin Cities house, embedding the colonial nexus in a Native history. It also establishes an artificial gendered divide for the story to follow, a story of feminine determination in the face of masculine exploitation: those oak trees, the 'finest that could be obtained', are destined, like Fleur, for the cities.

The symbolic parameters for this story could not be clearer. The exploitation in the dismissal of the claims of 'one Indian, just a woman' is underpinned by a description of the building of the house itself: 'The chimneys were constructed of a type of brick requiring the addition of blood, and so, baked in the vicinity of a slaughterhouse, they would exude when there was fire lighted a scorched, physical odor' (*FS* 7). Here, the blood of the slaughterhouse takes the figurative place of the blood of the construction workers. It invokes a chain of metaphors from the stripping of the land to the physical labour of its workers, which creates a layering of subjugation fraught with the hierarchical coda of race and class. Like that icon of nineteenth-century American literature, the Pequod in *Moby-Dick*, the house literally wears and inhabits the collateral damage of the owner's economic pursuits. For at the very least the house that is built as the product of that first moment of exploitation – metonymic of the whole colonial or even capitalist project – is infused with the blood of its labour.

In *Tracks* a simple ironic distinction is drawn between the substance of the contest for ownership (the lumber in this instance) and the documents of ownership (the lapsed land titles that are plastered on the inner walls of Fleur's cabin), a product *of* the lumber and one in a number of paper trails that both name the land as 'owned' *and* require its resources. That same relation persists in *Four Souls* but is also demonstrated via the human cost of this construction, preoccupying the reader's first view of Mauser's house. More importantly, it forges a truly global concatenation of colonial and economic subjugation:

Iron for the many skeleton keys the house would take, for the griddles, the handles of the mangle, for the locks themselves, the Moorish-inspired turned railings of the entrance and the staircase, was mined on the Mesabi Range by Norwegians and Sammi so gut-shot with hunger they didn't care if they were trespassing on anybody's hunting ground or not and just kept on digging deeper, deeper into the earth. (*FS* 7)

This connection with the Sámi, implicated along with other European peoples in the settlement of the Americas, is interesting, not least for the localised systems of colonisation that have occurred through the centuries in Scandinavia.[27] Like the Hmong in *The Antelope Wife*, the common experience of subjugation of indigenous peoples at least notionally transcends their otherwise localised conditions, and again locates the processes of economic globalisation in the late colonial model. Ironically, that one indigenous group is, however indirectly, involved in the exploitation of another, stages the book's central tension between narratives of agency, power, and responsibility.

It forecasts the paradox of power in indigenous–European relationships with which the novel ends, when Margaret Rushes Bear points out to Fleur that in seeking revenge against Mauser she has done even more damage by neglecting her family and community obligations. The bigger paradox is that it is precisely Fleur's strength – the single-mindedness diagnosed by Margaret as ' "put[ting] the heart of an owl under your tongue . . . brav[ing] all the old wisdom . . . scorn[ing] us" ' (*FS* 203) – that results in her weakness, shame, and emotional distance from her children. Margaret asks:

'How can they love a woman who has wasted her souls? How can they love a mother who forgot to guard their tenderness and her own? How can they love a woman who can suffer anything and do anything? Forget your power and your strength. Let the [Medicine] dress kill you. Let the dress save you. Let yourself break down and need your boy and your girl.' (206)

In performing a naming/healing ceremony for Fleur, Margaret provides the function that Fleur herself fails to offer her mute savant son, a failure that Margaret believes explains his own introversion: 'For sure, such a thing was no accident . . . "He's strange in the head because the spirits don't know him!" ' (200). In *Last Report* his strangeness is attributed to the possible loss of his *indis*, a small package containing a part of his umbilical cord, confirming that sense of his 'loss' to the gap in that maternal/ancestral connection (*LR* 261).

The implication, again, is that Fleur has neglected the specific ritual patterns of the Ojibwe in bringing him into the world.

So subjugation and indigeneity are only one aspect of the larger structures in which Mauser's house sits and it is to this broader context that Erdrich draws our attention momentarily:

> Water from the generous river. Fire trembling in beehive kilns. And sweat, most of all sweat from the bodies of men and women made the house. Sweating men climbed the hill and set the blocks and beveled the glass and carved the details and set down floors of wood, parquet, concrete, and alabaster. Women coughed in the dim basement of a fabric warehouse sewing drapes and dishcloths and hemming fine linen. One day overhead a flight of sandhill cranes passed low enough to shoot and the men on the crew brought down nearly a hundred to pluck and roast, eat, digest, and use up making more sweat, laying bricks. A lynx was killed near the building site. One claw was set in gold and hung off the watch fob of John James Mauser, who presented his wife with a thick spotted muff made to the mold of her tender hands. (*FS* 7)

Here, privilege quite literally comprehends all, subsuming the elements and even corporeal secretions into the stuff and substance of the building, and absorbing the natural terrain – fauna and flora – into the survival cycle of both. The crane and lynx, both clan totems, are expeditiously culled for the feeding of a workforce and adornment of the 'client's' wife. Their extra-textual significance is juxtaposed against the recipients of their sacrifice, the Mausers, for whom these animals serve a merely functional and decorative purpose. That chasm between the privileged few and their haunted denizens and the gulf of meaning between spiritual and material investment is reinforced as the narrative returns to that blood-infused brickwork:

> They had this house of chimneys whose bricks contained the blood of pigs and calves so that a greasy sadness drifted in the festive rooms. They had this house of tears of lace constructed of a million tiny knots of useless knowledge. This house of windows hung with the desperations of dark virgins. They had this house of stacked sandstone colored the richest clay-red and lavender hue. Once this stone had formed the live heart of sacred islands. Now it was a fashionable backdrop to their ambitions. (*FS* 8)

The 'fashionable backdrop' to the Mausers' ambitions signifies that network of interactions between the powerful and the powerless that finds its most entrenched metaphor in the plantation house: the rupture between its superficial artifice and its melancholy substance is palpable. The Mausers themselves are painted in terms that echo the rise of nineteenth-century manoeuvring classes (the *nouveaux riches*), particularly prominent at the fin-de-siècle but ever present into the modernist era in models such as Cather's Louie Marsellus (*The Professor's House*) or Fitzgerald's Gatsby (both 1925).[28] Their house becomes a monument to their 'degenerative' decadence.

For Fleur the house simultaneously serves as a manifestation of loss and a 'spectre' of the sequence of dispossessions on which it, and the economic success it represents, is founded:

> This house of beeswaxed mantels and carved paneling, of wooden benches set into the entryway wall and cornices and scrolls and heavy doors hung skilfully to swing shut without a sound – all this made of wood, fine-grained, very old-grown, quartersawn oak that still in its season and for many years after would exude beads of thin sap – as though recalling growth and life on the land belonging to Fleur Pillager and the shores of Matchimanito, beyond. (*FS* 9)

The life oozing from the structure foreshadows the spectral presence of Fleur herself. It is a presence that slowly yet surely ushers the Mausers and their dominion into self-destruction, but not without repercussions that suggest an authorial didacticism, casting a more vivid light on those 'oozing' memories that refuse to relinquish the relationship between a land and a people. It does become a treatise on the nature of revenge and the needfulness for temperance in the pursuit of reparation or restorative justice. Conversing about Fleur's long lineage and the Pillager heritage, Margaret admonishes her, emphasising her folly through a naming sequence:

> 'No matter what people call you [your name is no longer Fleur]. Your name was Leaves Her Daughter. White Woman. Zhooniyaa. Your name was All Wrong. All Too Different. Impossible. Your name was Sorrow like the dog your aunt slaughtered so her child should eat. Your name was Kills Him Once. Kills Him Again. Kills Him Over and Over. I'm not faulting you for your revenge, but what did it get you?' (206)

Finally returning the bones of her ancestors to Pillager land, Fleur truly comes home, a diminished shadow of her former self. More significantly, though, and certainly more overtly politically, *Four Souls* becomes a story of the power and importance of the land in Fleur's single-minded, if flawed, attempt to recover it. If Fleur's method is indeed a 'pyrrhic victory', undone by the individualism and essential compromise of her actions, her aim – and the lessons learnt through her pursuit – is central to questions of indigenous sovereignty.

Inextricable from this are the diminishing returns of the drive for acquisition, which eats away at the relationship of Nanapush and Margaret Rushes Bear back on the reservation, and leads, albeit through the comedic escapades we have come to associate with Nanapush, to greed, jealousy, and wanton acts of revenge. It is no coincidence that both Nanapush's and Fleur's stories essentially revolve around sex. Nanapush, still beset by fear of impotence and his general inability to provide, becomes jealous of Shesheeb, his ex-brother in law who 'went windigo' (102) and now appears to pursue Margaret. In Fleur's case, windigo itself becomes her rival as her intention to heal Mauser so as to destroy him is thwarted by her own instincts to seduce him. In both instances, one result of this inner conflict is alcoholism, and as Nanapush explains, 'I shared with Fleur the mysterious self-contempt of the survivor' (FS 21). Fleur essentially internalises her experiences in the cities, experiences she otherwise seems to adapt easily to, despite the alien landscape she initially perceives.

Polly Elizabeth celebrates the house for its technological precision, enhanced by, but separate from, nature:

> On the most exclusive ridge of the city, our pure white house was set, pristine as a cake in the window of a bakery shop. High on sloped and snowy grounds, it was unshadowed yet by trees. The roof, gables, porch, all chiseled and bored in fantastic shapes, were frosted with an overnight fall of gleaming snow. Clipped in cones and cubes, the shrubs were coated with the same lacquer, as was the fountain, frozen, and the white cast-iron lacework of the benches and the tea tables in the yard. (FS 11)

Even the use of the word 'lacquer' privileges process: an organic substance in origin, lacquer is *derived* from the natural world. As a metaphor for the snow it manages to abstract the substance to its effect. The artifice contrasts starkly with Fleur's impressions: 'For a long while she stood before a leafless box hedge, upset into a state of wonder at its square shape, amazed that it should grow in so unusual a fashion, its twigs gnarled in smooth planes' (FS 3). Then her fluid appearance into this world disrupts the rigidity of the household, as Fleur's sensuality contrasts with Placide Gheen Mauser's self-denial.

Placide's devotion to Karezza, a form of orgasm control, condenses female conduct writing, from the eighteenth-century domestic manual to Alice Bunker Stockham's *Karezza: Ethics of Marriage* (1896). Subtly the narrative presents another archetypal image of the late imperial mode as barren, repressed, degenerative. Intriguingly, as Fleur's seductive powers ensnare Placide's sexually frustrated husband, Fleur herself enters a process of degeneration (into acquisition, alcohol, self-contempt) that ironically inverts the staple narratives of colonial degeneration of, for instance, Robert Louis Stevenson's stories and travels in the south Pacific (1888–1894) or Joseph Conrad's *Heart of Darkness* (1902). Such intertexts are rife. First and foremost the novel self-consciously explores the terrain of those fin-de-siècle and early twentieth-century novels that take social, sexual, and racial 'health' as their topic. As such it gestures to domestic literature from the novel of manners through to late gothic – with hints of transgression and darkness – and the late naturalist or modernist novel of capital and instinct.

There are faint but deliberate echoes here of writers as diverse as Wilkie Collins, Emile Zola, Edith Wharton, and even André Gide. In the relationship between Mauser and his attendant, Fantan, we catch similar echoes of those archetypal partnerships between European men and mute(d) indigenes – Defoe's Crusoe and Friday, Cooper's Hawkeye and Chingachgook, Melville's Ishmael and Queeqeg, for instance – where though the 'power' resides with the coloniser, the vitality is largely to be found in the 'tragic' native. That essential tragedy is, of course, that these figures are so distant from their people, or are the 'last' of their kind, that they have literally to throw in their lot with their Euroamerican companions. In *Four Souls*, of course, no such tragedy ensues. Fleur's return ensures that for all the masquerading, this novel is first and foremost *her* story, an ironic reclamation of a classic European mode: at once a morality tale, a quest, a circular narrative of cause, effect, and consequence. Rushes Bear ensures that it is the indigenous narrative, not the 'colonial' one, that resounds once the book has been put down.

Outside looking in: repatriation and/of *The Painted Drum*

The Blue Jay's Dance, with its mix of maternal memoir and evocative longing for the plains from a New Hampshire farmstead, was first published in 1996. It has taken until 2005 for Erdrich to revisit that terrain in her fiction and it is perhaps no surprise that *The Painted Drum* also focuses partly on a mother–daughter relationship, this time

from the adult daughter's point of view. Just as *Blue Jay* evinces a sense
of displacement and self-sacrifice, in a landscape so far from the 'great
rolling sky of the plains' (*BJD* 92), so *The Painted Drum* presents two
mixed-blood women, Pillager descendants Faye and Elsie Travers,
remote from their originary community but rooted, unlike the
eponymous drum, which is destined, after its discovery in a house
clearance, to make the return trip home.

Faye finds the drum in the family home of Jewett Parker Tatro, on
the death of his last surviving grandson, John Jewett. Tatro is a
recurring – if peripheral – character, the Indian agent who buys the
Pillager land in *The Bingo Palace* and reappears in the card game in
Four Souls. Opportunistic, with an eye for an artefact, Tatro took family
(and sacred) items in lieu of unpaid bar bills. His family, apparently
aware of the special nature of many of these materials – largely
mundane but important nevertheless – has taken care of them in
the intervening years. Retreading the well-worn paths of mother–
daughter and broader family relationships, romantic relationships,
female and native identity, the novel also reengages with, and creates
anew, a number of narrative threads surrounding Ojibwe heritage.
The motif of beading so central to *The Antelope Wife* recurs in revenge
enacted by a wife and her love-rival against the man who duped them
both; we follow the creation, nature, and purpose of the drum itself;
and explore the significance of repatriation to both the repatriators
and the community of the drum's return. Alongside these are more
universal narratives of deaths and births; the losses of siblings,
spouses, children and parents; and the environmental presences of
memory. This latter is encapsulated by the unkempt orchard in which
Faye's sister Netta died. Faye's part-time lover Kurt Krahe prunes it,
symbolising the start of a process of reassessment, repatriation, and
reconciliation in which the drum is central. Taking the road – 'Revival
Road' – as both literal and metaphorical site of change and continuity,
as pattern and as chronotope; and going 'off road' as metaphor for the
tangled web of life ('Just look around you. Here is the way things
are. Twisted, fallen, split at the root. What grows best does so at the
expense of what's beneath': 25–26), *The Painted Drum* explores the
permutations of stories as they cross and connect time, generations,
and distances.

Speaking of his work, sculptor Krahe explains, 'I have in mind a
perception of balance, although the whole thing must be brutally
off the mark and highly dysphoric' (9). That sense of balance emits a

self-reflexive note, gesturing to the form of Erdrich's novels as well
as to the more emic sense of balance within *The Painted Drum*. In
the foreground it pertains to the four key present-day relationships:
between Elsie and Faye; Faye and Krahe; between Krahe and *his*
daughter, Kendra, and between Kendra and Davan Eyke. Of the first,
Faye reveals:

> It is difficult for a woman to admit that she gets along with her own
> mother – somehow it seems a form of betrayal, at least, it used to among
> other women in my generation. To join in the company of women, to be
> adults, we go through a period of proudly boasting of having survived
> our own mother's indifference, anger, overpowering love, the burden of
> her pain, her tendency to drink or teetotal, her warmth or coldness, praise
> or criticism, sexual confusions or embarrassing clarity. (20)

It is the tension behind this admission that then threatens the second,
where she reveals that 'openly becoming Krahe's lover would upset
the balance' (21). Indeed, each of these relationships teeters on the
brink of disaster; they are finely weighted balances that place the other
relationships under constant threat. Krahe's tense relationship with
Kendra leads to friction between himself and Faye, while the same
leads Kendra into the ultimately destructive relationship with Eyke.
When the two youngsters, chased by police, go hurtling off the road
to their deaths, the tension between Faye and Krahe intensifies,
magnified even through the story of Netta's premature death. Thus
the fragile tenor of these several relationships emphasises the individual weaknesses of the characters as well as their need for and
vulnerability around one another.

These fine, fickle threads that connect kin and kind in rural New
Hampshire also tie together the strands of the novel's narratives
around the central motif of the drum, itself an emblem of community.
The communally played big drum, around which the powwow has
generally revolved since it evolved from the spring gatherings of the
Dakota, is traditionally revealed to an individual in a dream and then
constructed according to the dream's revelation. Retained within
families, the drum proceeds from ceremony to ceremony with numerous careful rituals pertaining to it. Most importantly, of course, it
becomes the heartbeat of the gathering, the timekeeper of the dances,
and the centre of the social circle: 'The big drum creates a shared
heartbeat that resounds beyond the powwow arena out to the circle of
families and clans' and 'permeates all things, seen and unseen'
(Attachie et al. 2005: 110, 124).[29]

In the novel the drum effectively becomes the catalyst of, and vehicle for, a series of stories that trace its lineage from the point of its discovery through the history of the people from whom it originates. As a device it uniquely interacts with the fallout of those personal histories Erdrich documents elsewhere – alcoholism, lost love, death, and so on – charting an intimate journey of the drum (and by inference Faye's antecedents) from and back to the territory of their predecessors (and from and to a sense of Faye's Ojibwe roots). As such, and not least for the ethnographic detail of the drum itself, this novel more problematically than any of Erdrich's novels to date engages with the kind of cultural testimony David Treuer critiques in *Native American Fiction* (see Chapter 1). Alternatively, Cook-Lynn's misgivings about 'Native cultures [being] used like props' criticise the titillating nature of apparent cultural detail to non-Native audiences (1996b: 68).

Of course Treuer's critique calls not least for acknowledgement of the *literariness* of Native American literature. In that sense *The Painted Drum*'s narrative structure conforms to the literary devices of the picaresque or episodic novel and the story cycle, whose origins span numerous cultural traditions. One recent intertext for this kind of narrative device, exploring immigrant experience through the relayed ownership of an assortment of accordions, is E. Annie Proulx's *The Accordion Crimes*. There, the even more picaresque form of the novel is directly informed by the instrument's journey. In this case, however, the drum exceeds that role as Erdrich takes on the larger issue of patrimony and repatriation, almost self-consciously enlarging and exploring some of the tenets of Treuer's criticism of *Love Medicine* – particularly questions of nostalgia and cultural longing (2002) – explicitly 'conceded' by Erdrich's sense of 'unziemliches Verlangen' (Pearlman 1994: 152). As if to acknowledge the potential charges, a postscript note declares that 'no sacred knowledge is revealed' and that Erdrich 'check[s] carefully to make certain everything [she] use[s] is written down already' (277). Nevertheless, anxieties about the ways in which Native texts can reveal and inform, exoticise and objectify are implicated in these ethnographic details.

In a sense, then, the drum in this novel symbolises Faye Travers's cultural patrimony. 'What I love about my cultural patrimony', writes David Treuer, 'is the life it provides, not the material' (2002: 62). Although Treuer is more explicitly referring to language here, the ultimate movement of the drum from its removal and desacralisation, through Faye's rediscovery (and near-fetishisation) of it, back to the community of its origin is interesting in this light. Despite Faye's own cynicism, where she notes, 'I do not believe of course that the drum itself possesses a power beyond its symbolism and antiquity' (43), its presence in the community proves almost instantly positive. Whether self-conscious or not, the kind of dilemma to which Treuer turns his argument is implicit in the disparity between the representation of the drum's 'activities' and Faye's interpretation of its largely, if not merely, symbolic value. The question of repatriation has been a live issue throughout the world in recent decades, and a key factor in American–Indian relations since the passage of the Native American Graves Protection and Repatriation Act in 1990, which 'provides a process for museums and Federal agencies to return certain Native American cultural items – human remains, funerary objects, sacred objects, or objects of cultural patrimony – to lineal descendants, and culturally affiliated Indian tribes and Native Hawaiian organizations' (NPS 2009). Born of the controversy of the countless bones, sacred remains, and other sensitive items held by bodies such as the Smithsonian, NAGPRA has provided a mechanism – though not infallible – for the sensitive return of cultural goods.

That the movement of the drum participates in the politics of return at least theoretically speaks to those questions of control and legitimacy that have abounded in Native American Studies. In the sense that the drum is a vehicle for the stories shared within the novel – both the personal/family narratives of Faye, the Strings, and the Shawanos; the Pillager stories Bernard Shawano tells on the drum's return; and the history-in-continuity story of the String family's relationship to the drum – there is at least a notional sense of returning story to the cultural centre. Owned and stored for many years by Tatro before being harboured (respectfully but inappropriately) by Faye, the drum returns to community ownership. Its first act once returned is to 'save' Ira's freezing children, guiding her eldest child, Shawnee, to Bernard's house and then taking its place in the healing ceremony Bernard conducts for the youngest, Apitchi.

While several of these stories do indeed appear to impart the kind of fine cultural detail alluded to above they also participate in the political contexts of contemporary Native life. Faye's grandmother Niibin'aage, for instance, was taken away from her family by a teacher staying with Tatro and sent to the Carlisle Indian school, a familiar narrative of the disruptions produced by the Indian boarding school system. Ira's story itself, one of poverty and desperation, reflects the impoverished conditions in which many Native people both rural and urban still live. As live as these issues are, they also tread a thin line between empowerment – the return of the drum and its community-centred role – and victimology as it negotiates again that fraught history of allotment, Indian education, dislocation, and poverty. Necessary to drawing attention to the often difficult circumstances of Native life, the *em*placement of the drum within that nexus of stories is vital to understanding the affirmative movement back to the socio-political centres of the reservation. Tension exists between those two narrative strains of political efficacy/sovereignty and cultural 'colour'.

One such element, with which this section will close, echoes the 'mythical' patterning of *The Antelope Wife*. Hooked on the idea of snaring the antelope woman, the woman he comes to call Sweetheart Calico, Klaus Shawano describes his methods in the following terms:

> Once I get near enough I begin to fence them with my trader's talk – it's a thing I'm good at, the chatter that encourages a customer's interest. My goods are all top quality. My stories have stories. My beadwork is made by relatives and friends whose tales branch off in an ever more complicated set of barriers. I talk to each of the women, make pleasant comments, set up a series of fences and gates. (*AW* 27)

Where in *The Antelope Wife* the 'beading' of Klaus's words becomes a masculine trap, in *The Painted Drum* the literal beading of a dance outfit by his once rival wives becomes a somewhat macabre torment-to-the-death for Simon Jack:

> Sometimes they ran out of thread and continued to sew with grasses or wolf sinew or even with their own hair. It was only from necessity that they did this. They did not mean to bind him to them in an evil way. They did not mean any evil at all. They were only caught in what the story did to them. The story Simon Jack had set into motion . . . [I]f each woman beaded the bottom of one of his makizinan the way grieving widows bead the soles of their dead husband's, it was only the fault of Simon Jack again. (*PD* 144)

His betrayal of his first wife with Anaquot (Fleur's mother), rather than overcoming the women, which it initially threatens to do, draws them together in solidarity: 'The two women stitched each other still closer, became true sisters' (145). This action consolidates the source of the Pillager power that we witness in Fleur's actions elsewhere. Driven by union with another that leads to revenge, the delicate balance between power and abuse of that power is evident in Fleur's very early childhood. These sequences, including the presence of the spirit of Fleur's older sister, devoured by wolves when their mother, in panic, threw her from their sled, bespeak all of those elements of balance and chance – between life and death; over snap decisions taken; between control and loss of control; between action and the implications of the actions of others – that become almost recursive themes in Erdrich's later work. The symbolic movement in this text – the removal and return of the drum – carries its key political register; the power for good in respect of community.

Truth and legacy in *The Plague of Doves*

If *Four Souls* illuminates the complex interrelation of indigenous and Euroamerican (hi)stories, *The Plague of Doves*, plays out the inherent tensions and paradoxes of those relationships. Arriving just too late for lengthy analysis here, *The Plague of Doves* marks a shift and a decisive return to Erdrich's lyrical best. Rooted in an exploration of a single, traumatic event, the lynching of three Native people, one a thirteen-year-old boy, in North Dakota in 1897, the novel weaves together the stories of subsequent generations springing from, and touched by, the legacies of both lynched and lynchers. The generative complexity of that one event is incisively characterised by Noori in relation to the novel's opening scene, and the eponymous plague of doves:

> Erdrich's tales operate on many levels. The doves, for instance, are simultaneously historical realities, biblical signs, and political night-mares. Like the locusts that plagued Egypt, the birds – actually now-extinct passenger pigeons – descended in 1896 on the North Dakota town of Pluto. A biblical dove can be a sign of peace or of the Holy Ghost, and a flock is a message from God. Yet all that whiteness descending on Chippewa reservation farmland, hungry and destructive, is also a metaphor for the myth of manifest destiny. The people watching the doves and settlers arrive compare them: 'the murmurous susurration, the awful cooing babble, and the sight . . . of the curious and gentle faces.' (2008: 12)

As both the lynching and Noori's comments suggest, the novel once more opens up a fraught terrain, both nuanced and vexed, with a strong symbolic coda and a clear historical narrative of displacement and injustice. That sense of displacement and injustice, however, becomes internalised, less a focus of conflict than an examination of a collective past. As in *The Antelope Wife* or *Last Report* the emphasis falls on the mutually constituting/corrupting force of contact, this time turning to characters like Evelina, who is a descendant of both indigenous and settler lines. As Erdrich herself notes, 'We are all mixed up together. There's been so much finger-pointing and blame ... I'm a mixed background; so many people are, of this country. We all have mixtures in our backgrounds, now' (Baenan 2008).

Far from moving away from the politics suggested earlier in this chapter, however, this novel offers intense meditation on the generational implications of these events. While the one-time conflict is ultimately resolved in one character, the competition – and violence – over place, land, entitlement that said conflict entailed is far from reconciled. The possibilities for readings of the novel are equally multiple and complex, so this chapter will close with a single, simple focus, dwelling on the early stages of the historical contexts the novel portrays, in which the three key components of Evelina's mixed ancestry – the European émigrés, the Native victims of their ire, and the Métis guides who assist in the settlement of the land – come together. That those Métis are not cast as 'caught between' but rather as strong, autonomous agents carving out their place in this terrain is but one element of the new nuances Erdrich brings to this familiar tale of Indian–white relations.

Early on in the novel, the narrator's grandfather and great uncle revel in a spot of priest-baiting, drawing in the retired Father 'Hop Along' Cassidy; 'nothing made them happier than the chance to fling history into the face of a member of the hated cloth' (*PoD* 22). The history they fling is itself fraught, both personally and nationally:

> On the kitchen wall ... three pictures hung. John F. Kennedy, Pope John XXIII, and Louis Riel ... he was the visionary hero of our people, and the near leader of what could have been our Michif nation. Mooshum and our mother venerated him, even though Mooshum's parents had once lived in neat comfort near Batoche, Saskatchewan, and their huge farm would have passed to their sons, if not for Riel. (21)

As supporters of Riel, however, the Milk family are proud of having sustained losses in the cause of nationalist rebellion. Earlier priests' threats to excommunicate Riel's followers and betray them to their killers is the source of their priest-baiting (21). Louis Riel (1844–1885), of French and Native parentage and advocate of reform of the Catholic

Church, developed, in response to the refusal of his Catholic friends
to take his aspirations seriously, a more radical desire to 'break with
Rome, to establish on the soil of the New World a successor to the
Catholic Church, which had lost its spiritual vitality' (Flanagan 1979:
73).[30] That radical desire, joined with a sense of injustice and
dispossession, ended in the two armed rebellions over territory in
Manitoba, and one of the most famous executions of an indigenous
son in Canadian, if not North American, history. Long understood as
a patriot/traitor depending on viewpoint, Riel's place in the Canadian
mythic imagination is profound and complex, embodying the paradox
of split/balance that has so preoccupied Erdrich.

Described in *The Plague of Doves* as having gone to his death
'wearing moccasins and holding in his hand a silver-worked crucifix'
(22), Riel is thought by many to have 'set forth a pattern and paradigm
that became the template for all the major subsequent attempts to
order the many and various regional, Euro-American ethnics, Metis,
and Aborigines, as well as the various economic interests into some
kind of ordered Canadian identity' (Long 2008: ix). Immediately
following his execution in 1885, he represented French Catholic
subjection to Anglo-Saxon oppression. His Métis ethnicity, subsumed
under Quebois cultural identity (Reid 2008: 32), doubled his role as
radical national hero if, paradoxically, eliding that key component of
his identity and political cause. Figuring prominently in Métis and
indigenous writing as touchstone for resistance and reclamation
in the last few decades, he has gradually taken a more visible, if
background, role in Erdrich's work.[31] His multiple images, outlined
by Braz (2003) as including enemy and/or victim of confederation,
cultural mediator, martyr, and maverick, ensure the symbolic power of
his legacy for Erdrich's own ongoing examinations of the power
of perspective.

For Mooshum and his brother Shamengwa, deliberation on Riel's
legacy is always a double consideration of both politics and religion, for
victory territorially would also have meant the advance of Métis
Catholicism. Acknowledging his weaknesses as a war chief does not
detract from his strengths as a mystic:

> Both . . . insisted that if Louis Riel had allowed his redoubtable war chief
> Gabriel Dumont to make all of the decisions preceding and at Batoche,
> not only would he have won for the mixed-bloods and Indians a more
> powerful place in the world, but this victory would have inspired Indians
> below the border to unite at a crucial moment in history . . . The two

brothers also liked to speculate about the form that Metis Catholicism would have taken and whether they might have had their own priests ... Both agreed that Louis Riel's revelation, which he experienced upon learning of his excommunication and that of his followers, was probably sound. (30)

The prevailing motif of the novel, through various permutations, is that of settlement – the literal taking of one's place on the land as well as the cultural parameters that settlement lays down. Given that the Milk family are themselves doubly displaced, first as descendants of both European and indigenous lines, and then, most importantly, as Métis forced to flee across the border to escape persecution after the failed rebellion, Father Cassidy's response to Mooshum's question of whether he knows their history is incendiary: ' "I'm a Montana boy," said the priest. "I know how they put down the rebellion" ' (32). Mooshum's response is indicative of what was, and is, at stake:

'It was an issue of rights,' he cried, slapping the table. 'Getting their rights recognized when they had already proved the land – the Michifs and the whites. And old Poundmaker. They wanted the government to do something. That's all. And the government pissed about this way and that so old Riel says, "We'll do it for you!" ... If we had our rights, as Riel laid 'em out, Father Cassidy, you'd be working *for* us, not *at* us.' (33)

Shamengwa pipes in with, 'If Riel had won, our parents would have stayed in Canada, whole people. Not broken' (33), which not only reiterates the dislocating consequences of that loss, but echoes the moment of 'cracking apart' in others of Erdrich's novels.

Yet equally instructive is the emphasis in Mooshum's outburst of who 'they' actually are – 'the Michifs and the whites'. The Michifs *and* the whites. As Flanagan notes, 'The invitation to Riel from the inhabitants of the Saskatchewan valley was the result of discontent affecting all classes of the population: métis, English half-breeds, whites, and Indians' (1979: 121). The failure to fulfil the land issue promised the Métis in the 1870s was very much part of a wider failure that included the Cree (among whom Poundmaker was a leader), who also had treaty grievances, and serious economic hardship among white settlers who blamed railway monopoly and high freight charges, many of whom were also resentful of their territorial status (Flanagan 1979: 121–123). Both implicitly and explicitly, the turmoil around settler colonisation is presented as far more complex and finely wrought than any representation of contact-as-conflict might allow.

This treatment draws in many of the major themes of Erdrich's work, including the affective and *altering* nature of contact for both parties. Non-Native characters, whether presented as agents or pawns of the state, are equally implicated in the failures and flaws of the larger structures of the state. In this light, relations between Natives and whites, Natives and Métis, and Métis and whites are themselves more nuanced than the politics of division can account for.

While by no means co-operative, there is nevertheless a mutual element in the attempts to settle on, and survive in, the plains. This is exemplified by 'The Expedition' in which men of the families implicated in the lynching set out to survey northern lands with the help of the two Métis Peace brothers as guides. That this need to survive, undoubtedly competitive at times, results in the kind of violence on which the novel centres, that it can *breed* racism, is perhaps inevitable, but, as Erdrich repeatedly makes clear, failure to fully uncover the causes and consequences of that violence through the political need to focus on singular narratives can itself overshadow the broader injustices of human existence. Combining stories of resistance and revival with stories of honour, humour, cooperation, and collaboration, honouring the memory of Paul Holy Track, the thirteen-year-old boy brutally lynched in 1897, is not only a matter of apportioning blame. It also involves understanding the circumstances of that moment and exposing the ongoing ramifications for generations born of those violent meetings and enduring not as victims but as survivors of historical oppression. All of these things – and most importantly the responsibility of the teller, as the novel's final narrator Dr. Cordelia Lochrane, the surviving child of the house murders, attests – are bound intricately with the nature of the tale:

> When Pluto's empty at last and this house is reclaimed by earth, when the war memorial is toppled and the bank/café stripped for its brass and granite, when all that remains of Pluto is our collected historical newsletters bound in volumes donated to the local collections at the University of North Dakota, what then? What shall I have said? How shall I have depicted the truth? (308)

Early on in *Red on Red* Womack rejects '[t]he supremacist notion that assimilation can only go in one direction, that white culture always overpowers Indian culture, that white is inherently more powerful than red, *that Indian resistance has never occurred in such a fashion that things European have been radically subverted by Indians*' (2000: 12,

emphasis added). While Erdrich's work will never satisfy the particular
political demands of some commentators, it cannot be denied that her
recent novels in particular develop themes that speak to Womack's
latter point. Her stories *are*, in one sense, stories of Indian survival.
But so too are they stories of Euroamerican endurance, of the contact
zones and deeply intertwined histories of Native and European
presence on the plains. To say this is not simply to recast the old
'betwixt and between' narrative but rather to point to the ways in which
Erdrich's work, as it matures, has highlighted the common paths of
enmeshed communities at the same time as demonstrating their
differences, the discrete (as well as synthetic) cultural traditions on
which they draw in all their 'radical specificity' (Owens 1998: 45), and
the patterns of negotiation and exchange through which they develop
as communities and individuals. Responding both to the aesthetic
demands of the physical and psychological landscapes she deals with,
and to the static histories that have documented and fixed what she
emphasises as fluid and mutable territories, it is to the contingency
implicit in Cordelia Lochrane's aspirations that Erdrich repeatedly
turns. Through metaphors of breaking and healing, of cracking apart
and reforming, reforging, remembering that new truths displace old
truths, she both complicates and reconstructs the literatures and
histories with which she engages, and makes a significant contribution
to the rich and diverse body of Anishinaabe literature.

Postscript

Published just prior to this book going to press, in some respects
Shadow Tag takes a slightly different turn, into a much more compact
world. A claustrophobic domestic narrative, it negotiates some of
Erdrich's common themes – identity, human relationships, love,
family – in markedly different terms, focusing on the failing marriage
between husband and wife Gil and Irene and the broader repercussions for themselves and their children. The main narrative device also
makes a shift, from the contrapuntal 'spoken' narratives of *Tracks*, for
instance, to Irene's interwoven double diary, with its emphasis on a
very intimate, private, written mode, complemented by a third-person
narration. Here, she keeps a red and a blue notebook, the first a tease
for her husband Gil who, she knows, has discovered its hiding place.
That both Gil and Irene consider themselves Native American, without
having been brought up 'within' their cultures, speaks to those issues

of pan-Indian identity, and more particularly nostalgia, while emphasising a universality of human relationships perhaps more strongly than any of her other novels. For this is the story of intense relationship struggle, of mind games bordering on mental cruelty, of the battle between suffocating love and the need for space. In that respect it perhaps most closely evokes the complex and often twisted relationships of *The Antelope Wife* – Rozin and Richard Whiteheart Beads's in particular. It will inevitably encourage biographical readings but there is still a clear thread throughout of concerns highlighted in other novels: Irene and Gil's daughter, for instance, is named Riel, after Louis Riel, while their second son, Stoney, is named after Chief Stone Child, who led the Turtle Mountain Chippewa into Montana in the 1870s, and after whom (via a mistranslation), the Rocky Boy's Reservation in Montana is named. More pointed is Irene's dissertation on the nineteenth-century 'Indian painter' George Catlin, presented here as a shadow stealer. Alongside the protagonists' self-consciousness about their Native heritage, the novel lays clear emphasis on questions of ethics, and foregrounds aesthetics (all of the characters, including the children, at some point either paint or write), without letting either overwhelm the simple central story of a marriage falling apart while the family struggle to function. Less densely plotted than some of Erdrich's recent novels, *Shadow Tag* is no less intense, largely because of the painful intimacy of Irene's notebooks. The patterns of home and habit are finely wrought here, demanding close critical attention to its representation of familial dysfunction, and the strengths and corruptions of human character, even as their varying shades are vividly expressed through Gil's painting and Irene's diaries.[32]

Notes

1 In December 1862, 303 Dakota warriors were tried and sentenced for their part in what was called the 'Sioux uprising'. Thirty-eight of them were eventually hanged.
2 Louis Riel (like Cyprian himself, a mixture of French, Ojibwe, Cree, and possibly some English) led a rebellion against the newly formed Canadian Dominion's land surveyors (and their supporting troops) in Manitoba in 1869. In 1885, in Saskatchewan, he led a second failed rebellion, again provoked by land surveys, projected and real settlement, and the Canadian Pacific railroad, all of which disrupted the Métis way of life.

3 Beidler and Barton locate their line in 'woman who gets beads from Midass, who got them from Augustus Roy II in exchange for his wife, Zosie II' (2006: 43).

4 Ahokas points out that although the novel itself presents a series of binaries, characters such as Cally Roy work towards a reconciliation of difference and division.

5 See e.g. Little (2000), who refers to Theresa S. Smith's *The Island of the Anishnaabeg* (1995), an invaluable source alongside Callicott and Overholt (1982), Johnston (1982; 1990), and Vizenor (1998a). Readers might also be directed to Hallowell (1947), Vecsey (1983), Landes (1968), and Densmore (1929).

6 Theresa Smith explains this structure as a constitution of 'three parts: the body, the ego-soul (the part that leaves the body upon death), and the free or shadow-soul (the dream or traveling part)' (1995: 63 and 132).

7 Connie Jacobs notes the potential to be both benevolent and malevolent: 'Erdrich plays with these pan-tribal perceptions of the antelope people in *The Antelope Wife*: antelope as deceivers, the beauty of the antelope women, antelope people as guardians to humans, and the ability of the antelope people to transform themselves at will to human form. The motif of the mythological antelope people frames *The Antelope Wife* along with the story of the mythic twins and their often violent attempts to secure the perfect beads for their design, which turns out to be the stories of the three families' (2001: 171).

8 The dualities Castor mentions specifically are good and evil, light and dark, God and the devil, truth and falsehood, male and female, friend and enemy, all of which run throughout Erdrich's oeuvre.

9 Though rare, and scientifically unsubstantiated, reports of male breast-feeding occur in the global press from time to time, such as Hewlett's (2005) report in the UK *Guardian*, which tells of the Aka men's willingness to suckle their babies.

10 In *The Blue Jay's Dance* Erdrich identifies a sense of connection with life through maternity that she describes as 'the mystery of an epiphany, the sense of oceanic oneness, the great *yes*, the wholeness' (1996b: 148).

11 Erdrich's interest in Catholic mysticism is apparent all the way back to *Jacklight*. The irony in Erdrich's inversion of the image is palpable – she figures the maternal as saved by the child, rather than the maternal act of nurturing itself as salvation. Thus, she both subverts the normative assumptions outlined above, with a transgressive narrative from the Christian margins, and, in doing so, further subverts the Christian grand narrative by presenting Scranton as *colonial* 'savage' and Matilda as the civilising influence.

12 Erdrich's choice of 'profession' for the friends wonderfully illustrates the cannibalistic cycle of excess, breeding waste, which in turn can be turned into money, which fuels the desire for excess, and so on.

13 In fact, although we are never given the identity of the 'author' we might wonder if it coincides with Eleanor Schlick's biography of Sister Leopolda in *Tales*.

14 This is not extraordinary in the hagiographic archive (see Chapman 2007).

15 See also the closing chapter of Womack (2000); Williams (1984); Brant (1994); Jacobs et al. (1997); Roscoe (1998); Gilley (2006); and Tatonetti (2007).

16 As Goulet (1996) shows, in some instances even these ways of conceptualising Native gender variance owe more to the epistemic constructs that limit anthropologists than to indigenous ways of understanding gender and social behaviour. Trexler, however, has recently suggested that historical evidence prior to the twentieth century points to this 'figure as constructed through force by parental or tribal authority' (2002: 628). Trexler refers to 'berdache' throughout, a term that is largely denounced by Native two-spirits people and contemporary scholars of two-spirits, and gay and lesbian studies, as inappropriate and derogatory. Deriving ultimately from the Persian, 'barah', the word means ' "male prostitute", a "kept boy", a "catamite" ' (Forgey 1975: 2). Barak notes that the berdache among plains groups were both respected and ridiculed, marginal as well as special (1996).

17 See, for instance, Grim (1983), who describes Hole-in-the-Day's snake-vision as the source of his healing power; and Conway and Conway, who describe the importance of the giant serpents depicted in the Agawa pictographs as both natural enemies of the Thunderers and allies of Micipijiu, guards of the Great Lakes, the source of the paint used in the pictographs themselves, and as being covered with copper or silver (1990: 29). These serpents also appear frequently in the sacred scrolls related to the Midéwiwin (see Dewdney) and again, 'if a medicine man or woman gained some control over it, it could release great power' (Rajnovich 1994: 107).

18 Alison Chapman writes: 'just as the reader discerns the recognizable contours of the life of St. Cecilia, for instance, Erdrich wrenches the saint's life off into an unexpected, almost parodic, direction' (2007: 150).

19 Just as Erdrich's earlier novels 'survive' the Depression due to a mixture of their narrative insularity and their geographical location, Fidelis and his family seem utterly unaware of and untouched by the policy of internment of German American 'Enemy Aliens', a fact often suppressed in the popular memory, while internment of Japanese-American citizens remains well-known.

20 Fighting had ended on 11 November 1918 with the signing of the armistice by the allied forces and Germany. The Treaty of Versailles, formally ending the war, took place at the Palace of Versailles on 28 June 1919.

21 Numerous other common elements abound, such as the prevalence of weak men and strong women; a principal character who has frequent

visions (Delphine Watzka); a healer or medicine person – in this case a Braucher, or faith healer, whose practice originated in the German colonies in Russia; and a strong, if mysterious, Indian survivor (Step-and-a-Half).

22 Interestingly, Cyprian experiences no prejudice in the novel; indeed, his inability to 'settle' in a normative sense with a man is largely implicit both in his attempts to be a 'man' for Delphine and his itinerancy.

23 Native American service on behalf of other nations dates back to colonial warfare between the British and French, and between them and other Native tribes. The Ojibwe fought largely on behalf of the French during the French-Indian War and on behalf of the British during the War of Independence. Britten suggests that more than 17,000 Native peoples registered for service during the First World War, while other estimates vary between 5,000 (Boston Hampton Committee), 9,000 (Reverend Chief Red Fox Skiuhushu), 10,000, and 17,000 (Barsh 2001). Also see Camurat 1993.

24 Intensity of feeling against Germans reached fever pitch during the First World War, partly due to what Dobbert describes as a 'strident German immigrant nationalism' that left a residual effect in the run-up to the Second World War (1967). By summer 1918 half the states in the Union had restricted or banned outright the German language. The creation of the German American Bund by Fritz Kuhn in 1936, an organisation which 'tried to advance National Socialism in the United States', again caused alarm but was ultimately unsuccessful. See Kraus (1966); Dobbert (1967); and Bell (1970: 585), respectively. Echoing the terms of contemporary reclamation programmes, The German Quarterly printed a pamphlet in 1942 entitled 'The Study of German in This War and After', which argues: 'For the preservation of culture and for the sake of a well-informed war effort, we must prevent a declaration of war upon the German language' (1942: 179).

25 Totten defines these traits as including remarkable diligence and efficiency on the one hand, and a marked materialism and tendency to overwork 'their' women on the other (1985: 187).

26 The felling of Pillager timber in Tracks occurs in 1919 and The Last Report seems to date Fleur's return to spring 1933 (LR 260).

27 As Helander has noted, Norway is scattered with evidence of the subjugation of the Sámi people, much of which dates back to nationalist policies at a time when Norway was subject to domination by Sweden (2007).

28 Opportunist parvenue Marsellus represents all that the professor regrets (and yet can't entirely resist) about the modern era.

29 Not all nations use a central common drum, or drums. The Dane-Zaa in northeastern British Columbia, for instance, use smaller hand-held drums in their dreamers' dance tradition (Attachie et al. 2005).

30 Flanagan's early work on Riel was, by his own admission, more sympathetic to the Métis cause than his later, revised views in the controversial *Riel and the Rebellion* (1983), in which he suggests that the Métis' problems were substantially of their own making.

31 Cherokee writer Thomas King makes several allusions to Riel (*Green Grass, Running Water* (1993); *Truth and Bright Water* (1999)); Lee Maracle notes recognition of Riel's patriotism as a point of allegiance and historical correction in *I Am Woman* (1996 [1988]). Note, however, that Métis historians also stress the need to revisit this historical period with a broader view of the Métis community and not just the singular focus (Barkwell et al. 1999).

32 *Shadow Tag* is the third new book Erdrich has published since the earliest drafts of this book: evidence of her energy and prolificacy, and also a salient reminder of the sometimes Sisyphean task of staying up to date with a dynamic and ambitious author.

5

The writer's brief: collaboration, (auto)biography, and pedagogy

If, at this stage, a hint of unease is discernible in *this* writer's voice, it is not least because after four chapters, we have still only accounted for two thirds of Erdrich's output. As the title above suggests, this is somewhat of a 'portmanteau' chapter. As such its common themes are perhaps obliquely wrought at times, but they constitute the various ways in which Erdrich herself, and critics of Erdrich, examine the intricate symbiosis of her various 'spheres': writer, woman, mother, and in all roles, student *and* educator. This chapter, then, attempts to do several things. I will offer the briefest of overviews of Erdrich's working collaboration with Michael Dorris (insofar as it has been documented) in order, equally briefly, to address the revision process so key to her work. A glance at the reception of *The Crown of Columbus* (1991), the one novel published under both authors' names, will conclude the first section.[1] Rather than further explore speculative terrain, discussion will then turn instead to Erdrich's two memoirs, *The Blue Jay's Dance* (1995) and *Books and Islands in Ojibwe Country* (2003), to consider the ways in which she documents her influences, writing processes, and the importance of homes and families to her creativity. After considering collaboration and autobiography, the chapter will close with an examination of the pedagogical brief of Erdrich's children's writing. Having begun her publishing career with a children's textbook, *Imagination*, it is perhaps no surprise that Erdrich returned to the entertainment and education of children, beginning with *Grandmother's Pigeon* (1996), for younger children, to *The Porcupine Year* (2008), third in a planned series of novels for young adults.

Working together: collaborative vision and the work of revision

The story of Erdrich's collaboration with Michael Dorris has been frequently rehearsed. To summarise, Erdrich and Dorris arrived at Dartmouth College together in 1972, Erdrich an eventual English and Creative Writing major, Dorris the new director of the nascent Native American Studies programme. Having graduated from Johns Hopkins with her MA in Creative Writing, and with a number of jobs in between, Erdrich returned to Dartmouth (in 1979) to give a poetry reading, after which she and Dorris exchanged addresses. Although Dorris was to spend a year in New Zealand, the two established a correspondence that was eventually to lead to their marriage. Later still, Dorris (at the suggestion of one of his aunts) encouraged Erdrich to submit a short story for the 1982 Nelson Algren Prize: it was to be the winning 'The World's Greatest Fisherman'. Dorris continued to encourage Erdrich to expand the central elements of her story to novel length and, having decided that prose was a more comfortable vehicle for her narratives than poetry, Erdrich began the work.

Erdrich had been writing poetry, and indeed prose in the form of an apparently sprawling manuscript titled 'Tracks', long before Dorris encouraged her to develop her talents. There is no denying, however, as comments by the couple reveal, that the books we know as the *Love Medicine* tetralogy would not have existed in their current form without Dorris's input:

> Erdrich recalls the ordering of its parts as one of Dorris's most significant contributions to *Love Medicine*: ' "Scales" and "The Red Convertible" were written at the same time (I collected sentences over a period of time for them . . . But I let them sit a long time. . . . They didn't become a novel until Michael entered the picture. I did not see that the bunch of episodes was really a long, long story.' (Grantham 1985: 46)

During this early collaboration, the pair also co-wrote, under the pseudonym Milou North: ' "Michael plus Lou*i*se plus where we live. No one seemed to think it was a strange name, which is weird . . . The general theme was domestic crisis – money, an old flame showing up, that sort of thing. We thought it would make a lot of money. It didn't" ' (Grantham 1985: 45). While this close collaboration says something about the nature of their relationship – arguably few writers are willing to suspend authorial autonomy to this degree – it must again be noted that Erdrich subsequently also collaborated in pseudonymous fashion with one of her sisters, under the name Heidi Louise Erdrich.

Nevertheless, it captured the imagination of the literati when it was revealed that books published under the single name of Erdrich, and later Dorris, had been born of a collaborative process; interviewers have repeatedly tried to uncover the secrets of both the process and the marriage that could apparently withstand such ego-suppressing decisions. ' "The basis of the collaboration," says Dorris, "is talk" ': ' "weeks of conversation" about a character's looks, his clothes, her jewelry. "The details of clothes and action are invented and thought about between the two of us," says Erdrich. "Often Michael notices things about people I don't" ' (Grantham 1985: 44). Following conversation, the writing was driven by a process of drafting, editing, and redrafting, with Dorris insisting, ' "She knows her stuff well. I am a gentle reader, a sounding board" ' (Grantham 1985: 44). Further, the couple made clear (and this is readily identifiable in *The Crown of Columbus*) that Dorris's life experience was as integral to the fiction as Erdrich's:

> Sometimes, says Dorris, he contributes 'whole episodes.' 'Sister Leopolda in the "St. Marie" story was a character I knew well in the fourth grade – the closet, the shoe, the window-stick. And suddenly that appeared, susbsumed, as a story. Louise said, "The complete image popped out of my head." But I recognized it.' (Grantham 1985: 46–47)

And yet he was always clear in interview that his role was not that of creator but editor; their decision not to co-publish was 'based on Dorris's firm idea of his editorial status, reading "with pencil in hand" ' (Grantham 1985: 47). This latter point is corroborated by Rothstein, who reports: 'Authorship, Ms. Erdrich says, goes to the person who does the first draft.' There is a minor hint of scandal behind these early probings, generative of both fascination and suspicion. The couple, however, never tried to deny this collaboration and were always careful to acknowledge the respective partner in a given book's dedication.

The centrality of Dorris to this whole process returns us to that fraught ground identified in Chapter 1, for Dorris's own claim to Modoc ancestry was itself contentious. Since his suicide there have been few writing in his defence and Erdrich's early expressions of allegiance, though sincere, were brief and focused primarily on the accusations of child abuse. The narrative, therefore, is largely one-sided but it cannot go without being told since those first five novels at least, held by so many at the time to 'set the pace' for Native American literature, owed so much to his input. Again, Cook-Lynn most vocally highlights what she sees as a series of deceptions in his character: his claim to Modoc ancestry, when there is no record of any Dorris ever having been registered on the Klamath tribal rolls (2001c: 78); his claim to be an anthropologist when Cook-Lynn could only validate an MA in Fine Arts (2001b: 70); and his refutation of those abuse claims, despite allegations by four of his five living children on the Hennepin County Attorney records (2001c: 74). I am unable to clarify the veracity or otherwise of any of these claims. Cook-Lynn identifies no personal reason necessarily to assassinate *his*, or Erdrich's, character; her diatribe is in the service of protectionism. She asserts the primacy of tribal citizenship and sovereign rights; the need to protect the vulnerable and maligned, as she saw the mother of 'Adam' in Dorris's hands; the importance of developing tribal solutions to tribal problems; and the danger of both claiming and accepting authority on the basis of 'vague and ambivalent assertions carefully cloaked in a kind of secrecy that rises out of prejudice' (2001c: 78). No doubt fuller literary biographies of these figures will do more justice to the complexities of this issue: what is abundantly apparent, however, is the way in which such controversial and possibly mendacious contexts to Dorris's contributions considerably complicate those claims to representation and representativeness made about the early books.

Whatever its merits and demerits, this unconventional authorship seems to go hand in hand with the revision process itself – an equally unconventional attitude Erdrich has taken to the nature of the novel. As most readers are aware, she took the bold step in 1993 of reissuing an expanded and slightly modified version of *Love Medicine*. The revisions significantly alter emphasis in the novel, the ramifications of which have been elaborated by Allan Chavkin and others (2000). Changes to the later work – even minor ones such as the titling of *The Bingo Palace*, which had been provisionally titled *American Horse* – and of course the inflections later novels place on earlier narrative events, further signify the ongoing mutations and permutations of the creative process. *Last Report* had also been planned, according to Krumholz (2007), as a revised and expanded reissue of *Tracks*. These changes and shifts are not unique to Erdrich but, framed by the 'romantic' collaboration, they have been played out more publicly and with greater immediacy than may otherwise have occurred.

The complexities of Erdrich's work, alongside these questions of editorship and revision, have led several commentators into an almost archaeological excavation of the minutiae of the fiction. Within the web of interleaving, parallel, and conflicting stories that consti- tute the 'North Dakota series', critics such as Beidler and Barton have identified inconsistencies, particularly in the geography, that might further unsettle the stability of the North Dakotan community Erdrich constructs. In their commentary on *The Antelope Wife*, for instance, Beidler and Barton go to some pains to define and explain the geographical locale, a cartographic endeavour that by their own explanation is no mean feat and requires a number of decisions that arguably transcend the evidence of the texts themselves. They note, for instance, that 'Although the fictional reservation site is ambiguous from novel to novel, its location in *Love Medicine* is rather precise' – in North Dakota not far from Canada (2006: 10). Asserting that it seems to be in much the same place in *The Bingo Palace*, they 'thus placed the fictional reservation on the map in approximately the same location as the Turtle Mountain Indian Reservation' (10–11). I have already mentioned some of the problems associated with this kind of geo- graphical precision in Chapter 3 and it is the stuff, really, of a whole different study. What is more interesting is that despite the com- plication of that location in *Tales of Burning Love*; despite the compli- cations they identify as to the location of the towns of Hoopdance and Argus relative to the reservation (11–13); and despite the specific assertion not to identify the reservation with Turtle Mountain in the author's disclaimer in *Last Report*, the impulse to map, order, and above all *fix* this fictive terrain is compelling.

Beidler and Barton decide to do so by placing the reservation in 'approximately the same location' as Turtle Mountain, in spite of their own caution that 'Readers should not be upset by the indeterminate location of the reservation and Argus. Erdrich *did not want us to identify the reservation in her novels with the Turtle Mountain Indian Reservation and thus, apparently purposefully, included some inconsistencies*' (13; emphasis added). Every instructor who has ever used Erdrich's fiction in the classroom has no doubt experienced the frustration of students' insistence on straightening out the curves and bounces of Erdrich's game. It occurs, often, at the expense of the purposeful destabilising those inconsistencies perform. There is a clear tension here between the desire to make sense of the chaos – the apparently inchoate mess of characters' lives and relationships and the indeterminacy bordering on ethereality of the 'ground' on which they are drawn – and the flexibility, the fluidity, and the essential contradictions of what 'is, after all, a fictional world. Like Garrison Keillor's Lake Wobegon, it need not be expected to coincide exactly with real locations in real states' (13). The other tension that exists – and this is more pertinent to the various genealogical charts that Beidler and Barton and, in more recent novels, the publishers have provided – is between the constant human need to make sense of our own lives (which do not come, after all, with a neat set of instructions) and the means of doing so.

As Beidler and Barton's genealogies also make clear, Erdrich's net-works of relations are highly complex and, at times, highly confusing. The sheer number of 'bit part' actors, for instance, from Two Hat, identified by Beidler and Barton as 'Man under whose window a fox barks' in *The Bingo Palace* (343), to Zozed Bizhieu, reservation gossip who appears briefly in *Last Report*, engenders a sense of the transitional and transitory. The majority of Erdrich's characters, in fact, function partly as narrative devices, but more significantly in contribution to the quantitative sense of community. Other characters reappear in different masks. Take the Pauline–Leopolda transform-ation, for instance; readers of *Love Medicine* will always be shocked by the different inflection *Tracks* imposes on the relationship between Leopolda and Marie. And others still become easily conflatable/confused outside the confines of the text(s) in which they appear. The Shawano family tree, for example, can become particularly confusing in *The Antelope Wife*, not to mention in relation to the Shaawano family in *The Painted Drum*: 'We are not given particular links between these Shaawanos and the Shawanos of *The Antelope Wife* . . . but both families come from a people whose name means "south"' (Beidler and Barton 2006: 316).

In essence the choice is between understanding relations and interactions through charts, maps, and tables, or through stories. The former is the result of hard labour – and we can see the results of that labour, of course; the second is a matter of involvement, absorption, immersion in a world, or series of worlds, that echoes (if it falls short of mimicking) the incoherent complexity of life itself. As much as this sounds like a bifurcation of western scientific rationalist and Native spiritual revelatory modes, such is not my intention. Indeed, the comparison most readily available to us is entirely novelistic. For what is at stake too is the notion that authorial intent and authorial determinism are one and the same; that the author's conscious choices and unconscious instincts are readily available for our scrutiny and that we can second guess their mind when we search for 'truths' in their fiction.

Many readers of course are put in mind of Faulkner, whose Yoknapatawpha County offers useful comparison with the complexities, colour, and detail of Erdrich's fictional terrain. That comparison is also useful here, since Faulkner repeatedly revised and revisited Yoknapatawpha and numerous inconsistencies exist in his work. One such example, Faulkner's character Ikkemotubbe, is described as Issetibbeha's father in the story 'Red Leaves' but her nephew elsewhere (Padgett 2000). Furthermore, those who seek to compare Yoknapatawpha with the real Lafayette County in the Mississippi Delta, for instance, find inconsistencies in topography. Judging the layout of Jefferson a reasonable match for Oxford, Faulkner nevertheless 'plays fast and loose with the cemetery' (Brown 1962: 652), hazing the 'edges' where his fictional reconstructions of a real place meet. Few authors have created as concrete and minutely detailed a location as Faulkner and Erdrich, with so many recurring characters, and perhaps we should rather be amazed at the general consistency rather than critical of those few anomalies. Some of them are no doubt inadvertent, while others serve to properly steer the present course of the *fiction*; and most of them, after all, arise from that very same revisionist process described above:

> Readings of *The Sound and the Fury* have been complicated by William Faulkner's unusual, extensive 'supplementing' of the novel . . . He wrote about the Compsons in a few short stories and *Absalom, Absalom!* in the 1930s, added a long Appendix in 1946 . . . and commented on the novel at length in several interviews and in classroom discussions at the University of Virginia during the 1950s. (Burton 2001: 604)

These changes and inconsistencies are, quite naturally, the kinds of things that worry students and that therefore preoccupy their instructors. Perhaps, however, we should emphasise the essential fluidity of definition and persisting vitality in these works, and highlight the fundamentally fictive worlds they create. Rather than seeking provenance, authority, or authenticity from the authors (collaborators or otherwise) and their intentions, the texts invite us to embrace their very ambiguities, to refrain from closing off possibility. Such closure in itself goes against the grain of Erdrich's highly fluid, organic prose style, not to mention the spirit, as Hafen sees it, of Native storytelling

(2001b). The revision process is, in many ways, a fruitful part of this, because as I have suggested above, revision does not always mean refinement or correction. It is clear, as Erdrich's oeuvre expands, and as that abundant cast grows and changes, that the inconsistencies and ambiguities, inadvertent errors aside,[2] are every bit as revealing as the hard and fast detail.

The fortunes of *Columbus*

That sense of fluidity is an interesting note in what concentrated analyses of the collaboration might discern as a contrapuntal motion between Dorris's and Erdrich's narrative voices and styles. Charles Trueheart notes, for instance:

> 'If the books that bear their different names are a reliable measure of individual style, they don't write indistinguishably. Michael's narratives seem carefully invented and then set down, one foot before the other; Louise's stories seem received from the ether, and allowed to pass through her onto the page. Dorris is vernacular, Erdrich is oracular.' (qtd. in Karell 2002: 37)

That concentrated analysis is still wanting (and indeed I turn to other aspects of the collaborative question here) but it is clearest in that text that has been presented in the most immediate terms as a jointly written piece. Karell herself asserts:

> Their only cosigned novel, *The Crown of Columbus*, delves into this contradictory stance: as a metaphor for the individual, privileged author, Columbus rapidly deconstructs into a variety of Columbuses – one for every season, reason, and politicized agenda – all without losing 'his' overwhelming cultural cachet as an enduring emblem of individual discovery whose diary reflects his unique literary achievement. Key characters in the novel work and write collaboratively, revealing the competitions, power inequities, manipulations, utopian desires, and potential rewards of collective creativity. (2002: 32)

Returning to that idealised literary marriage, this interpretation speaks more of a struggle – that proverbial balancing match in evidence throughout the fiction – than of an easy equilibrium.

Ironically, the one novel Erdrich and Dorris have published under both names has arguably been the least well received of their combined fictional output. It tells the story of Vivian Twostar, assistant professor in Native American Studies at Dartmouth, and her lover (then ex-lover), fellow academic and poet Roger Williams. The plot travels to the Bahamas, where Twostar is investigating the contents of some lost pages of Columbus's diary, which she discovered in the archives of the Dartmouth library. Along with some oyster shells combining clues coded in Hebrew, Twostar is convinced she is about to locate the whereabouts of a treasure linked to Columbus's expedition. Williams, meanwhile, is highly cynical towards her work, not least because it contradicts his own research and undermines his aesthetic interest, revealed by an ongoing epic poem on Columbus. The plot thickens as their guide, Henry Cobb, attempts to murder Twostar, hoping to cash in the treasure himself. Meanwhile, Twostar's second child, the baby Violet, drifts off to sea in a dinghy and Williams himself is caught by a riptide and ends up in a bat-infested cave reciting his poem. The novel climaxes in the discovery of Christ's crown of thorns and a series of cathartic moments: the bonding between Williams and the couple's daughter Violet; between Williams and Nash (Twostar's first-born son from a first, failed, marriage); revived love between the couple; and Twostar's long-desired and hard-won tenure.

At first glance, then, the book's plot reads like a revisionist history crossed with a set of overdetermined Romance/Adventure films. The novel was written to coincide with the quincentennial of Columbus's 'discovery', and the uncharitable interpretation, encouraged by Harper and Row's decision to advance the couple $1.5 million, was of rampant commercialism. Arguments as to the aesthetic, educational, and political merits of this book can go either way and early reviews certainly cast critical eyes over its content and the manner of its publication. A widespread view was that it was compelling entertainment but not to either author's standard; Elson was particularly scathing: 'Curiously, the talent pooling has spawned a novel with as much spontaneity as if it had been plotted by a computer'. A series of comments in *Entertainment Weekly* described it as 'cultivated corn', 'a puree of pastiche and cliché', 'well-meant mush', climaxing in Klepp's description of Williams's Columbus poem as '16 cruel and unusual pages' (1991). A slightly more insightful, if still damning, critique was offered by *New York Times* reviewer Robert Houston: 'It's as if in hoping to disguise any didactic intent, it tries on too many costumes – domestic comedy, paperback thriller, novel of character, love story – and finally decides that, unable to make up its mind, it will simply wear them all at once' (1991). A local review of a reading the couple gave prior to publication in the college town of Hanover, New Hampshire, is particularly positive, which suggests that the couple themselves still conveyed the charm and talent their readers admired even if the finished article did not do the same for critics. Similarly, where many critics assert the critical and ultimate commercial failure of the novel, Craig points out that within four days, The Crown of Columbus, backed by a significant publicity machine, was eighth on the UPI bestseller list (1991).

Whether one sees the book as a materialist vehicle or as a parody (even a self-reflexive parody) of the mainstream clichés usually yielded by the generic conventions the authors exploit, it makes for entertaining if also frustrating reading, and invites some investigation of the collaborative process. Beidler and Hoy, in twinned reviews, have found the novel's strength to be in its collaboration and polyvocality and in 'the playful self-reflexivity with which they have chosen to respond to the parallel importunities and inducements proffered them, as prominent Native writers, in the advent of the Columbus quincentennial' (Hoy in Beidler and Hoy 1991: 51). Beidler notes:

> Rather than being disappointed, it may be that we should thank our lucky twostars that The Crown of Columbus is not predictably 'Indian' in its treatment of Columbus. Instead of trying to portray Columbus as the greedy, hateful, heartless barbarian slave trader he no doubt was, our authors – when they do not ignore him altogether – portray him as the inevitable accident of history. (Beidler in Beidler and Hoy 1991: 49)

Beidler's assertions of an almost apolitical perspective are not endorsed by Hoy, nor by the novel itself, which enacts a radical revision of Columbus and, implicitly, the colonial narrative. So where Beidler enthuses that 'Because our Indian authors have refused to let their novel drift into predictable anger at European exploitation of Indians, we have a novel of considerably more universality' (1991: 49), he seriously underplays that subversive element. Hoy tends towards reading a reclamation of history (albeit flawed, even failed), in which the anti-colonial narrative effectively plays second fiddle to a sensational, melodramatic rom-com adventure story. That 'yarn' nevertheless weaves a series of intriguing and variously successful subtexts. The jury, clearly, is still out but one element of the scenario is absolutely, indeed vitally, clear: the historical terrain of the European New World narrative is ripe for subversion, available to parody, and quite capable of being turned, by accomplished Native authors, into a field of play. Vizenor's *The Heirs of Columbus* (1991) resists direct comparison but it must be noted that Erdrich and Dorris are not the only Native authors to take an ironic look back (and forwards) at Columbus.

Working apart: autobiography and affiliation

As central as the personal and working relationship with Dorris was to Erdrich's early career, both of her memoirs deal with even more generative relationships: those between mother and child, and author and place. Responding to Erdrich's statement that 'I am probably an easterner who mistakenly grew up in the Midwest', Cook-Lynn asks, 'How can one be a tribal nationalist and "set the pace" if one claims no connection to the land either in one's personal life or in one's fiction?' (1993: 28). This, to readers of Erdrich, may at first seem counter-intuitive to the determining presence of the land in her fiction. What is most interesting, though, is the consistency of this kind of authorial statement that repeatedly places Erdrich outside that which she is objectifying, in search, if you like, of *em*placement. So in *The Blue Jay's Dance*, from the vantage point of her New Hampshire farmhouse, Erdrich writes:

> I want to fly, to breathe the great rolling sky of the plains. I want to scatter the lovely colors of the nest. But loving this family as I do, I do the opposite.
> Instead, I sink roots . . . I literally transplant myself into this ground. (*BJD* 92)

In *Books and Islands* she makes a similar statement that seems simultaneously to disavow while reluctantly embracing a specific space. Expressing the contradictions between a sense of belonging to place and belonging to family or heritage; the internal tensions that go to form character; and the recurring negotiations between individual (chosen) and cultural and social (imposed) identity that express something far more complex than ideological stances permit, she writes: 'The islands are really incidental. I'm not much in favour of them. I grew up on the Great Plains. I'm a dry-land-for-hundreds-of-miles person, but I've gotten mixed up with people who live on lakes' (*B&I* 4). Later she comes round to a personal investment:

> And even now, as I am writing in my study, and as I am looking at photographs I took of the paintings, I am afflicted with a confusing

nostalgia. It is a place that has gripped me. I feel a growing love. Partly, it is that I know it through my baby and through her namesake, but I also had ancestors who lived here generations ago. (80)

The casual disavowal of place in the earlier comment gathers depth and dimension in the context of the autobiographical writing as a whole. Some readers will be disconcerted by aspects of *Books and Islands*, with its sense of pastness and its occasional ethnographic quality (Stirrup 2006), but there is also a fundamental honesty in this kind of admission. Though she clearly claims a connection, Erdrich openly negotiates the process of resisting and romanticising the active presence of this terrain; in claiming Ojibwe heritage, she does, in effect, come out of the journey with a clearer sense of what is at stake, of what it *means* to claim Ojibwe identity and of the rights and responsibilities that accompany the claim. Perhaps, there, its individualised narrative conjures the 'departure *and* return, separation *and* (re)integration' implicit in tribal diaspora, the double movement that Justice sees as intrinsic to narratives of motion and migration, and continuity rather than discontinuity (2008: 164).

In relation to the broader themes and nuances of these memoirs, Cook Lynn's demand for an emplaced tribal nationalism, as powerful as that call is, and as compellingly as it is made by many Native scholars, obscures the equally powerful interrogations of self as woman, self as mother and wife, self as writer, and self as *out* of place that drive *Blue Jay* in particular and, joined by self in relation to ancestry, figure the key chord of *Books and Islands*. In the latter, focused on a journey Erdrich takes with her youngest daughter, Nenaa'ikiizhikok, into 'Ojibwe Country' in northern Minnesota and southern Manitoba, it is Erdrich's exploration of Kiizhikok's patrimony as the daughter of Tobasonakwut (Peter Kinew) that motivates the journey. In *The Blue Jay's Dance* it is the journey itself – of pregnancy, birth, and the birth year – that takes centre ground. The hormonal 'victory' over intellect and autonomy, the sleep-depriving, physically draining bond between mother and child that Erdrich describes as 'all jam the first few months after a baby is born' (*BJD* 113) but that precipitates a loss 'of the ability to focus, . . . that in turn saws on the emotions, wears away the fragile strings of nerves' (*BJD* 113), produces a paradoxical sense of all-consuming fulfilment *and* desolation:

> Most days, I can't get enough distance on myself to define what I am feeling . . . I'm being swallowed alive. On those days, suicide is an idea

too persistent for comfort. *There isn't a self to kill,* I think, filled with dramatic pity for who I used to be. . . . once I've established that I have no personal self, killing whatever remains seems hardly worth the effort. (*BJD* 114, author's emphasis)

The balancing act between self and selflessness, sanity and depression is palpable. The older mother of *Books and Islands,* mother to an infant-toddler rather than a baby, reflects less on this consuming self-abnegation; seems more content, in the later journey of discovery, to give herself up to the nurture full time. Not that the mother of *Blue Jay* is a reluctant mother; but she expresses in this memoir the internal conflicts that possess most mother–daughter relationships in her fiction, that maintain a constant battle between being individuals and belonging to one another, teaching one another. Feminist critics in the 1980s identified the mutually constitutive mother–daughter relationships in writing by Chinese-American women as providing a much needed model in western thought for the autonomy and agency of the daughter in apposition to the mother figure. While Erdrich's relationships do not quite match this model – indeed, sit closer to the (self-)eliding model – there is no doubt that the awesome power of the bond is a fully constitutive element of her own character development, not merely as a 'mother' but as a woman influenced and inspired by another and by the 'role' that other imposes upon her. 'Mothering', she writes, 'is a subtle art whose rhythm we collect and learn, as much from one another as by instinct' (*BJD* 161).

Intriguingly, in *Blue Jay,* writing is a wholly solitary affair – the contrast with the collaborative ideal depicted by many of those early biographical sketches is keen. The battle to find space and time for the solitary creative act despite all the distractions and demands is intense. On the one hand, motherhood shapes and informs the literary product:

Writing as a mother shortly after bearing, while nurturing, an infant, one's heart is easily pierced. To look full face at evil seems impossible, and it is difficult at first to write convincingly of the mean, the murderous, the cruelty that shadows mercy and pleasure and ardor. But as one matures into a fuller grasp of the meaning of parenthood, to understand the worst becomes a crucial means of protecting the innocent. A mother's tendency to rescue fuels a writer's careful anger. (*BJD* 146)

On the other hand motherhood is a barrier, a complication: 'Writing is reflective and living is active – the two collide in the tumultuous business of caring for babies' (*BJD* 6). The two are described, in their own terms, as a 'woman's work', somehow exclusive and yet combined, another blurred boundary in the Erdrich archive.

Rita Ferrari suggests Erdrich 'uses the concept of the border as metaphor and narrative strategy for a newly imagined negotiation of individual and cultural identity' (1999: 145), a concept that may be mapped on to the idea of the cultural encounter in *Books and Islands*, which effectively constitutes the book's own discursive terrain. There are effectively two 'encounters' in the book. Embodied by both the people (Tobasonakwut et al.) and the islands, *Books* explores the collision of apparently dichotomous systems of knowledge represented by environmentalist Ernst Oberholtzer's library and the petroglyphs of Lake of the Woods. More provocatively, it also addresses a literal territory, Ojibwe country, and the artificial border that cuts it into the distinct legislative territories of the US and Canada. At the border Erdrich describes the US guard's suspicion, to her great surprise, of her maternity:

> suddenly, as though to trip me up, [the guard] shoots the question, 'And who is this?' at me, indicating Kiizhikok. Each time, gasping the strategy, I shoot straight back, 'My daughter!' Each time, Kiizhikok grips me even tighter . . . Eventually, the sharp-eyed woman clears us. We've passed some mother/daughter test. (*B&I* 100–101)

This test of maternity, the sudden rigidity of the border site in contrast with those fluid boundaries, subtly underlines the historical processes against which indigenous people advocate: Ojibwe country, an ancient territory, sits awkwardly within the spectral bounds of two 'new' nation states that split and continually attempt to redefine the Anishinaabe. Almost paradigmatic in Erdrich's work, the literal and metaphorical border space is always-already implicated in a process of mapping – the cartographic project of the colonial power and, more significantly, a more recently identified process of literal and symbolic remapping: 'The surge in mapping discourses in Native women's writing constitutes an exciting direction in Native literary studies – an emphasis on local, Indigenous knowledges embedded in literature as a means of asserting, maintaining, and advocating political and cultural sovereignty' (Johnson 2007: 116). The passage northward essentially retraces – and replaces – those colonial routes Erdrich follows, going back *beyond* the colonial moment. This retracing does not simply offer another American palimpsest, but partially erases the

imposed surface narrative, rearticulating territory in a modern
'pilgrimage' of sorts, where 'stories of pilgrimage . . . are seldom the
account of individual movement . . . they are braided accounts that
entwine themselves with the destinies of communities, generations,
tribal nations, the ecosystems of a region, the spiritual inheritance
of a people' (Blaeser 2003: 85–86). Erdrich's return southward, in
reminding us so forcibly of the authority that, in this instance, continues to assert control over the female (indigenous) body, reinforces
the power of that alternative reality, the colonial cartographic dominion
writ large.

There are several other examples of what we might see as the
explicatory mode of this ancestral tracing. Describing language
acquisition in a way that echoes much recent discussion, including
Ojibwe language specialist Anton Treuer's, about the revivification of
Anishinaabemowin, Erdrich writes:

> Ojibwemowin is one of the few surviving languages that evolved to the
> present here in North America. . . . Its philosophy is bound up in
> northern earth, lakes, rivers, forests, and plains. Its origins pertain to the
> animals and their particular habits, to the shades of meaning in the very
> placement of stones. Many of the names and songs associated with these
> places were revealed to people in dreams and songs. (*B&I* 85)

Language and culture are inextricably linked, so by feeding Kiizhikok
a diet of books in which she has replaced the English with
Ojibwemowin, Erdrich both seeks connection to the land through
language and attempts to establish connection to culture both for and
through her daughter's patrimony. That selfsame process of coming
to know the land and language establishes an awkward double
narrative. It initiates, in the text, an unfurling awareness of implicit
sovereignty issues as Erdrich describes language acquisition as a
process of awakening to the vitality of Ojibwe culture in language that
was no real part of her own upbringing: 'I thought Ojibwemowin was
a language for prayers . . . I had no idea that most Ojibwe people on
reserves in Canada, and many in Minnesota and Wisconsin, still spoke
English as a second language' (81). But at the same time, it performs
another kind of nostalgia and evokes a romanticism, often encoded in
self-conscious awareness of her other heritage, when having described
the purpose of tobacco offerings, she writes, 'There was a time when
I wondered – do I really believe all of this? I'm half German. Rational!
Does this make any sense? After a while such questions stopped

mattering' (16). Holm outlines in Silko criticism a 'covert romantic desire for the concrete relationship between Native language and land' (2008: 201) noting how it can, in fact, obscure sovereignty, the material politics of the land and its communities giving way to a neutered symbolism. Those lyrical quotations above about Erdrich's connections to the Midwest echo this sense of a spiritual, mythic, above all non-threatening coda. This reflects the metaphysical qualities of the environment in Erdrich's work – the animated freezings and soulful quests across vast terrain – in contrast with the more directly political manoeuvres around the ownership of land in Fleur's ongoing story.

But *Books* takes a more difficult turn in directly confronting the failure of the Jay Treaty's promise of free passage as well as her own sense of initial alienation in Ojibwe country. These explorations begin to shift the tone from pseudo-spiritual symbol to sovereign issue, grating directly against the geographical and legal delimitations that the nation state imposes. Although it remains problematic in its cultural relativism, this is recognised in her claims for continuity between traditional Ojibwe means of recording history and stories and the book: 'The Ojibwe had been using the word *mazinibaganjigan* for years to describe dental pictographs made on birchbark, perhaps the first books made in North America . . . People have probably been writing books in North America since at least 2000 B.C. Or painting islands' (*B&I* 5). An apparent claim to the 'Indigenous firstness' of her own art (a claim which is either reductive, or hubristic, or, well, sublimely insightful)[3] this nevertheless – and far more provocatively – engenders a powerful statement of what it means to be an *American* writer. 'For an American writer', she notes, 'it seems crucial to at least have a passing familiarity with [Ojibwemowin], which is adapted to the land as no other language can possibly be' (85). The other associations she names, in such literary affiliates as W.G. Sebald, George Eliot, G.K. Chesterton, and Laurence Sterne, among others, are in their turn mediated by *this* necessity, a 'return and reaffirmation' of indigenous primacy (Holm 2008: 247, qtg Ortiz). It may not convince politically but it does illuminate just what is at stake in this journey, this territorial claim to the mutually influential and interwoven importance of Ober's books and Tobasonakwut's islands to her own connection with that earth, that clay, of the North Dakotan plains.

Writing for children

The double emphasis in *Books and Islands* – on movement into what can best be described as *specifically* cultural terrain, with its emphatic markers not only of place but of historical and spiritual connection with that place; and on the switching between author as student and mother as educator – arguably connects the memoir most closely with Erdrich's children's fiction. She has published five books for children to date, beginning with a picture book, *Grandmother's Pigeon* (1996), the later *Range Eternal* (2002), and the first three in a planned series of novels for young adults, *The Birchbark House* (1999), *The Game of Silence* (2005), and *The Porcupine Year* (2008). It is on the novels that I will focus attention but the picture books are notable for their basis in early memories (*Range Eternal*) and surreal forays into the imagination (*Grandmother's Pigeon*), foregrounding the importance of home, family, and story. Erdrich joins a long line of Native authors of children's fiction – many of them intentionally so, others by default. Charles Eastman's *Indian Boyhood* (1902) was written first for his own children but, as Dykema-VanderArk points out, also reflects the prevailing opinion of its moment that Native Americans were in an 'arrested' evolutionary state, a 'child race' (2002: 10). That opinion has seen Native texts, particularly myths and legends, generally packaged as children's literature, or folklore. Trafzer's review of a number of publications of Native American children's literature, for instance, strikingly demonstrates the relationship between Indian myth and children's writing – the majority of the books he reviews are retellings, reshapings, or reclamations of oral traditional stories (1992).

Beyond the common association of Native American stories with the children's market, Trafzer's review makes two other things perfectly clear. The first is that many stories common to the various oral traditions of Native peoples were indeed intended to edify and educate – are, in other words, appropriate and often intended for children. The second is that it is incumbent on Native peoples themselves to displace the often well-intentioned but problematically monolithic views of Native cultures propounded by the children's literature market. 'Some authors', notes Stewart, 'continue to depict American Indian culture as foreign, as something "other" that must be brought into the fold of American culture rather than celebrated for its distinction' (2002: 181). And Dorris himself lamented that Native people themselves 'continued to be treated as if they were the property

of children' (qtd in Stewart 2002: 181). Clearly there are two intertwined issues here that many Native writers have attempted to
address: there is a general appetite for children's writing that engages
with the lives and histories of Native peoples; but such writing comes
with an ethical imperative to deal in far more nuanced fashion with the
realities of those lives and histories. Among those writers best known
for adult fiction, Erdrich joins Abenaki writer Joe Bruchac, Chickasaw
writer Linda Hogan, and Kiowa writer N. Scott Momaday, among
others, in producing work intended, or deemed suitable, for children
and young adults. Drawing on Momaday, Trafzer notes, 'From the
elders children learned the power and magic of words, and the children were to listen and learn, not with careless attention but with all
their senses' (1992: 381). These writers, then, step into an imperative
mode in many Native cultures – interaction with the young – that we
rarely see among other literary constituencies; and more importantly,
assuming they do it 'well', their works enter a field clearly beset by
problematic representations of Native peoples.[4]

The Birchbark House has been described by Rolo as an attempt to
write an Indian *Little House on the Prairie* (1935). Laura Ingalls Wilder's
popular novels, which followed on from the original *Little House in the
Big Woods* (1932) and have long been staples of American children's
literature, are problematic for the Native American communities
mis-/unrepresented in them and all but ignored in the TV spin-off.
Osage Dennis McAuliffe, Jr., begins a scathing review of Wilder's best-
known book with the pronouncement that 'The tens of millions of
adoring fans of . . . Wilder's books and of the television series based on
them should be grateful that the Osages didn't dismember her when
they had the chance' (McAuliffe 2005: 49). He continues:

> Little Laura Ingalls, her sisters and their beloved Ma and Pa were illegal
> squatters on Osage land. She left that detail out of her 1935 children's
> book, *Little House on the Prairie*, as well as any mention of ongoing
> outrages – including killings, burnings, beatings, horse thefts and grave
> robberies – committed by white settlers, such as Charles Ingalls, against
> Osages living in villages not more than a mile or two away from the
> Ingalls' little house.

Yet the book's narrative structure, set around the homestead of the
Ingalls family and the surrounding community, is an obvious draw to
a writer whose work focuses on the interactions between individuals
and community. Erdrich's decision to mirror this in *The Birchbark*

House appears to be partly didactic, an attempt to redress the balance of historical inaccuracy and introduce children to the humanity carefully concealed behind stereotypes: 'I read the Little House books as a child and so have my children. I love their humor and warmth, but am disturbed by Ma's racism. . . . I didn't write this book as an answer but hope it will be perceived as an enlargement of the view encompassed in Laura's world' (*Kidsreads* 1999).

The educational intent, also an act of cultural recovery/respect, is made clear by the use of Ojibwe words throughout – including an explanation that Ojibwemowin was originally a spoken language, which precedes a glossary of terms at the end of the novels – and the declaration: 'The name Omakayas appears on a Turtle Mountain census. I am using it in the original translation because I've been told those old names should be given life . . . Dear reader, when you speak this name out loud you will be honouring the life of an Ojibwa girl who lived long ago' (*BBH* 229). Beyond the didactic, it is clear in the acknowledgements that the text's historicism is also a continued exploration of family history: 'My mother, Rita Gourneau Erdrich, and my sister Lise Erdrich, researched our family life and found ancestors on both sides who lived on Madeline Island during the time in which this book is set . . . This book and those that will follow are an attempt to retrace my own family's history' (*BBH* 229). That attempt bears further witness to the centrality in Erdrich's work of the mutually constructing relationships between individuals and larger kinship/community groups.

Coming *from* a particular place, family, community, and tribe, Erdrich is also, in a sense, tracing a return to that group. This work stresses the importance of what Bevis calls 'homing in', where the 'centripetal movements of the characters back to traditional centers of culture' (Wilson 2007: xi) might more accurately be seen as the author's own journey back to a sense of emplacement. In returning, she is also, in essence, returning the stories, or perhaps they, themselves, are 'migrating home'.[5] Notwithstanding my earlier objection to Connie Jacobs's assertion, Erdrich self-consciously establishes the centrality of storytelling in Ojibwe tradition as a tool to both educate and entertain here; her own role as 'storyteller' and the pedagogic quality of the children's books is paramount. McNab claims, 'it is the continuity provided by Aboriginal storytellers, like Erdrich, through their songs that will enable Aboriginal people to continue on their spirit journeys and to survive as Omakayas did' (2004: 34 and 39). And of course the naive pose in the narration of the children's stories, mimicking a process of knowledge discovery that is made to measure for its equally naive audience, speaks directly to the process of mediation that preoccupies Ruppert, allowing each group 'access' to the mores and belief systems of the other.

Individual stories within the novels also perform a vital function in Omakayas's education. Told by a member of the older genera-tion, either these stories illustrate a personal event that will aid in the instruction of the children as they learn about Ojibwe customs, beliefs, and history, or they recount a family or tribal story that again engages the young with the tribal past. 'Deydey's Ghost Story' (*BBH* 59–64), for instance, is told as a reward for the girls' protection of the corn crop, and differs markedly from the 'adisokaan stories' that Nokomis strictly reserves for winter. Deydey's story, partly recounted in entertainment, tells of his narrow escape from evil ghost sisters, a story of courage and quick-wittedness. Nokomis's stories, such as 'Nanabozho and Muskrat Make an Earth' (*BBH* 162–164) and 'The Little Person' (*GS* 103–110), while entertaining and absorbing, are purposeful. After the Muskrat story, outlining the importance of this little animal in its relationship with Nanabozho just as the earth was being formed, the narrator confides, 'Omakayas knew that her Nokomis told her this story for a larger reason than just because she asked for it' (*BBH* 164). As if hearing, Nokomis then tells Omakayas, 'If such a small animal could do so much . . . your efforts are important, too' (*BBH* 165). Similarly, 'The Little Person', a tale about Nokomis's spirit helper, is in turn designed to remind Omakayas of the importance of performing required tasks as she continues on her path to becoming a healer.

These stories, then, speak to Erdrich's apparent concern to instruct readers. As elders are instructing their youngers, so we as readers are being instructed in the history of mid-nineteenth-century Ojibwe, still semi-nomadic but clearly touched by white society, the winter camp close enough to town for Angeline and Omakayas to go to school for a new form of instruction. Historical grounding empha-sises this instruction through the backdrop of an 1847 smallpox epidemic, which Erdrich claims is historically documented. Small-pox ravaged this area of the Great Lakes (most extensively in 1837) and was certainly a danger that announced the presence of the Old World settlers. The other clear historical circumstance is the presence of the Catholic mission headed by Father Baraga. From 1843 Bishop

Frederick Baraga was located in L'Anse, on Keweenaw Bay, having arrived at L'Arbre Croche (Michigan) in around 1831. More pointedly, he was the author of the first comprehensive grammar and dictionary of Ojibwemowin, an activity that occupies him in *The Game of Silence*. Similarly, the trader is called Cadotte, presumably after the French-Ojibwe Michel Cadotte, son of Jean Baptiste and owner of an extensive trading post on Madeline Island. A certain poetic liberty is taken here, however, as Cadotte died in 1837, thirteen years after his business had been passed down to his sons-in-law, the brothers Lyman Marquis and Truman Abraham Warren.

Alongside Omakayas's own historicity one further aspect of this historical contextualisation is worth mentioning, and this is the degree to which Erdrich draws on other texts in order to map out the detail. This is a part of the process she clearly relishes, explaining that her material is derived from conversations with elders on Madeline Island and her own textual research. Beidler has attempted to establish direct correlation between *The Birchbark House*, *Tracks*, and John Tanner's captivity narrative, the 1994 edition of which includes an introduction written by Erdrich (Beidler 2000a). In recent novels, meanwhile – *The Last Report on the Miracles at Little No Horse* and *The Painted Drum* in particular – Erdrich names specific textual resources in notes at the ends of the books (respectively, Kenneth Woodward's *Making Saints* and Diane Wood Middlebrook's *Suits Me: The Double Life of Billy Tipton*, and Thomas Vennum's *The Ojibwe Dance Drum: Its History and Construction*). Intriguingly, the 'sources' perform an authentication and validation of Erdrich's own narratives, highlighting Tanner's first-hand account, Tipton's secret life as a woman passing as a man, and of course the verity and veracity of depictions of the drum, while in the latter case they also seem to exonerate the author from charges of cultural betrayal: 'As in all of my books, no sacred knowledge is revealed. I check carefully to make certain everything I use is written down already' (*PD* 277).

From source to substance

Just as the *Little House* books chart the Ingalls family's migration from the Wisconsin woods to the open prairies of Wisconsin, and the Minnesota and Dakota plains, detailing the domestic life and family relationships through the young Laura's eyes, so Erdrich's stories tell of migration (or displacement) and the domestic scene through the eyes of Omakayas, or Little Frog, the young Ojibwe girl. The structure of all three books is the same: a brief introductory chapter – 'The Girl from Spirit Island' (*BBH*), and 'Prologue' (*GS* and *PY*) – opens into a number of chapters divided into four key sections tracking the seasons.

In *The Birchbark House*, that opening chapter describes the discovery by *voyageurs* of a baby girl, the only survivor of a bout of smallpox on Spirit Island.[6] As the voyagers paddle away, fearful of the disease, one of them speculates that his wife, Tallow, will return to rescue this baby girl. This first instance of the impact of settlement, and the death and displacement of the Ojibwe by disease, recurs in the prologue to *The Game of Silence*, wherein that baby, now the young girl, Omakayas, is the first to spot the arrival of the Raggedy Ones, twice displaced from their lands by whites, and then from their allotted destinations by resident *Bwaanag* (Dakota and Lakota). The seasonal cycle and the domestic setting, against this foreboding backdrop, enable the author to explicate the daily cycles and rituals of the Ojibwe in their unique environment just as that cycle is facing the encroaching threat of westward-moving white settlement. The 1840s was a period of increasing relocation of tribes of the northeast culture area to destinations further westward and into the Great Plains, and in all three of *The Birchbark House*, *The Game of Silence*, and *The Porcupine Year* we witness a community increasingly aware of its vulnerability.

Importantly, though, and despite this backdrop, the narrative focuses more acutely on the inner life and experiences of Omakayas as she discovers, develops, and matures. Having been the sole survivor of the smallpox epidemic on Spirit Island, Omakayas, who we rejoin seven years later with her adopted family on Madeline Island, becomes a 'transformer': 'That Omakayas is the last person left alive among her people after a smallpox epidemic makes her a transformer in history, a person imbued with medicine power from birth who is able to transform events as they take place' (McNab 2004: 37). Alongside her rescuer, Old Tallow, who is also favoured with this gift, she becomes a healer when her new community are struck down with smallpox after the visit of an infected voyager, saving all but her tiniest brother, Neewo, from the ravages of the disease. McNab draws attention to the presence of birds in Omakayas's stories – from the birds that keep her alive with their song as a baby, to Andeg, the raven she befriends when she nurses his wing, broken in nets she and Angeline placed to protect the corn crop ('Andeg', *BBH*). Birds, significantly, are 'the spirit protectors of the bears in the clan system'

(McNab 2004: 37–38) and by establishing this relationship between clan membership, role in the community, and the natural world Erdrich subtly instructs her readers in the basics of Ojibwe clan structure. In another instance of such 'instruction', Omakayas has a frightening but safe encounter with a pair of bear cubs (her 'brothers') and their mother in *The Birchbark House* ('Old Tallow' and 'Pinch', *BBH*). In these depictions Erdrich stresses positive practices such as adoption and care for the vulnerable, and the strength and endurance of her characters.

Descriptions of the nature and division of labour are, unsurprisingly for novels that focus so clearly on the domestic routine, also key. We learn, in this sense, something about how the semi-nomadic Ojibwe organised themselves, and the ways this small group maintains that organisation under pressure. The books are organised into the four seasons as this is how the Ojibwe year itself, and, by necessity, their movements between different locations, was organised. Thus, chapter one of *The Birchbark House* describes the building of the eponymous lodge as the family prepare to move from their winter cedar cabin at LaPointe on Madeline Island, or *Moningwanaykaning*, the Island of the Golden-Breasted Woodpecker. Summer is characterised by hunting and fishing (for eating, trading, and caching for the lean months), playing and gathering in the woodlands, protection of the corn crop, and the preparation and tanning of hides, a job Omakayas greets with disgust, while Mikwam, or Deydey (daddy), her half-French adopted father, goes off on trapping expeditions.

Fall sees a move to the rice camps for the annual wild rice harvest, 'a part of the year everyone looked forward to because there would be cousins to play with, games in the rice camps, the pleasures of talk, feasting' (*BBH* 88). The remainder of the fall season is spent preparing supplies and tools for the winter, and overhauling the birchbark canoes. As the cold begins to creep in, the family leave the birchbark house and head back to the cedar cabin at LaPointe. Winter is inevitably the most uncomfortable of seasons in the Great Lakes, a season of survival and stories. The men hunt and trap while the women turn their attention to preparing hides, mending and creating new costumes, dolls, and other functional items, the winter's length punctuated by the winter gathering dance.

In *The Game of Silence* winter is also a season of games and role-plays for the children but in *The Birchbark House* it is a time of great tragedy. A lone *voyageur* visitor dies of smallpox, and despite their

attempts to eradicate the disease, burning his belongings and conducting a sweat lodge for themselves, it does transfer to other
members of the band. Smallpox is an invasive precursor of white
territorial claims (in that the disease was historically brought in by the
advance guard of missionaries, traders, and map makers) that partly
led to relocation of the Ojibwe to equally contested Dakota lands.
The Game of Silence makes this threat clear, opening with the arrival of
the 'raggedy ones' and continuing, later, to contextualise the undermining of sovereignty: ' "We signed a paper that said they could take
the trees. We signed a paper that said they could take the copper *from*
the earth," said the old chief Bizhiki, disturbed, "we didn't say they
could take the earth" ' (20). The discussion between these new visitors
and Omakayas's band continues, framed by the 'game of silence', an
endurance test set the children, with rewards for those who can remain
quietest while the adults discuss difficult matters. Explanation of the
changing circumstances of the Ojibwe continues within this context:

> The ogimaa or the president of all of the chimookomanag had sent a
> message to the leaders of the Ojibwe. That message was simple. They
> must leave their homes . . .
>   'There was a time when we had no quarrel with the Bwaanag [Lakota
> and Dakota],' said Deydey. 'They lived in their part of the world and we
> in ours. We even traded with them. But as the chimookomanag push us,
> so we push the Bwaanag. We are caught between two packs of wolves.'
> (21)

Arguably this is the most contentious pedagogical aspect of these texts,
a view of settlement that mirrors, as much as it redresses, the one-
sidedness of texts like the *Little House* series. The Ojibwe had been a
very powerful force, benefiting from close alliance with the French and
more or less aggressively moving westward before this moment, while
the Seven Fires Prophecy locates these events *within* Ojibwe patterns
of knowledge, rather than presenting the Ojibwe simply as victims of
external actions.[7]

This is not, however, to diminish the importance of the insertion of
Native voices in an otherwise white-dominated history of the Midwest,
and in fact, one other instance of mirroring humorously provides a
lesson in objectification. The Break-Apart Girl is a young white girl,
resident in the town closest to the winter village. Alongside the school
to which Angeline and later Omakayas are sent to learn the 'tracks'
the white man makes; alongside the missionary presence and the

efforts of Father Baraga to transcribe an Ojibwe lexicon; and alongside
the proximity of traders and the threat of sickness, Break-Apart Girl is
evidence of the massive changes at mid-century, covertly encoding
Manifest Destiny. Named for her pinched waist that looks as though
she might snap in two, she becomes, inevitably, the other in this story.
Erdrich inverts the ethnographic gaze, acknowledging that this
nineteenth-century Euroamerican girl will be as much other to the
twenty-first-century child as she is to Omakayas, allowing Omakayas
to describe (often with shock, horror, and pity) her curious dress,
including the constricting shoes that deform her feet and the corsets
that explain her nickname. These sequences serve several purposes.
We witness the gulf of cultural understanding between these children,
who balk at one another's clothing, run scared of certain customs, and
repeatedly mispronounce one another's names. Set against this,
however, is the affinity that permits these children to play together, to
find a common language in their shared environment.

In another ironic challenge to the rhetoric of freedom-in-civilisation
that Manifest Destiny, implicit in the encounter, carries, we see the
Break-Apart Girl 'liberated' by the time she spends with the Ojibwe
children:

> With a daring look, the Break-Apart Girl pointed at the remotest part of
> the beach. She took off running. . . . The Break-Apart Girl took off her
> dress, too [. . .Omakayas] couldn't help notice, though, that along with
> the dress the Break-Apart girl had shed a stiff, short garment that had fit
> around her waist, pinching it tight. Without this thing, the Break-Apart
> Girl was shaped just like any girl and she seemed happy to run and play,
> to dive into the water. (GS 133)

Underneath the cultural apparel, then, there exists a common
humanity. Both the Ojibwe girls and this white girl have things the
other desires (which, at its simplest and most avowedly romantic,
include freedom and companionship on the one hand, chickens and
bright fabrics on the other). Both are equally strange to the other, and
yet mutually attracted. And both are presented as innocent parties
in a game being played out by their elders. On the one hand the
comparison serves to emphasise the discrete cultural values of
the Ojibwe girls, demonstrating while celebrating their difference.
On the other, the implicit subnarrative of the irresistible temptation of
western culture is unavoidable, given that the audience knows how
the story – at least the hegemonic narrative – turns out. The role of

'multicultural' literature in the classroom – as a means to help children accommodate difference – is writ large in this kind of relativistic representation.

It is also a source of discomfort. The Ojibwe, whether intentionally or not, are portrayed simplistically at times as victims of the white man's whim – not least here, drawing on those stereotypes of the carefree natural man and the simplistic Indian attracted and appeased by beads and bright cloths. This is not to say that Erdrich presents them as victims *per se*. Indeed, her emphasis is on survival; they are survivors of illness, the elements, and territorial and cultural incursion. Yet, the victimhood of the Ojibwe is implied by two scenarios. The first, in relation to the Break-Apart Girl, is when Omakayas wonders why they are being driven off: 'The Break-Apart Girl was so friendly, so good to them. Surely she did not want them to leave! Omakayas wanted to ask her why the others, the big chimookomanag, wanted her people to go off into dangerous territory, but the idea was too complicated to get across by signs' (*GS* 132). While exhibiting the relative powerlessness of the Ojibwe at this point in history and although the naivety of the childish questions is compelling, it is deeply reductive of the political and historical processes, not to mention the hugely complex interrelationships between different groups of Natives and whites, of this time. One might not expect these issues to be dealt with in a children's book, but they nevertheless raise the spectre of the kinds of elisions and attitudes that embody the *Little House* flaws. In relation to both of these broad issues, Rice notes: 'A major difficulty confronted by contemporary Native American literature is to navigate between the uniqueness of Indian experience and its similarities to Euramerican culture. Children's literature in particular risks engendering confusion or oversimplifying matters in depicting Native experience' (2002: 246). The balance Erdrich needs to strike – the cause, perhaps inevitably, of such compromises – is between that inner complexity (Omakayas is bothered, but psychologically unaffected as yet, by cultural contact) and the simplification of that exceptionally complex outer world.

The second stereotype comes through in the kind of language that the older members of the group in particular use. Describing the precariousness of their situation to her granddaughter, Nokomis says, '"Listen, my little one, . . . for I'm going to tell you the truth. The chimookomanag we see here are only the first drops of rain. A storm of them lives past the sunrise, in the east. They can flood us like a river"' (*GS* 29). This kind of stylised narrative is highly evocative of transcriptions of Native stories and speeches, materials that are often inseparable from the romanticised clichés of Indians embedded in nature, what David Treuer calls '"culturally derived" expressions' (2006: 80). It echoes, too, an older text, *Night Flying Woman* (1983) by the Ojibwe educator Ignatia Broker, which has a similarly 'unsophisticated' feel to its narrative register. The recent reprint of that text carries an endorsement on the front, which reads 'One of my favorite books – LOUISE ERDRICH, author of *Love Medicine*'. Like *The Birchbark House, Night Flying Woman* is an evocative story and a testament to strength and continuity. The stylised nature of the language, however, treads a fine line between evoking a past in the attempt to find an adequate idiom for recovered and *translated* voices, and the reinforcement of stereotypes. This is, of course, a far bigger dilemma that goes well beyond the pages of children's books.

In his earlier essay, 'Reading Culture', Treuer focuses particularly on the function of myth and language in Native fiction, arguing that they are 'not conveyors of cultural sensibilities or cultural truths' but that they 'embody . . . they inscribe, the longing for culture' (2002: 61). Unlike the example Treuer uses, *The Antelope Wife*, in Erdrich's young adult fiction Ojibwe words and phrases remain untranslated in the body of the text, leaving the reader free to use the glossary at the back of the book. The pedagogic intent behind this is apparent, speaking somewhat to the sense that 'Some authors continue to depict American Indian culture as foreign, as something "other" that must be brought into the fold of American culture rather than celebrated for its distinction' (Stewart 2002: 181). I would argue that in establishing 'distinction' through language, rather than through arcane cultural reference, Erdrich goes some way towards a meeting point between these demands. That said, historical fiction is itself a problematic vehicle for navigating this terrain. Again, Stewart notes that 'Bishop suggests an over reliance on historical fiction propagates the myth of the "vanishing Indian", and Reese decries the lack of depictions of contemporary Native Americans' (2002: 182). The tension between the more universal, or timeless, aspects of the young adult novels and the persistent denial by external bodies of the commensurability of indigenous peoples with modernity, is best encapsulated by those decisions over the 'translation' of reported speech and the use of Ojibwe.

Treuer would not, I suspect, be persuaded by Beidler and Barton's assertion that Ojibwe language use in Erdrich's adult fiction is strategic, intended to frustrate, to exclude, or to encourage her readers 'to struggle to learn at least the rudiments of the language, and so help to keep it alive' (2006: 376). If Treuer is right, that language use is too rudimentary, too arbitrary and, in almost every case, is translated either directly or by its context. The glossaries in the children's books, however, negate the first two 'strategies', while making the third a genuine likelihood. But Treuer dismisses Erdrich's earlier language use as a poor reflection of 'active' (verb-based), Ojibwemowin, concerned that an incredibly beautiful, primarily active language is 'reduced to a few nouns, simple phrases, and the like' (2002: 55), and that rather than functioning as effective communication between people, it merely provides 'lexical nuggets' used 'more like display'. Erdrich has admitted that her knowledge of Ojibwe is 'at the level of a dreamy four-year-old-child's' (Beidler 2000a: 54). With regret, I cannot yet claim any higher level of expertise than that, but the glossaries do seem again to contain a disproportionate number of nouns, suggesting a similar lack of sophistication.

This raises an important question regarding the major significance of language learning among Native communities – namely, where does one begin? On the one hand the imperative to learn languages that are threatened with extinction is clear, particularly as those languages are said to 'carry culture'. Doing so does require expert guidance; it also, naturally, requires tolerance; as with that earlier question of representation, Erdrich has not, at least in the documentary record, claimed expertise. It is imperative, once again, that critics do not mistake signs of culture for the cultural sign. The pedagogic purpose of language use in the young adult fiction, then, in the light of increasing Ojibwe language programmes in schools in Minnesota, Wisconsin, and elsewhere, is clear alongside the *primacy* accorded the language in *Books and Islands* and Erdrich's ambition for Kiizhikok to be raised bilingual. In that latter text, strategies of language use suggest (whether or not they can enforce) the kinds of strategies of decolonisation that other writers, such as Gloria Bird, have written of, wherein language, and particularly the ability to see and describe the world through indigenous languages, is central (1998). There is an increasing market for bilingual and all-Native language texts for children and young adults; Erdrich's glossaries therefore move beyond performing as 'at best . . . a "gang sign," and, at worst, as static, dioramic museum pieces' (Treuer 2002: 55).

The sting in Treuer's critique of the adult fiction, however, is also worth brief consideration here, where he argues, 'we have created narratives that bleed out our rich cultural specificities into the world, translated and trammelled' (2002: 61). This section began with the suggestion that Erdrich was, to some degree, instructing her readers in aspects of Ojibwe culture, as well as the historical circumstances of the area and period in which her books are set. Those manners and customs to which Erdrich draws the attention of her readers include the subjects of 'adisokaan stories, meant only for winter' (*BBH* 59), tobacco and other offerings (both books, *passim*), hide preparation and fasting rituals (*GS* 59), canoe making (*GS* 67–73), wild rice collection (*GS* 78), the Midewiwin (e.g. *GS* 100), and many other instances of the cultural and social lifeway of the historical Ojibwe. On the one hand, Erdrich's narration performs the traditional storyteller's role of instruction as suggested above, following Tallow, Yellow Kettle, and Nokomis; it also brings Ojibwe political and social structures to the foreground, depicting active players not woodland shadows. Erdrich is, unusually, described as a 'spiritual leader' by McNab (2004: 34 and 39). The message is affirmative, empowering, but one wonders if this notion risks, as Treuer iterates, encouraging her readers to mistake the fiction for culture, treating narrative as manifestation of cultural knowledge. While the optimistic sense of pedagogical importance of this work to Native, particularly Ojibwe, readers is clear in both Erdrich's and McNab's intentions, it nevertheless proceeds in tense balance with an inherent exoticism; although it opens up history, some might argue it reinforces that sense of *pastness* inherent in an ethnographic reconstruction. This does some small disservice to McNab's larger point – that it is necessary to know something of Ojibwe heritage, particularly clan structure, to fully appreciate the work; certainly, said knowledge will inevitably produce a more nuanced reading of the complex cultural signs in interesting interplay in these books. Treuer's caution, however, is that we beware mistaking the semiotic intarsia, as beautiful as it is, for life itself.

It is a stretch to attempt to tie all three elements of this chapter together. There are, though, loose common threads relating to the relationship the individual has to community, and the questions of roles and responsibilities that both individuals and their communities occupy. In so far as the modern author performs an 'ethical' function, the emphasis on responsibility in Native writing is significant. From the overt commercialism of *The Crown of Columbus* and the 'collective responsibility' Erdrich and Dorris took for the early work; through the focus in the memoirs on the parent–child relationship – the role of motherhood in nurturing and educating; to the various ways in which the memoirs and young adult novels in particular visit questions of Ojibwe culture and historical experience, it is impossible to ignore the bonding function of stories in Erdrich's work, and the importance of generating and renewing narratives of Native survival and continuation on the woodlands, lakes, and plains of Ojibwe Country. Through all of this it is the story, the histories, and the way they are remembered and recounted, as well as the *processes* of that recounting, that take centre stage.

Notes

1 The other 'book' published under both names is the short travelogue, *Route Two*, which describes the authors' journeys from New Hampshire to Washington along the US highway of the same name. It is a fascinating read, but its brevity (thirty-four pages) and the focus below on Erdrich's single-authored memoirs mean it has not quite made the cut.

2 Interestingly, Erdrich does, 'in tandem with Trent Duffy, her copy-editor', keep a timeline in order to avoid inadvertent errors. This careful attention to detail perhaps makes extant inconsistencies even more intriguing.

3 Erdrich is not the first to refer to such mnemonic systems as 'writing' systems but the knowledge economy they participate in is significantly different to the knowledge systems that depend solely on the written text. The images themselves can be appreciated but they require very specific, and sometimes restricted, sets of knowledge for interpretation and are, in a more literal sense, communal in both origin and purpose.

4 Jon Stott noted in 1995 that only 20 per cent of texts for children that represented Native peoples were actually written by Native Americans (Stewart 2002: 181). Numerous new figures and presses have entered the scene since then, including bilingual presses such as Kiva and Clear Light (Hopi), Cherokee Publications, Willowisp (Cree), and Press Pacifica (Hawaii). One hopes, then, that the situation has altered, but clearly a lot of ground needs to be made up.

5 In the introduction to her collection of Anishinaabe prose, Blaeser notes both that 'Stories keep us migrating home' and 'stories construct intricate patterns of home' (1999b: 3 and 4).

6 *Voyageurs* were licensed fur traders, employees usually of one of the major trading companies.

7 Ojibwe oral history suggests the appearance of a *miigis* shell initiated their migration some five hundred years ago (see Vizenor 1998a: 21; and see Benton-Banai (1979) for more on Ojibwe migration and the Seven Fires Prophecy).

6

Conclusion? Tradition, translation, and the global market for Native American literatures

As the span of this book hopefully suggests, Erdrich's career thus far has been both distinguished and varied. The prolific nature of her output, and the variety of modes in which she writes, make a comprehensive overview of her achievement difficult and, inevitably, reductive. It is clear, to this author at least, that serious critical studies of Erdrich's later books – particularly *Master Butcher* and *The Plague of Doves*, both especially rich, dense texts – are now needed to complement the abundant archive of criticism on the earlier works. Long-term readers have witnessed the maturing of a strong voice in American letters, a voice deserving of regular reappraisal. It is striking that the range and sheer quantity of Erdrich's writing remains unknown even by some of her critics. I have made only brief mention of *Route Two*, the short travelogue she co-wrote with Dorris, for instance. Her introductions, forewords, and prefaces to a number of texts, such as *The Broken Cord*, John Tanner's *The Falcon*, *Edward S. Curtis: The Women*, Desmond Hogan's *A Link with the River*, along with her chapter on North Dakota in the recent *State by State: A Panoramic Portrait of America* and her guest editorship of 1993's *The Best American Short Stories*, all also speak in interesting ways to the positioning of Erdrich as a diverse and profuse *American* author. Extracts of Erdrich's work, whole stories, and shorter abridgements, have been produced in a variety of formats, from college anthologies to general interest short story readers. In 2003 she collaborated with four Minnesota artists in a beautiful, limited edition *Winter Reader* in which her writing was interwoven with a number of original artworks in paper. As already noted, she has collaborated with Dorris as Milou North, and with her sister Heid as Heidi Louise.

Alone, and with those collaborators, she has written for publications as diverse as *Redbook, Ms., The New Yorker,* and *Woman,* among many others. And in January 2009 HarperCollins released *The Red Convertible: Selected and New Stories,* in which Erdrich herself repackages many well-known stories, first published in magazines before reappearing as chapters in novels, alongside a few new ones and thus lays full claim in book-length publication to the short story form.

If chapter 5 seemed to take an ambivalent turn, it is precisely because the position Erdrich's writing occupies in Native American Studies is caught between lavish praise and vituperative criticism. Outside the reviews, there are few dissenters to the lyrical quality of her prose – although critics, like readers, tend to dwell on writing that pleases them. The same cannot be said for the thematic bases of Erdrich's narrative arcs, or for the claims that are made for her/their representativeness. Here, critics, particularly Native critics, more readily pick up what they find problematic, even distasteful, about her brand. If such commercial language is provocative, it is intended to be. It very much reflects Cook-Lynn's concerns about Dorris's enterprise, for instance, not least because he also became Erdrich's literary agent. It reflects David Treuer's objections to the easy, often clichéd cultural assumptions about her work. The jacket blurb to *Books and Islands* stands as partial testament to such colouration: 'In this world, where her Ojibwe ancestors have lived for centuries, otter and moose still flourish, and ancient sturgeon leap in a glittering sunlit flash'. The book, as I have already mentioned, is published by *National Geographic.* Replete though that organisation's flagship magazine is with exotic glossy photos, one would hope it would be alert to the politics of indigenous representation. Where, both in the book and in their blurb, is the Anishinaabe polity? Are they subsumed into the picturesque image of moose and sturgeon, like them 'just the backdrop to what Erdrich summons to life: the long, elemental tradition of storytelling that is in her blood'? There is a prioritisation here that grates, loudly, against those earlier assertions of Erdrich's status as tribal storyteller. For which tribal storyteller is land, the natural environment, ancestry, merely a backdrop? Which tribal storyteller blanks out the tribal community in favour of evocative stylings? Whatever the flaws of *Books and Islands,* it is not Erdrich I am accusing here: it is the publicity machine. Generated by marketers but partly, too, the responsibility of critics, it creates a number of hackneyed clichés, labels by which to sell books, ultimately obscuring both the nature of the work and the realities of its social and political contexts.

These are not, generally, claims Erdrich makes herself, as noted in Chapter 1. And as Lischke and McNab observe, 'To understand stories, one must understand the spirit of the stories and the spirit of the person and the family who is telling them' (2006: 191). That spirit has been repeatedly revealed in interview in Erdrich's ambivalent resistance to labels such as 'Native American' or 'women's' writing. Similarly, she notes herself that she is 'on the edge, [has] always been on the edge, flourish[es] on the edge, and [doesn't think she] belong[s] anywhere else' (qtd in Chavkin and Chavkin 1994: 230). What, though, of the responsibility to respond to those claims made on one's behalf? For some, the problem is not so much whether Erdrich claims to be representative; it is the fact that this is how she is popularly portrayed. Intentional or not, her 'saga of an inadequate Chippewa political establishment and a vanishing Anishinabe culture suggests the failure of tribal sovereignty and the survival of myth in the modern world' for Cook-Lynn (1996b: 125–126). I don't entirely agree with that analysis but it does suggest a responsibility in the light of claims for Erdrich's representativeness, the privileging of the *ethnic* signifier in her 'Chippewa landscape' (the concept, not the book), or her status as *tribal* storyteller.

Such overstatements are often unhelpful in coming to a complex understanding of a narrative, and to the real work of tribal politics. A final example, from the same jacket blurb, makes the point more elegantly: 'At once an affirmation of a rich, resonant Native American past and a clear-eyed, open-hearted vision of a different and wider world, *Books and Islands in Ojibwe Country* is an irresistible self-portrait of a writer who speaks from America's heart'. On the one hand, this answers an earlier question: the book doesn't deal with the Anishinaabe polity because it is a 'self-portrait' (ironically anathema to 'tribal' modes). On the other, it admirably demonstrates several problems, implying that Native America remains only in a state of *pastness*, of *narrowness*. There is a sense of hope here of course, in that in declaring Erdrich to be speaking from 'America's heart' maybe the editors recognise the provocatively political point that 'Ojibwe country' transcends the imaginary line between the USA and Canada. Or maybe they recognise the still powerful position of North America's middle-west in the rearticulation of lines of political importance by its indigenous peoples. Whether they do or not, this 'region', after all, is spring-source for more published writers than any other tribe except perhaps the Cherokee has yet produced. Anishinaabe writing is actively engaged in narratives of contemporary Native experience, in the assertion of indigenous sovereignty, and in reimagining the storied existence of the USA and Canada.

This book does not seek to 'define' Erdrich or close down criticism of her work. Rather, it is a critical attempt to engage fully with the breadth of her writing and to consider the varied texture of its reception. The first edition of *Love Medicine* was translated into eighteen languages, the tetralogy as a whole into at least fourteen. Among other prizes, *Love Medicine* won the National Book Critics Circle Award; *The Antelope Wife*, intriguingly given this discussion about context, won the World Fantasy Award for 1999; and Erdrich was a 2009 Pulitzer Prize finalist with *The Plague of Doves*. Dawkins (1985) notes that Jane Fonda called to enquire about the film rights for *Love Medicine* and Erdrich and Dorris dined with Philip Roth and Clare Bloom. Roth, along with Toni Morrison and Angela Carter, has commended Erdrich's work in numerous publicity bites. Meanwhile several other Native writers, including Linda Hogan, Susan Power, and (notwithstanding his criticisms) David Treuer reveal her influence in their writing. This high praise and its truly global impact acknowledge Erdrich's work for exactly what she aspires to, namely, in her own words, 'excellence, the qualities that shine out and endure' (qtd in Chavkin and Chavkin 1994: 231).

If not here, then where?

Native American literary criticism has changed significantly since Ziff wrote that 'the process of literary annihilation would be checked only when Indian writers began representing their own culture' (1991: 173). Suggesting that Native people played no part whatsoever in the development of US literary culture in the eighteenth and nineteenth centuries, such attitudes to earlier Native literature have long been challenged. Warrior (Osage) has been responsible, alongside others, for opening up the hinterland of Native print practice, identifying what he sees as the continuous intellectual traditions of eighteenth- and nineteenth-century writers often dismissed as performing acts of colonial ventriloquism. This kind of reclamation is central to current trends in tribal literary nationalism, which complicate the earlier authenticity/identity politics through rigorous engagement with a set of aesthetics that foregrounds the political in relation – indeed in opposition – to colonialism and racism.

While it is difficult (though not impossible) to align Erdrich with such moves for many of the reasons already stated, nevertheless many of the key concerns of the latest 'ethical turn' in Native Literary Studies speak loudly to Erdrich's work. The connection between literature and liberation, grounded in the Native community, is central to Womack's call for tribe-specific criticism. He discusses the idea of insider/outsider in terms of a postmodernism in which Native and non-Native literatures are continually deconstructing one another, surely a net outcome of many of Erdrich's narrative forays? The continued discussion of these terms among native communities, so often interpreted by outsiders, also stands at the heart, often in subtle ways, of Erdrich's various reprisals of hegemonic representations of Natives; representations that refuse to limit identity to the imposed taxonomies of *either* colonising or tribal authorities. Indeed, Womack's claim that Native people are not 'mere victims but active agents in history, innovators of new ways, of Indian ways, of thinking and being and speaking and authoring in this world created by colonial contact' (2000: 5–6) explicitly resounds in those demonstrations of the ways in which identities are not prescribed but grown into, developed, proffered. In all of these examples we can also, can we not, discern in Erdrich's work an echo of 'Radical Indigenism' which would 'dare to suggest that American Indian cultures contain tools of enquiry that *create* knowledge' (Garroutte 2003: 107). The parallel readings of Pauline/Fleur in part resist assumptions of the superiority of Western over Native epistemologies and hermeneutic modes. But where Womack seeks to negotiate a specific tribal intellectual tradition, Erdrich's tribal specificity is part of her attempt to 'articulate. . . the universality and connectedness of the human race' (Lischke and McNab 2006: 193) or in her own words to write about 'American experience in all its diversity' (qtd in Ruoff 1999: 184).

This latter of course is one degree of separation from the tribal nationalists, who also resist the notion that Native authors are involved first and foremost in acts of writing back to colonial centres – a feature, admittedly, of several of the readings in this book. Nevertheless Erdrich's work engages, even if it doesn't necessarily 'promote', the issues this discourse establishes. Weaver argues that many Native texts work towards asserting an autonomous and distinct Native identity in community for the benefit and inclusion of all Native peoples. Such an argument, though possible, may be contentious relative to Erdrich's work. But Weaver's emphasis on 'The need for collective survival in diverse, often quite harsh environments', noting that 'Tribal communities are wholly defined by family relationships, whereas non-Indian communities are defined primarily by residence or by agreements with sets of intellectual beliefs' (1997b: 50), coincides more directly with her project. This is a view reinforced by many other Native writers and critics, as Owens testifies when he asserts that Native writers 'write with a "consciousness of responsibility as a member of a living Native American culture" and community' (Owens 1992, qtd by Weaver 1997b: 51). This sense of community is posited in what commentators identify as a 'geomythology', defined by the 'bioregionality' of worldview and religion that vary according to natural environment (Weaver 1997b: 50). Further to this, emphasizing the political importance of such activity, Baldridge (Cherokee) asserts, '[i]dentifying and attacking the enemy is a time-honored means to gain respect and admiration within one's community' (1996: 85).

In the introduction I suggested that Erdrich's writing was fundamentally orientated towards community. Shifting this claim from the aesthetic to the political, Weaver notes, 'Communal, identity-producing potential exists in any contemporary Native text'. For Weaver, literature has become a means of ensuring what he calls the 'continuance' of the people. Hobson is hopeful that by 'making literature, like the singers and storytellers of earlier times, we serve the people as well as ourselves in an abiding sense of remembrance' (Hobson 1979: 11). Continuance presupposes a living present, indeed takes that living present as a given, rather than embalming a body politic with a static sense of 'traditional' culture. Vizenor argues that '[s]tories are a circle of believable dreams and oratorical gestures showing the meaning between the present and the past in the life of the people. The stories change as the people change because people, not facts, are the center of the anishinabe world' (2001: 69). There is some vacillation around this point in Erdrich criticism. It is difficult to confidently make such a clear 'tribal' claim for the fiction, given the multitude of explicitly other contexts she engages and her willingness to present 'community' as frequently *incoherent* and even, occasionally, malevolent. The patterns of allegiance, affiliation, and coalition that form and persist in her work nevertheless speak to the power and proximity of bonds between humans and other entities. I suppose I am saying Erdrich is *not* necessarily an indigenist writer, nor is she clearly a tribal nationalist; but I am also asking whether efforts to politicise her work in relation to broader human community necessarily diminish the specific politics of Anishinaabe sovereignty discernible in her work. Can these features be reconciled? Is she, for instance, testing the limits of self-governance in the face of state and federal legislative power rather than undermining it through the negative portrayal of council leaders in *Love Medicine*? Does *Four Souls*, in simultaneously establishing and testing a broader postcolonial paradigm for the consideration of Anishinaabe dispossession and its reverberations, itself implicitly understand that moment within a global indigenist frame? And does the apparent multiculturalism of *The Antelope Wife* explicitly give way to the primacy of Ojibwe identity, the one constant in its motley cast of hyphenated characters?

Cook-Lynn's sense is that mixed-blood writers pander to and confirm dominant expectations of their Euroamerican audiences, that they fail to demonstrate anger. I would hope I have shown that, although there are few moments that can be interpreted in singularly polemical terms, anger – as well as confusion – is abundant. This speaks also to Silko's suggestion that the work becomes apolitical in its obsessive play with form and language. Again, I would hope I have demonstrated that, though Erdrich is not an activist, her work is political. Indeed, although it is more pronounced in recent writings, issues such as the importance of Ojibwemowin to self-identity first appeared in *Love Medicine* where Marie returns to the 'old language', recognising 'how comfortless words of English sounded in her ears' (263). That the recent work modifies the somewhat dismissive tone of 'old' language is perhaps instructive. The transnational turn in literary criticism also bears some reflection. The transnational, for instance, is exemplified in *Books and Islands* in the shared ('hemispheric') indigeneity and in the specific nexus of relationships across the border-lines, as shown by Erdrich's trip into Ojibwe country, a terrain that conceptually redraws the map but whose crossing by someone who can claim connection to its original inhabitants is thwarted by the nation state boundary. In so doing, it also challenges the conceptual

scope of the 'transnational' – in so far as it implies cross-border relationships – as it draws attention to the affiliations and common
material realities impeded by the imposition of the border. Beyond
'transcending' territorial delimiters, it seeks, provocatively, to recast
them, including the parameters of Native nationhood, taking them
beyond reservation borders and into a precolonial territory. The
persistence of that territory, and Erdrich's memoir, are clear reminders
to both US and Canadian governments of that prior claim. Alternatively, *The Master Butchers Singing Club* sharply defines the transatlantic weave in her family tapestry, that continued connection
to Europe which is palpable even in – or perhaps specifically because
of – the distant wilds of the Great Plains. These are all questions of
affiliation: literary, familial, and political.

In terms of advocacy, Erdrich has also written in support of Leonard
Peltier (2000b), also a source for Gerry Nanapush, revealing a political
commitment most recently illustrated by her refusal of an honorary
degree from the University of North Dakota because of its use of an
Indian mascot (*Bismarck Tribune* 2007). Speaking about *The Plague of
Doves*, Erdrich herself makes clear connections between its depictions
of vengeance and the 'hunger for vengeance' in the aftermath of 9–11
(Baenen 2008). In a small but significant way, Peltier himself fed the
appetite for blame after the deaths of two FBI agents at Pine Ridge
Reservation in 1973. Erdrich attended the trial in 1977 in Fargo,
North Dakota, and describes the compelling factors for doing so in
affably self-deprecating terms: 'Now, here were my friends dressed in
flamboyant vests, beads and black hats hung with eagle feathers. I, too,
wore a hat, a brown Italian fedora, only my feather was a blue macaw's.
On the basis of our hats, rather than any political awareness, I joined
the crowd . . . and became immediately drawn into the trial' (2000b).
Like so much of her writing, beyond that 'surface', as she describes
her political leanings, beyond the veneer of narrative play and the
subtleties of craft, lay a nascent politicism. And it is that wilful naivety,
feigned or otherwise, that draws us all, author and reader, to the
substance of lived experience. 'I changed the hours in my job so that
I could sit through the trial and listen carefully', she continues; having
done so, she claims confidence that 'not one scintilla of hard evidence'
tied Peltier to the crime. Most importantly, given what she says above
about 9–11, she believes:

The court system had been influenced, as had I, by the black hats and the feathers and the aura of paranoia. Only to me, these things were attractive. To others, the mood at the back of the courtroom and the drum beating in the street outside were threatening. No one at the time was capable of impartiality.

This document, which goes on to reiterate accusations of corruption and coercion by the FBI, was published at an important juncture, less than a month before Bill Clinton's final review of sentences as president.[1] 'As long as Leonard Peltier is imprisoned', she insists, 'our country's relationship with its Native people is stained by ongoing dishonour . . . our own human rights statements are undermined by hypocrisy'. As separate as these public comments and her fictions are, there is a clear correlation in both forms of writing of a desire to see justice fully enacted and to use, though infrequently, the public platform afforded her by the commercial success of her work to draw attention to injustice. Infrequent though they are, these outwardly political statements by Erdrich that demonstrate not only her own politics but also her self-positioning with regard to America and its global standing, do, I believe, shed a stronger light on the politics of Erdrich's fiction than others have discerned. That her writing has rarely been solely predicated on, or polemically directed against, singular politico-historical issues is more testament to her artistry than evidence of apoliticism. Erdrich is not an ideologue and even in these two instances, both particularly pertinent to Native American politics, she returns us, as ever, to the human cost. She returns, past the bigger political contest, to compassion for Peltier's now frail condition and the personal price she feels he has paid on behalf of others. And she returns to the human cost in the UND logo case, to the students who have suffered under its divisiveness while trying to study for their degrees: 'I've known how painful it is for [Indians] to have dealt with the divisiveness that this logo has caused' (2000b; qtd also in Louwagie 2007).

These are specifically Native-related cases, but as in her fiction, Erdrich often seeks that universal experience – whether it be suffering, injustice, or inequality – that speaks well beyond cultural borders, to the concrete rather than the abstract or theoretical. The directness of these appeals is in stark contrast to the abstraction that Silko identifies in *The Beet Queen* (see Chapter 3). Yet it is precisely that universalism

– her continued assertion that 'we're all mixed now' – that is often at the root of others' disquiet. Since Silko first accused Erdrich of a 'fairytale' apoliticism in 1986 the political, and at times polemical, nature of Erdrich's writing has changed significantly. As suggested in Chapter 4, the deeply racially motivated and violent tensions made explicit in *The Plague of Doves* speak to a Midwest settled on violent grounds while simultaneously addressing, as suggested above, the nature of contemporary events in our post 9–11 world. In 'local' terms that violence is made manifest in the landscape and the environment, and is deeply internalised. That Erdrich chooses, throughout her adult fiction at least, to frequently begin at that point of contact, in a late colonial moment in which the Native communities she depicts have apparently exhausted their ability to resist those external forces that confine them to a small patch of land somewhere in the Minnesota–North Dakota borderlands, ensures that her readers are always aware, not of pristine culture, but of the strategies of survivance that have seen a people endure, adapt, and persist against stark odds. There is, clearly, a certain romance in this interpretation of Erdrich's work. It is a romance not dissimilar to the lack of racial tension in *The Beet Queen*; it is a romance that David Treuer rejects; and yet it admits of one thing above all else; namely that the Midwest, as Cather showed before Erdrich, provides a rich canvas for the playing out of human struggle in all its dimensions. But the stakes are higher; this is no mere test of stamina, there is no other homeland to which to return. That her later work revisits that terrain with a much more pronounced political edge to it, and a keener eye for the devastating and often paradoxical legacy of communities, values, lifeways, and economies clashing, 'cracking apart', merging, and reforming speaks to a clear sense of the development of the work and its relationship to the socio-political milieu.

In global terms, however, there is a mixture of naivety, and certainly tragedy in the implications of a contemporary analogue in *The Plague of Doves*, as suggested by Erdrich herself. Her later books all pursue, to varying degrees, the theme of vengeance with consequences that range from emotional paucity, through neglect, to miscarriage of justice. If we are to take the author at her word we might conclude that vengeance, unreasonable or not, is both circumstantial and inevitable: we do not look beyond our present moment and yet, as Erdrich repeatedly shows us through her generational fiction, our actions today will have a profound effect on generations hence. It speaks to responsibility – we must always look ahead to consider the ramifications of our actions before we act. These, of course, are the political truths to which literature opens our eyes. The 'message' needs no cultural 'costume' for its power and importance.

There is echo and contrast in all of this, not least in the afore-mentioned 'contests' and dialogues between European-oriented discourses, and tribal nationalist and indigenist discourses, in the wider debate about the shape of American literature. Asserting distance between nation state ideology and the practice of literary criticism, Dimock refers to Janice Radway's appraisal of the field:[2] 'Radway's challenge to the "container" model turns the United States from a discrete entity into a porous network, with no tangible edges, its circumference being continually negotiated, its criss-crossing pathways continually modified by local input, local inflections' (2007: 3). At one level Erdrich's work speaks to this fluid sphere of negotiated practice, setting it perhaps in contradistinction to the tribalist concerns of Womack, Warrior, and others. On another level, however, it sits slightly less easily with what Dimock asserts as the principal lessons of 9–11 and Hurricane Katrina: 'Territorial sovereignty, we suddenly realize, is no more than a legal fiction, a man-made fiction . . . the nation is revealed to be . . . an epiphenomenon, literally a superficial construct, a set of erasable lines on the face of the earth' (2007: 1).

In this context, Erdrich's work joins the work of so many other Native artists in redrawing the sovereign territories – whether they be political, geographical, cultural, or intellectual – of America's indigenous population. *The Plague of Doves*, in fact, clearly traces the cartographies of midwestern settlement, while powerfully reinscribing indigeneity – through its Métis and Anishinaabe characters – back into that narrative. Or, more forcibly, it absorbs that settlement narrative into a longer Native history of belonging. This echoes in part the accommodations of an earlier cosmopolitanist, Arnold Krupat. In *Red Matters* Krupat writes, 'you just can't understand America, more specifically the United States, without coming to terms with the indigenous presence on this continent' (2002: viii). The interconnections he establishes between these principal modes of discourse suggests a somewhat radicalised status for Native literatures within the larger nation. A wholly 'ethnocritical' take on Erdrich's work might stress the anti-colonial aspect of her work; an indigenist reading, those elements of the work that can only be fully explored and embraced through a total (insofar as that is possible for non-Native readers) understanding of Anishinaabe thought and culture; and a nationalist reading, those efforts to assert claims to sovereignty, or at the very least autonomy of representation. A combination of the three approaches, where each heavily stresses the local and the particular, could in turn speak against the deterritorialising concerns of Dimock and others. Although Native literatures benefit from, and participate in, pan-indigenous networks of relation, cultural sovereignty in Native terms is expressed precisely *through* relations to land, returning us perhaps to Radway's 'criss-crossing pathways continually modified by local input, local inflections' and stopping short, way short, of Dimock's 'set of erasable lines'.

In this sense Erdrich, in her moment, is very clearly part of the continued construction of American national discourse, inflected, as well as reflected on, by her cast of Anishinaabe characters, the most memorable of whom – such as Nanapush – stand as testament to the history they participate in. If the tribal nationalist project can be seen itself to be at least secondarily involved in moderating – even forcing the recalibration of – that historical discourse, which surely it can, then there is no reason why the two need to be seen as mutually exclusive. There are, of course, other contexts that should (and no doubt will in time) be brought to bear. No significant study has as yet compared Erdrich's work to the range of writing by Métis authors in the US and Canada for instance. Given the unique position of the Métis between the tribal cultures from which they sprang and the French (and other European) travellers with whom they mixed, peoples who Cook-Lynn scathingly notes 'were and probably still are seen by native peoples as those who were *already converts* to the hostile and intruding culture simply through their marriage into it' (1996a: 35), such comparisons might speak instructively to the 'fluidity and split' of Erdrich's explorations of identity. That repeated motion of splitting and reconciling has itself set the tone in the late twentieth century for the representation of community and for narrative consideration of what that most nebulous of entities does; how it is organised; how it performs, outside the institutional frameworks of 'town hall', 'tribal council', or 'church'. Whatever the contexts in which we understand Erdrich's works, their importance, and their endurance, is undeniable.

Notes

1 On 20 January 2001 outgoing president Bill Clinton granted 140 pardons and commuted 36 sentences. These actions, along with earlier commutations in 1999, caused some controversy. See *House Committee*. Supporters of Peltier were aggrieved at Clinton's refusal to pardon him after twenty-four years in jail: they had believed, prior to 20 January, that a pardon was likely. Very strong opposition from the FBI was one of several reasons for the ultimate decision.

2 In fact, Dimock goes much further than Radway in her rejection of the idea of 'nation' as 'disciplinary' centre.

Bibliography

Works by Louise Erdrich

1981. *Imagination* (reading reinforcement skilltext series). Westerville, OH: C.E. Merrill.

1987. w. Michael Dorris, 'Sea to sea on route 2', *New York Times Magazine*, 15 March, 30–31, 44–48.

1988. w. Dorris, 'Who owns the land?', *New York Times Magazine*, 4 Sept., 32–35, 52, 54, 57, 65.

1989a. Foreword to Michael Dorris, *The Broken Cord: A Family's Ongoing Struggle with Fetal Alcohol Syndrome*. New York: Harper.

1989b. Preface to Desmond Hogan, *A Link with the River*. New York: Farrar, Straus.

1990. Introduction (w. Dorris) to Charles A. Eastman and Elaine Goodale Eastman, *Wigwam Evenings: Sioux Folk Tales Retold*. Lincoln and London: University of Nebraska Press.

1991. w. Dorris, *Route Two*. Northridge, CA: Lord John Press.

1992 [1991]. w. Dorris, *The Crown of Columbus*. London: Flamingo.

1993. Guest ed., *Best American Short Stories 1993*. Boston: Houghton Mifflin.

1994a [1984]. *Love Medicine* (rev. and expanded). London: Flamingo.

1994b [1986] *The Beet Queen*. London: Flamingo.

1994c [1988] *Tracks*. London: Flamingo.

1994d. Preface to John Tanner, *The Falcon: A Narrative of the Captivity and Adventures of John Tanner*. New York: Penguin.

1995 [1994]. *The Bingo Palace*. London: Flamingo.

1996a [1984]. *Jacklight*. London: Flamingo.

1996b. *The Blue Jay's Dance: A Birth Year*. London: Flamingo.

1996c. *Tales of Burning Love*. London: Flamingo.

1996d. *Grandmother's Pigeon*. New York: Hyperion.

1998. *The Antelope Wife*. London: Flamingo.

2000a [1999]. *The Birchbark House*. London: Dolphin.

2000b. 'A time for human rights on Native ground', *New York Times*, 29 Dec., http://query.nytimes.com/gst/fullpage.html?res=9403E1D71F38F93AA157 51C1A9669C8B63&sec=&spon=&partner=permalink&exprod=permalink [last accessed 01.02.09].

2001a [1989]. *Baptism of Desire*. London: Perennial.

2001b. 'Where I ought to be: a writer's sense of place' in Wong 2001, 43–50.

2001c. *The Last Report on the Miracles at Little No Horse*. New York: HarperCollins.

2002. *The Range Eternal*. New York: Hyperion.

2003a. *The Master Butchers Singing Club*. London: Flamingo.

2003b. *Original Fire: Selected and New Poems*. New York: HarperCollins.

2003c. *Books and Islands in Ojibwe Country*. Washington, DC: National Geographic.

2003d. *Winter Reader 2003–2004* (biographical essays by Minnesota Center for Book Arts) 6 Dec. Text by Louise Erdrich, artwork by five Minnesota papermakers.

2004a. *Four Souls*. New York: HarperCollins.

2004b. 'Extending our experiences to one another'. *Tribal College Journal* 16: 1 (fall).

2005a. *The Game of Silence*. New York: HarperCollins.

2005b. *The Painted Drum*. New York: HarperCollins.

2006. 'A writer's beginnings'. *Smithsonian* 37: 5 (Aug.), 20–22.

2008a. *The Plague of Doves*. New York: HarperCollins.

2008b. *The Porcupine Year*. New York: HarperCollins.

2009. *The Red Convertible: Selected and New Stories*. New York: HarperCollins.

2010. *Shadow Tag*. New York: HarperCollins.

Secondary sources

Acoose, Janice, Lisa Brooks, Tol Foster, Leanne Howe, Daniel Heath Justice, Phil Carroll Morgan, Kimberly Roppolo, Cheryle Suzack, Christopher B. Teuton, Sean Teuton, Robert Warrior, and Craig Womack. 2008. *Reasoning Together: The Native Critics Collective*. Norman: University of Oklahoma Press.

Adams, Heather and Layli Phillips. 2006. 'Experiences of Two-Spirit lesbian and gay Native Americans: an argument for standpoint theory in identity research'. *Identity: An International Journal of Theory and Research* 6: 3, 273–291.

Ahokas, Pirjo. 2004. 'Transcending binary divisions: constructing a postmodern female urban identity in Louise Erdrich's *The Antelope Wife* and Zadie Smith's *White Teeth*'. *American Studies* 119 (*Sites of Ethnicity: Europe and the Americas*), 115–129.

Allen, Chadwick. 2000. 'Postcolonial theory and the discourse of treaties'. *American Quarterly* 52: 1, 59–89.

Anderson, Eric. 2007. 'South to a red place: contemporary American Indian writing and the problem of Native/Southern studies'. *Mississippi Quarterly* 60: 1, 5–32.

Anishinaabeg Today. www.whiteearth.com/page/AnishinaabegToday.xml [last accessed 21.03.09].

Anzaldúa, Gloria. 1999. *Borderlands/La Frontera: The New Mestiza*. San Francisco: Aunt Lute Books.

—— and Cherrie Moraga eds. 1984. *This Bridge Called My Back: Writings by Radical Women of Color*. New York: Kitchen Table, Women of Color Press.

Appleford, Rob. 2005. '"Close, very close, a *b'gwus* howls": the contingency of execution in Eden Robinson's *Monkey Beach*'. *Canadian Literature* 18: 4, 85–101.

Armstrong, Jeannette C. ed. 1993. *Looking at the Words of Our People*. Penticton: Theytus Books.

Ashcroft, Bill. 2001. *Post-colonial Transformations*. London: Routledge.

Ashcroft, Bill, Gareth Griffiths, and Helen Tiffin. 1989. *The Empire Writes Back: Theory and Practice in Post-Colonial Literatures*. London: Routledge.

Attachie, Tommy, Dennis Hastings, and Robin Ridington. 2005. 'The songs of our elders: performance and cultural survival in Omaha and Dane-Zaa traditions' in Dunham et al. 2005: 110–129.

Attwater, Donald. 1983 [1965]. *The Penguin Dictionary of Saints*. 2nd edn, rev. and updated by Catherine Rachel John. London: Penguin.

Austenfeld, Thomas. 2006. 'German heritage and culture in Louise Erdrich's *The Master Butcher's Singing Club*'. *Great Plains Quarterly (GPQ)* 26, 3–11.

Baenen, Jeff. 2008. 'A dark event inspires Erdrich's new novel'. *News from Indian Country* (May). http://indiancountrynews.net/index.php?option=com_content& task=view&id=3557&Itemid=79 [last accessed 12.04.09].

Bak, Hans. 1992. 'Toward a Native American "realism": the amphibious fiction of Louise Erdrich' in Versluys 1997, 145–170.

—— 1997. 'Circles blaze in ordinary days: Louise Erdrich's *Jacklight*' in Castillo and Rosa 1997, 11–27.

Baker, Houston A. ed. 1982. *Three American Literatures: Essays in Chicano, Native American, and Asian-American Literatures for Teachers of American Literature*. New York: MLA.

Baldridge, William. 1996. 'Reclaiming our histories' in Treat 1996, 83–92.

Baraga, Frederic. 1992 [1878]. *A Dictionary of the Ojibway Language*. St. Paul: Minnesota Historical Society Press. Orig. pub. as *A Dictionary of the Otchipwe Langauge*. Montreal: Beauchemin and Valois.

Barak, Julie. 1996. 'Blurs, blends, berdaches: gender mixing in the novels of Louise Erdrich'. *Studies in American Indian Literature (SAIL)* 8: 3, 49–62.

—— 2001. 'Un-becoming white: identity transformation in Louise Erdrich's *The Antelope Wife*'. *SAIL* 13: 4, 1–23.

Barkwell, Lawrence J., Leah Dorion, and Warren R. Prefontaine. 1999. 'Deconstructing Métis historiography: giving voice to the Métis people' in *Resources for Métis Researchers*. Saskatoon: Gabriel Dumont Institute. www .saskpublishers.sk.ca/sampler/spotlight/gdi2.htm [last accessed 12.01.09].

Barnett, Marianne. 1988. 'Dreamstuff: Erdrich's *Love Medicine*'. *North Dakota Quarterly (NDQ)* 56: 1, 82–93.

Barnouw, Victor. 1950. *Acculturation and Personality among the Wisconsin Chippewa*. Menasha, WI: American Anthropological Association.

—— 1977. *Wisconsin Chippewa Myths and Tales*. Madison: University of Wisconsin Press.

Barry, Nora Baker. 2000. 'Fleur Pillager's bear identity in the novels of Louise Erdrich'. *SAIL* 12:2, 24–38.

—— and Mary Prescott. 1989. 'The triumph of the brave: *Love Medicine*'s holistic vision'. *Critique: Studies in Contemporary Fiction* 30: 2, 123–138.

Barsh, Russel Lawrence. 2001. 'War and the reconfiguring of American Indian society'. *Journal of American Studies (JAS)* 35: 3, 371–410.

Bataille, Gretchen. 1993. '*The Beet Queen*: images of the grotesque on the Northern Plains' in Fleck 1997, 277–285.

—— ed. 2001. *Native American Representations: First Encounters, Distorted Images, and Literary Appropriations*. Lincoln: University of Nebraska Press.

Beder, Sharon and Jasmin Sydee. 2001. 'Ecofeminism and globalism'. *Democracy and Nature*, 281–302.

Beidler, Peter G. 1992. 'Three student guides to Louise Erdrich's *Love Medicine*'. *American Indian Culture and Research Journal (AIC&RJ)* 16: 4, 167–173.

—— 2000a. 'The facts of fictional magic: John Tanner as a source for Louise Erdrich's *Tracks* and *The Birchbark House*'. *AIC&RJ* 24: 4, 37–54.

—— 2000b. Review of *The Birchbark House*. *SAIL* 12: 1, 85–88.

—— 2002. ' "The earth itself was sobbing": madness and the environment in novels by Leslie Marmon Silko and Louise Erdrich'. *AIC&RJ* 26: 3, 113–124.

—— and Helen Hoy. 1991. 'Two views of *the Crown of Columbus*'. *SAIL* 3: 4, 47–55.

—— and Gay Barton. 2006. *A Reader's Guide to the Novels of Louise Erdrich* (Rev. and expanded). Columbia and London: University of Missouri Press.

Belgarde, Scott, Les LaFountain, and Orie Richard. 2007. 'Who I am'. www.tmbci.net/PDF/WhoIAm.pdf [last accessed 29.07.09].

Bell, Leland V. 1970. 'The failure of Nazism in America: the German American Bund, 1936–1941'. *Political Science Quarterly* LXXXV: 4, 585–599.

Benjamin, Walter. 2001 [1974]. *On the Concept of History*. Gesammelten Schriften I: 2. Trans. Dennis Redmond. Frankfurt am Main: Suhrkamp Verlag.

Benton-Banai, Edward. 1979. *The Mishomis Book: the Voice of the Ojibway*. St. Paul: Indian Country Press.

Berninghausen, Tom. 1998. '"This Ain't Real Estate": Land and Culture in Louise Erdrich's Chippewa Tetralogy' in Roberson 1998, 190–210.

Bird, Gloria. 1998. 'Breaking the silence: writing as "witness"' in Ortiz 1998, 26–48.

Bismarck Tribune. 2007. 'Author Louise Erdrich rejects UND honor', 21 April. www.bismarcktribune.com/articles/2007/04/21/news/state/132278.txt [last accessed 21.07.09].

Blaeser, Kimberly M. 1993. 'Native literature: seeking a critical center' in Armstrong 1993, 53–61.

—— 1996. *Gerald Vizenor: Writing in the Oral Tradition*. Norman and London: University of Oklahoma Press.

—— 1997. 'Like "reeds through the ribs of a basket": Native women weaving stories'. *AIQ* 21: 4, 555–565.

—— 1999a. 'Centering words: writing a sense of place'. *Wicazö Sa Review* 14: 2, 92–108.

—— 1999b. *Stories Migrating Home*. Bemidji: Loonfeather Press.

—— 2003. 'Sacred story cycles: pilgrimage as re-turn and re-telling in American indigenous literatures'. *Religion and Literature* 35: 2–3, 83–104.

Bonetti, Kay. 1986. *Louise Erdrich and Michael Dorris Interview with Kay Bonetti* (sound recording), American Audio Prose Library.

Boureau, Alan. 2000. *The Myth of Pope Joan*. Chicago: University of Chicago Press.

Brant, Beth. 1994. *Writing as Witness: Essay and Talk*. Toronto: Women's Press.

Braz, Albert. 2003. *The False Traitor: Louis Riel in Canadian Culture*. Toronto: University of Toronto Press.

Brehm, Victoria. 1996. 'The metamorphosis of an Ojibwa Manido'. *American Literature* 68: 4, 677–706.

Britten, Thomas A. 1998. *American Indians in World War I: At War and At Home*. Albuquerque: University of New Mexico Press.

Brogan, Kathleen. 1996. 'Haunted by history: Louise Erdrich's *Tracks*'. *Prospects* 21, 169–192.

Brown, Calvin S. 1962. 'Faulkner's geography and topography'. *PMLA* 77: 5, 652–659.

Brown, Peter and Michael Irwin eds. 2006. *Literature and Place: 1800–2000*. Oxford and New York: Peter Lang.

Brozzo, Shirley. 2001. 'Food for thought: a postcolonial study of food imagery in Louise Erdrich's *The Antelope Wife*'. *SAIL* 17: 1, 1–15.

Bruchac, Joseph W. III. 1993 [1982]. 'A good day to be alive: some observations on contemporary American Indian writing'. *SAIL* 5: 2, 13–16.

—— 1994. 'Whatever is really yours: an interview with Louise Erdrich' in Chavkin and Chavkin 1994, 94–104.

Buell, Lawrence and Wai Chee Dimock eds. 2007. *Shades of the Planet: American Literature as World Literature*. Princeton and Oxford: Princeton University Press.

Buenker, Joe. 'Louise Erdrich: publications and criticism (the online guide)'. www.west.asu.edu/jbuenke/erdrich/index.html [last accessed 19.07.09].

Burdick, Debra A. 1996. 'Louise Erdrich's *Love Medicine, The Beet Queen*, and *Tracks*: an annotated survey of criticism through 1994'. *AICɑRJ* 20: 3, 137–166.

Burton, Stacy. 2001. 'Rereading Faulkner: authority, criticism, and *The Sound and the Fury*'. *Modern Philology* 98: 4, 604–628.

Butler, Alban. 1883. *Lives of the Saints*. London and Dublin: J.S. Virtue and Co. Ltd.

Bynum, Caroline Walker. 1982. *Jesus as Mother: Studies in the Spirituality of the High Middle Ages*. Berkeley and London: University of California Press.

Callender, Charles and Lee M. Kochems. 1983. 'The North American berdache', *Current Anthropology* 24:4, 443–470.

Callicott, J. Baird and Thomas W. Overholt. 1982. *Clothed-in-Fur and Other Tales: An Introduction to an Ojibwa World View*. New York: University Press of America.

Camurat, Diane. 1993. *The American Indian in the Great War: Real and Imagined*. Unpub. master's thesis, Paris. http://net.lib.byu.edu/~rdh7/wwi/comment/camurat1.html [last accessed 30.05.07].

Caron, John. 2004. 'Fargo, North Dakota newspapers'. www.fargo-history.com/other2/newspapers.htm [last accessed 13.02.09].

Carpenter, Kristen A. 2006. 'Contextualising the losses of Allotment through literature'. *North Dakota Law Review* 82: 3, 605–626.

Carpenter, Lynette and Wendy Kolmar eds. 1991. *Haunting the House of Fiction*. Knoxville: University of Tennessee Press.

Carter, Lyn. 2006. 'Postcolonial interventions within science education: using postcolonial ideas to reconsider cultural diversity scholarship'. *Educational Philosophy and Theory* 38: 5, 677–691.

Castillo, Susan. 1991. 'Postmodernism, Native American literature and the real: the Silko–Erdrich controversy'. *Massachusetts Review* 32: 2, 285–294.

—— 1996. 'Women aging into power: fictional representations of power and authority in Louise Erdrich's female characters'. *SAIL* 8: 4, 13–20.

—— and Victor M.P. da Rosa eds. 1997. *Women in Native American Literature and Culture*. Porto: Fernando Pessoa University Press.

Castor, Laura. 2004. 'Ecological politics and comic redemption in Louise Erdrich's *The Antelope Wife*'. *Nordlit* 15, 121–134.

Chapman, Abraham ed. 1975. *Literature of the American Indians*. New York: New American Library.

Chapman, Alison A. 2007. 'Rewriting the Saints' lives: Louise Erdrich's *The Last Report on the Miracles at Little No Horse*'. *Critique* 48: 2, 149–167.

Chapman, Mary. 1995. '"The belly of this story": storytelling and symbolic birth in Native American fiction'. *SAIL* 7: 2, 3–16.

Charles, Ron. 2004. '*Four Souls: A Novel*'. *Christian Science Monitor*, 29 June. www.powells.com/review/2004_08_02.html [last accessed 16.04.07].

Chavkin, Allan. 2000. 'Vision and revision in Louise Erdrich's *Love Medicine*' in Wong 2000, 211–219.

—— ed. 1999. *The Chippewa Landscape of Louise Erdrich*. Tuscaloosa: University of Alabama Press.

—— and Nancy Feyl Chavkin. 1994. *Conversations with Louise Erdrich and Michael Dorris*. Jackson: University Press of Mississippi.

Christie, Stuart. 2009. *Plural Sovereignties and Contemporary Indigenous Literature*. New York: Palgrave Macmillan.

Clarke, Joni Adamson. 1992. 'Why bears are good to think and theory doesn't have to be murder: transformation and oral tradition in Louise Erdrich's *Tracks*'. *SAIL* 4: 1, 28–48.

Clute, John. 1995 [1988]. 'Janus-faced fables' in *Look at the Evidence: Essays and Reviews*. Liverpool: Liverpool University Press, 126–128.

Conway, Thor and Julie Conway. 1990. *Spirits on Stone: the Agawa Pictographs*. San Luis Obispo: Heritage Discoveries.

Cook-Lynn, Elizabeth. 1993. 'The American Indian fiction writer: "Cosmopolitanism, Nationalism, the Third World, and First Nation Sovereignty"'. *Wicazö Sa Review* 9: 2, 26–36.

—— 1996a. *Why I Can't Read Wallace Stegner and other Essays: A Tribal Voice*. Madison: University of Wisconsin Press.

—— 1996b. 'American Indian intellectualism and the new Indian story'. *AIQ* 20: 1, 57–76. Rept. in Mihesuah 1998, 111–138.

—— 2001a. *Anti-Indianism in Modern America: A Voice from Tatekeya's Earth*. Champaign: University of Illinois Press.

—— 2001b. 'Letter to Michael Dorris' in Cook-Lynn 2001a, 69–71.

—— 2001c. 'A Mixed-Blood, tribeless voice in American Indian literatures: Michael Dorris' in Cook-Lynn 2001a, 72–90.

Cornelia, Marie. 2004. 'Shifting boundaries: reflections on ethnic identity in Louise Erdrich's *The Master Butchers Singing Club*'. *Glossen Sonderausgabe* special issue 19. www.dickinson.edu/glossen/heft19/cornelia.html [last accessed 02.04.07].

Cornell, Daniel. 1992. 'Woman looking: revis(ion)ing Pauline's subject position in Louise Erdrich's *Tracks*'. *SAIL* 4: 1, 49–63.

Cox, Jay. 1997. 'Muting white noise: the subversion of popular culture narratives of conquest in Sherman Alexie's fiction'. *SAIL* 9: 4, 52–70.

Cox, Karen Castellucci. 1998. 'Magic and memory in the contemporary story cycle: Gloria Naylor and Louise Erdrich'. *College English* 60: 2, 150–172.

Crabtree, Claire. 1987. 'Salvific oneness and the fragmented self in Louise Erdrich's *Love Medicine*' in Schirer 1987, 49–56.

Craig, William. 1991. 'An exploration of discovery'. *Valley News*, 19 April.

Cutchins, Dennis. 2000. 'Sugar cane and sugar beets: two tales of burning love'. *SAIL* 12:2, 1–12.

Daly, Bo and T. Reddy eds. 1991. *Narrating Mothers: Theorizing Material Subjectivities*. Knoxville: University of Tennessee Press.

Daniele, Daniela. 1992. 'Transactions in a Native land: mixed blood identity and Indian legacy in Louise Erdrich's writing'. *Rivista di Studi Nord Americani* 3, 59–71.

Dawkins, Young. 1985. 'The stuff of great fiction'. *Dartmouth Alumni Magazine* (March), 22.

DeBahJiMon. www.llojibwe.org/divisions/administration/ debahjimon.html [last accessed 26.06.09].

Debo, Angie. 1995 [1970]. *A History of the Indians of the United States*. London: Pimlico.

Deloria, Vine, Jr. 1969. *Custer Died for your Sins: An Indian Manifesto*. Norman and London: University of Oklahoma Press.

—— 1996. 'Vision and community: a Native American voice' in Treat 1996, 105–114.

DeMallie, Raymond J. and Douglas Parks eds. 1987. *Sioux Indian Religion: Tradition and Innovation*. Norman and London: University of Oklahoma Press.

Densmore, Frances. 1929. *Chippewa Customs*. Washington: Government Printing Office.

DePriest, Maria. 2008. 'Once upon a time, today: hearing Fleur's voice in *Tracks*'. *Journal of Narrative Theory* 38: 2, 249–269.

Derounian-Stodola, Kathryn Zabell ed. 1998. *Women's Indian Captivity Narratives*. London: Penguin.

Desmond, John F. 1994. 'Catholicism in contemporary American fiction'. *America* 170: 17, 7–11.

Dewdney, Selwyn. 1975. *The Sacred Scrolls of the Southern Ojibway*. Toronto and Buffalo: University of Toronto Press.

Dimock, Wai Chee. 2007. 'Planet and America, set and subset' in Buell and Dimock 2007, 1–16.

Dobbert, G.A. 1967. 'German-Americans between new and old Fatherland, 1870–1914'. *American Quarterly* 19: 4, 663–680.

Dorman, Robert L. 2006. 'From the middle of nowhere to the heartland: the Great Plains and American regionalism' in Brown and Irwin 2006, 179–198.

Downes, Margaret J. 1996. 'Narrativity, myth, and metaphor: Louise Erdrich and Raymond Carver talk about love'. *Multi Ethnic Literatures in the United States (MELUS)* 21: 2, 49–61.

Dunham, Gary H., Clyde Ellis, and Luke Eric Lassiter eds. 2005. *Powwow*. Lincoln: University of Nebraska Press.

Durrell, Lawrence. 1954. *The Curious History of Pope Joan*. London: Derek Verschoyle.

Dutta, Pratima. 2003. 'Erdrich's "The Red Convertible"'. *Explicator* 61: 2, 119–121.

Dykema-VanderArk, Tony. 2002. '"Playing Indian" in print: Charles A. Eastman's autobiographical writing for children'. *MELUS* 27: 2, 9–30.

Egerer, Claudia. 1997. *Fictions of (In)Betweenness*. Göteborg: Göteborg University Press.

Elson, John, '1+1<2' unnamed source, document located in Erdrich's alumni file, Rauner Special Collections, Dartmouth College.

Enochs, Ross. 1996. *The Jesuit Mission to the Lakota Sioux: Pastoral Theology and Ministry, 1886–1945*. Lanham, MD: Sheed and Ward.

Erdrich, Heid E. 2005. *The Mother's Tongue*. Cambridge: Salt.

Farrell, Susan. 1999. 'Colonizing Columbus: Dorris and Erdrich's postmodern novel'. *Critique* 40: 2, 121–135.

Fast, Robin Riley. 1995. 'Borderland voices in contemporary Native American poetry'. *Contemporary Literature* 36: 3, 508–536.

—— 1999. 'Resistant history: revising the captivity narrative in "Captivity" and *Blackrobe: Issac Jogues*'. *AIC&RJ* 23: 1, 69–86.

Fergusson, Suzanne. 1996. 'The short stories of Louise Erdrich's novels'. *Studies in Short Fiction* 33: 4, 541–555.

Ferrari, Rita. 1999. ' "Where the maps stopped": the aesthetics of borders in Louise Erdrich's *Love Medicine* and *Tracks*'. *Style* 33: 1, 144–165.

Fixico, Donald L. 2000. *The Urban Indian Experience in America*. Albuquerque: University of New Mexico Press.

Flanagan, Thomas. 1979. *Louis 'David' Riel: Prophet of the New World*. Toronto: University of Toronto Press.

—— 1983. *Riel and the Rebellion: 1885 Reconsidered*. Saskatoon: Western Producer Prairie Books.

Flavin, James. 1991. 'The novel as performance communication in Louise Erdrich's *Tracks*'. *SAIL* 3: 4, 1–13.

Flavin, Louise. 1989. 'Louise Erdrich's *Love Medicine*: loving over time and distance'. *Critique: Studies in Contemporary Fiction* 31: 1, 55–64.

—— 1995. 'Gender construction amid family dissolution in Louise Erdrich's *The Beet Queen*'. *SAIL* 7: 2, 17–24.

Fleck, Richard F. ed. 1997 [1993]. *Critical Perspectives on Native American Fiction*. Pueblo, CO: Passegiata Press.

Fleischner, Jennifer. 1994. *A Reader's Guide to the Fiction of Louise Erdrich*. New York: HarperCollins.

—— and Susan Ostrov Weisser eds. 1994. *Feminist Nightmares, Women at Odds*. New York: New York University Press.

Forgey, Donald G. 1975. 'The institution of Berdache among the Northern American Plains Indians'. *Journal of Sex Research* 11: 1, 1–15.

Foster, Tol. 2008. 'Of one blood: an argument for relations and regionality in Native American Literary Studies' in Acoose et al. 2008, 265–302.

Freeman, John. 2008. 'Louise Erdrich: secrets in the Indian file'. *Independent*, 6 June. www.independent.co.uk/arts-entertainment/books/features/louise-erdrich-secrets-in-the-indian-file-841027.html [last accessed 16.12.09].

Friedman, Susan Stanford. 1994. 'Identity, politics, syncretism, Catholicism, and Anishinabe religion in Louise Erdrich's *Tracks*'. *Religion and Literature* 26: 1, 107–133.

Frost, Robert. 1915. *A Boy's Will*. New York: Henry Holt. www.bartleby.com/ 117/16.html [last accessed 22.07.08].

Furlan, Laura. 2007. 'Remapping Indian country in Louise Erdrich's *The Antelope Wife*'. *SAIL* 19: 4, 54–76.

Garroutte, Eva Marie. 2003. *Real Indians: Identity and the Survival of Native America*. Berkeley and Los Angeles: University of California Press.

George, Jan. 1985. 'An interview with Louise Erdrich'. *NDQ* 53, 240–246.

German Quarterly. 1942. XV: 4, 179–182.

Giles, James, Connie Jacobs and Greg Sarris eds. 2004. *Approaches to Teaching the Novels and Poetry of Louise Erdrich*. New York: MLA.

Giles, Paul. 1992. *American Catholic Arts and Fictions: Culture, Ideology, Aesthetics*. New York and Cambridge: Cambridge University Press.

Gilley, Brian Joseph. 2006. *Becoming Two-Spirit: Gay Identity and Social Acceptance in Indian Country*. Lincoln: University of Nebraska Press.

Gish, Robert F. 1999. 'Life into death, death into life: hunting as metaphor and motive in *Love Medicine*' in Chavkin 1999, 67–83.

Gleason, William. 1987. '"Her laugh an ace": the function of humor in Louise Erdrich's *Love Medicine*'. *AIC&RJ* 11: 3, 51–73.

Gould, Janice. 1995. 'American Indian women's poetry: strategies of rage and hope'. *Signs* 20: 4, 797–817.

Goulet, Jean-Guy A. 1996. 'The "Berdache"/ "Two-Spirit": a comparison of anthropological and Native constructions of gendered identities among the Northern Athapaskans'. *Journal of the Royal Anthropological Institute* 2: 4, 683–701.

Gourneau, Patrick, or Aun nish e naubay. 1971. *History of the Turtle Mountain Band of Chippewa Indians* (pamphlet).

Grantham, Shelby. 1985. 'Intimate collaboration, or, what *The Wall Street Journal* calls "a novel partnership"'. *Dartmouth Alumni Magazine* (March), 43–47.

Gregory, Leslie. 1998. 'Native American humor: powerful medicine in Louise Erdrich's *Tracks*'. *Ampersand* 1: 2. http://itech.fgcu.edu/&/issues/vol1/ issue2/erdrich.htm [last accessed 08.05.07].

Grim, John A. 1983. *The Shaman: Patterns of Siberian and Ojibway Healing*. Norman: University of Oklahoma Press.

Grödal, Hanne Tang. 1990. 'Words, words, words'. *The Dolphin* 18, 21–26.

Gross, Lawrence W. 2002. 'The comic vision of Anishinaabe culture and religion'. *AIQ* 26: 3, 436–459.

—— 2005. 'The Trickster and world maintenance: an Anishinaabe reading of Louise Erdrich's *Tracks*'. *SAIL* 17: 3, 48–66.

Gunn Allen, Paula ed. 1996. *Song of the Turtle: American Indian Literature 1974–1994*. New York: Ballantine Books.

—— 'American Indian fiction 1968–1983'. www2.tcu.edu/depts/prs/amwest/html/wlr1058. html [last accessed 01.08.06].

—— and Patricia Clark Smith. 1996. *As Long as the Rivers Flow: the Stories of Nine Native Americans*. New York: Scholastic Press.

Hafen, P. Jane. 1996. 'Sacramental language: ritual in the poetry of Louise Erdrich'. *GPQ* 16: 3, 147–155.

—— 1999a. '"Repositories for the soul": driving through the fiction of Louise Erdrich'. *Heritage of the Great Plains* 32: 2, 53–64.

—— 1999b. 'Louise Erdrich'. *Twentieth Century American Western Writers: Dictionary of Literary Biography*. Vol. 206. Ed. Richard H. Cracroft. Detroit, MI: Bruccoli, Clark, Layman, Inc., 85–96.

—— 2001a. '"We Anishinaabeg are the keepers of the names of the earth": Louise Erdrich's Great Plains'. *GPQ* 21: 4, 321–332.

—— 2001b. Review of *A Reader's Guide to the Novels of Louise Erdrich* (Beidler and Barton) and *The Chippewa Landscape of Louise Erdrich* (ed. Chavkin). *GPQ* 21: 2, 71–72.

—— 2003. *Reading Louise Erdrich's Love Medicine*. Boise, ID: Boise State University Western Writers Series.

Hallowell, Irving A. 1947. 'Myth, culture, and personality'. *American Anthropologist* 49: 544–556.

Hasketh, John. 1923. 'History of the Turtle Mountain Chippewa'. *Collection of the State Historical Society of North Dakota* 5, 85–124.

Helander, Kaisa. 2007. 'The theory of toponymic silence and indigenous Sámi place names during the growth of the Norwegian Nation state' at *Language, Silence, and Voice in Native Studies*, University of Geneva, July.

Henry, Michelle. 2004. 'Canonizing Craig Womack: finding Native literature's place in Indian Country'. *AIQ* 28: 1/2, 30–51.

Herman, Matt. 2003. 'The Krupat-Warrior debate: a preliminary account'. *Culture and the State: Disability Studies and Indigenous Studies* 2, 60–65.

Hessler, Michelle R. 1995. 'Catholic nuns and Ojibwa shamans: Pauline and Fleur in Louise Erdrich's *Tracks*'. *Wicazö Sa Review* 11: 1, 40–45.

Hewlett, Bob. 2005. 'Are the men of the African Aka tribe the best fathers in the world?', 15 June. http://guardian.co.uk/parents/story/0,3605,1506843,00.html [last accessed 08.05.07].

Hickerson, Harold. 1962. 'The Southwestern Chippewa: an ethnohistorical study'. *The American Anthropological Society, Memoir 92* 64: 3, part 2 (June).

Hilger, Sister Mary Inez. 1939. *Chippewa Indian Families: A Social Study of One Hundred Fifty Chippewa Indian Families of the White Earth Reservation of Minnesota*. Washington DC: The Catholic University of America Press.

—— 1959. 'Some customs of the Chippewa on the Turtle Mountain Reservation of North Dakota'. *North Dakota History* 26: 3, 123–132.

Hobson, Geary. 1979. *The Remembered Earth*. Albuquerque: University of New Mexico Press.

Hoffman, Walter J. 1891. 'The *Midewiwin*; or "Grand Medicine Society" of the Ojibwa'. Washington, DC: *Bulletin of the Bureau of American Ethnology*. Seventh Annual Report, 1885–1886 (143–300).

Holm, Sharon. 2008. 'The "lie" of the land: Native Sovereignty, Indian literary Nationalism, and early Indigenism in Leslie Marmon Silko's *Ceremony*'. *AIQ* 32: 3, 243–274.

Holt, Debra C. 1987. 'Transformation and continuance: Native American tradition in the novels of Louise Erdrich' in Schirer 1987: 149–161.

Horne, Dee. 2004. 'A postcolonial reading of *Tracks*' in Giles et al. 2004, 191–200.

House Committee on Government Reform. 2002. 'Justice undone: clemency decisions in the Clinton White House', March 14.

Houston, Robert. 1991. 'Take it back for the Indians'. *New York Times*, 29 April.

Howard, James H. 1952. 'The Sun Dance of the Turtle Mountain Ojibwa'. *North Dakota History* 19, 249–264.

Huang, Hsinya. 2004. 'Disease, empire, and (alter)Native medicine in Louise Erdrich's *Tracks* and Winona LaDuke's *Last Standing Woman*'. *Concentric: Literary and Cultural Studies* 30: 1, 37–64.

Huggan, Graham. 2001. *The Postcolonial Exotic*. London: Routledge.

Hughes, Sheila Hassell. 2000. 'Tongue-tied: rhetoric and relation in Louise Erdrich's *Tracks*'. *MELUS* 25: 3/4, 87–116.

—— 2001. 'Falls of desire/leaps of faith: religious syncretism in Louise Erdrich's and Joy Harjo's "Mixed-Blood" poetry'. *Religion and Literature* 33: 2, 59–83.

Jacobs, Connie. 2001. *The Novels of Louise Erdrich: Stories of Her People*. New York: Peter Lang.

Jacobs, Sue-Ellen, Wesley Thomas, and Sabine Lang eds. 1997. *Two-Spirit People: Native American Gender Identity, Sexuality, and Spirituality*. Chicago: University of Illinois Press.

Jahner, Elaine. 1993 [1977]. 'Indian literature and critical responsibility'. *SAIL* 5: 2, 7–12.

James, Bernard J. 1961. 'Social-psychological dimensions of Ojibwa acculturation'. *American Anthropologist* 63: 4, 721–746.

Jaimes, M. Annette. 1992. 'The art of pandering: review of *The Crown of Columbus*'. *Wicazö Sa Review* 8: 2, 58–9.

Jarvis, Brian. 1998. *Postmodern Cartographies: The Geographical Imagination in Contemporary American Culture*. London: Pluto.

Jaskoski, Helen. 1987. 'From the time immemorial: Native American traditions in contemporary short fiction' in Logsdon and Mayer 1987, 54–71.

—— 1991. Review of *Baptism of Desire*. *SAIL* 3: 4, 55–57.

Johnson, Kelli Lyon. 2007. 'Writing deeper maps: mapmaking, local Indigenous knowledges, and literary nationalism in Native women's writing'. *SAIL* 19: 4, 103–120.

Johnston, Basil. 1982. *Ojibway Ceremonies*. Toronto: McClelland and Stewart.

—— 1990 [1976]. *Ojibway Heritage*. Lincoln and London: University of Nebraska Press.

—— 1995. *The Manitous: The Supernatural World of the Ojibway*. New York: Harper Perennial.

Jones, Malcolm. 1985. 'Life, art are one for prize novelist' in Chavkin and Chavkin 1994: 3–9.

Jones, Peter (Kahkewaquonaby). 1861. *The History of the Ojebway Indians: with Especial Reference to their Conversion to Christianity*. London: A.W. Bennett.

Justice, Daniel Heath. 2008. ' "Go Away, Water!": kinship criticism and the decolonization imperative' in Acoose et al. 2008, 147–168.

Kakutani, Michiko. 2004. 'A mystic with revenge on her mind', *New York Times*, 6 July, 7.

Karell, Linda K. 2002. *Writing Together/Writing Apart: Collaboration in Western American Literature*. Lincoln and London: University of Nebraska Press.

Keenan, Deirdre. 2006. 'Unrestricted territory: gender, Two Spirits, and Louise Erdrich's *The Last Report on the Miracles at Little No Horse*'. *AIC&RJ* 30: 2, 1–15.

Kidsreads. 1999. 'Louise Erdrich on *The Birchbark House*'. www.kidsreads. com/authors/au-erdrich-louise.asp [last accessed 20.07.09].

King, Thomas. 1993. *Green Grass, Running Water*. New York: Houghton Mifflin.

—— 1999. *Truth and Bright Water*. Toronto: HarperCollins.

Kirch, Claire. 2005. 'Marching to the beat of her own drum'. *Publishers Weekly* 252: 37 (19 Sept.), 38–39.

Klepp, L.S. 1991. 'Columbus, bye bye'. *Entertainment Weekly*, 3 May, 50–51.

Kolmar, Wendy K. 1991. ' "Dialectics of connectedness": supernatural elements in novels by Bambara, Cisneros, Grahn, and Erdrich' in Carpenter and Kolmar 1991, 236–249.

Kraus, Michael. 1966. *Immigration: the American Mosaic*. Princeton: D. Van Nostrand Co. Inc.

Kroeber, Karl. 1993 [1987]. 'Oral narrative in an age of mechanical reproduction'. *SAIL* 5: 2, 72–88.

—— 1986. (as ed.) Introductory note to Silko 'Artifact'. *SAIL* 10: 4, 177–179.

—— ed. 1997. 'Louise Erdrich's *Love Medicine*', a compilation of extracts by various authors in Fleck 1997, 263–276.

Krumholz, Linda. 2007. 'Saints and tricksters: translation and conversion in Louise Erdrich's *The Last Report on the Miracles at Little No Horse*'. Unpub. paper, *Native American Literature Symposium*, 8–10 March.

Krupat, Arnold. 1989. *The Voice in the Margin: Native American Literature and the Canon*. Berkeley and Oxford: University of California Press.

—— 1992. *Ethnocriticism: Ethnography, History, Literature*. Berkeley and Oxford: University of California Press.

—— 1996. *The Turn to the Native: Studies in Criticism and Culture*. Lincoln and London: University of Nebraska Press.

—— 2002. *Red Matters: Native American Studies*. Philadelphia: University of Pennsylvania Press.

Lafitau, Father Joseph Francis, trans. William N. Fenton and Elizabeth R. Moore. 1977. *Customs of the American Indians Compared with the Customs of Primitive Times*, Vol. II. Toronto: The Champlain Society.

Landes, Ruth. 1937. *Ojibwa Sociology*. New York: Columbia University Press.

—— 1968. *Ojibwa Religion and the Midéwiwin*. Madison, Milwaukee, and London: University of Wisconsin Press.

—— 1997 [1938]. *The Ojibwa Woman*. Lincoln and London: University of Nebraska Press.

Larson, Sidner. 1993. 'The fragmentation of a tribal people in Louise Erdrich's *Tracks*'. *AIC&RJ* 17: 2, 1–13.

—— 1997. 'Fear and contempt: a European concept of property'. *AIQ* 21: 4, 567–577.

—— 2000. *Captured in the Middle: Tradition and Experience in Contemporary Native American Writing*. Seattle and London: University of Washington Press.

—— 2000. 'The real thing: an essay on authenticity'. *Wicazö Sa Review* 15: 2, 75–78.

Levi, Sister Carolissa M. 1956. *Chippewa Indians of Yesterday and Today*. New York: Pageant Press.

Lincoln, Kenneth. 1982. 'Native American literatures: "old like hills, like stars"' in Baker 1982, 80–167.

Lischke, Ute and David T. McNab. 2006. 'Storytelling and cultural identity: Louise Erdrich's exploration of the German/American connection in *The Master Butchers Singing Club*'. *European Journal of American Culture* 25: 3, 189–203.

Little, Jonathan. 2000. 'Beading the multicultural world: Louise Erdrich's *The Antelope Wife* and the sacred metaphysic'. *Contemporary Literature* 41: 3, 495–524.

Logsdon, Loren and Charles W. Mayer. 1987. *Since Flannery O'Connor: Essays on the Contemporary American Short Story*. Macomb: Western Illinois University Press.

Long, Charles. 2008. 'Editor's foreword' in Reid 2008, ix–x.

Lott, Sandra W., Norman McMillan, and Maureen Hawkins eds. 1993. *Global Perspectives on Teaching Literature: Shared Visions and Distinctive Visions*. Urbana, IL: National Council of Teachers of English.

Louwagie, Pam. 2007. 'Sioux logo debate is in tribes' hands'. *Star Tribune*, 26 Oct. www.startribune.com/sports/11720126.html [last accessed 12.01.09].

Magalaner, Marvin. 1989. 'Of cars, time, and the river' in Pearlman 1989, 95–108.

Magoulick, Mary. 2000. 'Women weaving the world: Louise Erdrich's *The Antelope Wife* as myth' (part of unpub. diss.). www.faculty.de.gcsu.edu/ ~mmagouli/antwife.htm [last accessed 21.08.08].

Manley, Kathleen E.B. 1994. 'Decreasing the distance: contemporary Native American texts, hypertext, and the concept of audience'. *Southern Folklore* 51: 2, 121–135.

Maracle, Lee. 1996 [1988]. *I Am Woman: A Native Perspective on Sociology and Feminism.* Vancouver: Press Gang Publishers.

Maristuen-Rodakowski, Julie. 2000. 'The Turtle Mountain reservation in North Dakota: its history as depicted in Louise Erdrich's *Love Medicine* and *The Beet Queen*'. in Wong 2000, 13–26.

Markowitz, Harvey. 1991. Review of *The Crown of Columbus. Magill Book Reviews*, 9 Sept.

Matchie, Thomas. 1996. 'Louise Erdrich's "Scarlet Letter": literary continuity in *Tales of Burning Love*'. *NDQ* 63: 4, 113–123.

McCafferty, Kate. 1997. 'Generative adversity: shape-shifting Pauline/ Leopolda in *Tracks* and *Love Medicine*'. *AIQ* 21: 4, 729–751.

McAuliffe, Dennis, Jr. 2005. 'Little House on the Osage prairie' in Seale and Slapin eds, 2005, 49–52.

McCay, Mary A. 1993. 'Cooper's Indians, Erdrich's Native Americans' in Lott et al. 1993, 152–167.

McKenzie, James. 1986. 'Lipsha's good road home: the revival of Chippewa culture in *Love Medicine*'. *AIC&RJ* 10: 3, 53–63.

McKinney, Karen Janet. 1998. 'False miracles and failed vision in Louise Erdrich's *Love Medicine*'. *Critique* 40: 2, 152–160.

McNab, David T. 2004. 'Of bears and birds: the concept of history in Erdrich's autobiographical writings' in Giles et al. 2004, 32–41.

McNally, Michael D. 2000. *Ojibwe Singers: Hymns, Grief, and a Native Culture in Motion.* New York and Oxford: Oxford University Press.

Medicine, Beatrice. 1987. 'Indian women and the renaissance of traditional religion' in Demallie and Parks 1987, 159–171.

Meyer, Melissa L. 1994. *The White Earth Tragedy: Ethnicity and Dispossession at a Minnesota Anishinaabe Reservation, 1889–1920.* Lincoln and London: University of Nebraska Press.

Mihesuah, Devon. 2004. 'Finding empowerment through writing and reading, or Why am I doing this? an unpopular writer's comments about the state of American Indian literary criticism'. *AIQ* 28: 1 and 2, 97–102.

—— ed. 1998. *Natives and Academics: Researching and Writing about American Indians.* Lincoln and London: University of Nebraska Press.

Mink, Joanna Stephens and Janet Doubler Ward eds. 1993. *Communication and Women's Friendships: Parallels and Intersections in Literature and Life.* Bowling Green, OH: Popular Press.

Mitchell, David. 1987. 'A bridge to the past: cultural hegemony and the Native American past in Louise Erdrich's *Love Medicine*' in Schirer 1987, 162–170.

Mitchell, Jason P. 2000. 'Louise Erdrich's *Love Medicine*, Cormac McCarthy's *Blood Meridian*, and the (de)mythologizing of the American West'. *Critique* 41: 3, 290–304.

Momaday, N. Scott. 1969. *The Way to Rainy Mountain*. New York: Ballantine Books.

—— 1975. 'The man made of words' in Chapman 1975, 96–110.

—— 1999 [1968]. *House Made of Dawn*. New York: Harper Perennial.

Morace, Robert A. 1999. 'From sacred hoops to bingo palaces: Louise Erdrich's carnivalesque fiction' in Chavkin 1999, 36–66.

Murray, David. 1990. *Forked Tongues: Speech, Writing and Representation in North American Indian Texts*. Bloomington and Indianapolis: Indiana University Press.

—— 2001. 'Representation and cultural sovereignty: some case studies' in Bataille 2001, 80–97.

Nabokov, Peter. 1993 [1978]. 'American Indian literature: a tradition of renewal'. *SAIL* 5: 2, 21–28.

Nagel, James. 2001. *The Contemporary American Short-Story Cycle: The Ethnic Resonance of Genre*. Baton Rouge: Louisiana State University Press.

Nichols, John G. and Earl Nyholm. 1995. *A Concise Dictionary of Minnesota Ojibwe*. Minneapolis and London: University of Minnesota Press.

North Dakota State University. newspapers archive. www.lib.ndsu.nodak.edu /ndirs/collections/newspapers/index2.htm [last accessed 01.06.07].

Noori, Margaret. 2008. 'The shiver of possibility'. *Women's Review of Books* 25: 5, 12.

NPS (National Park Service). 2009. 'National NAGPRA', U.S. Department for the Interior. www.nps.gov/history/ nagpra/ [last accessed 21.04.09].

O'Hagan, Kathleen. 1995. *Pauline of Matchimanito: Une Femme Windigo. Reading Louise Erdrich's Religious Mixed-Blood*. Unpub. master's thesis, Dartmouth College.

Olson, Karen. 2001a. 'The complicated life of Louise Erdrich'. *Book* magazine May/June. http://search.barnesandnoble.com/Birchbark-House/Louise-Erdrich/e/9780786814541#ITV [last accessed 18.03.09].

—— 2001b. 'Meet the writers: Louise Erdrich'. *Book* magazine May/June. www.barnesandnoble.com/writers/writerdetails.asp?userid=2TH3X2Y63 W&cid=929573#bio [last accessed 17.08.06. Content now removed].

Onion, Pat. 2006. 'Crossing over: mediating between cultures in American Indian literature'. Maine Humanities Council. www.mainehumanities.org/ programs/talk-crossing-over.html [last accessed 31.03.09].

Ortiz, Simon. 1981. 'Towards a National Indian literature: cultural authenticity in nationalism'. *MELUS* 8: 2, 7–12.

—— ed. 1998. *Speaking for the Generations: Native Writers on Writing*. Tucson: University of Arizona Press.

Owens, Louis. 1987. 'Acts of recovery: the American Indian novel in the '80s'. *Western American Literature* 22: 1, 53–57.

—— 1992. *Other Destinies: Understanding the American Indian Novel*. Norman and London: University of Oklahoma Press.

—— 1998. *Mixedblood Messages: Literature, Film, Family, Place*. Norman and London: University of Oklahoma Press.

—— 2000. 'Erdrich and Dorris's Mixed Bloods and multiple narratives' in Wong 2000, 53–66.

—— 2001. 'As if an Indian were really an Indian: Native American voices and postcolonial theory' in Bataille 2001, 11–25.

Padgett, John B. 2000. 'A Faulkner glossary'. *William Faulkner on the Web*. www.mcsr.olemiss.edu/~egjbp/faulkner/glossaryi.html [last accessed 01.04.03].

Pasquaretta, Paul. 1996. 'Sacred chance: gambling and the contemporary Native American Indian novel'. *MELUS* 21: 2, 21–33.

Pearlman, Mickey, ed. 1989. *American Women Writing Fiction*. Lexington: University of Kentucky Press.

—— 1994. 'Louise Erdrich' in Chavkin and Chavkin 1994, 151–156.

Pheasant, Kenny Neganigwane. 2007. 'History of the Anishinaabek'. *Anishinaabemdaa*. www.anishinaabemdaa.com/history.htm [last accessed 23.09.09].

Pittman, Barbara L. 1995. 'Cross-cultural reading and generic transformations: the chronotope of the road in Louise Erdrich's *Love Medicine*'. *American Literature* 67: 4, 777–792.

Pollack, Harriet ed. 1995. *Having Our Way: Women Rewriting Tradition in Twentieth-Century America*. Lewisburg: Bucknell University Press.

Purdy, John. 1997. 'Betting on the future: gambling against colonialism in the novels of Louise Erdrich' in Castillo and Rosa 1997, 37–56.

Quehenberger-Dobbs, Linda. 1996. 'Literature, the imagination and survival: Louise Erdrich's *Love Medicine* tetralogy'. *Arbeiten Aus Anglistik und Amerikanistik* 21: 2, 255–265.

Quennet, Fabienne C. 2001. *Where 'Indians' Fear to Tread?: a Postmodern Reading of Louise Erdrich's North Dakota Quartet*. Münster: Lit.

Rader, Dean. 2002. 'Word as weapon: visual culture and contemporary American Indian poetry'. *MELUS* 27: 3, 147–167.

—— 2003. 'Engaged resistance in American Indian art, literature and film'. *Peace Review* 15: 2, 179–186.

—— 2004. '"Sites of unification": teaching Erdrich's poetry' in Giles et al. 2004, 102–113.

Rainwater, Catherine. 1990. 'Reading between worlds: narrativity in the fiction of Louise Erdrich'. *American Literature* 62: 3, 405–422.

—— and William J. Scheik eds. 1985. *Contemporary American Women Writers: Narrative Strategies*. Lexington: University of Kentucky Press.

Rajnovich, Grace. 1994. *Reading Rock Art: Interpreting the Indian Rock Paintings of the Canadian Shield*. Toronto: Natural Heritage/Natural History Inc.

Ramírez, Susan Berry Brill de. 1999. *Contemporary American Indian Literatures and the Oral Tradition*. Tucson: University of Arizona Press.

Rawson, Josie. 2001. 'Louise Erdrich'. *Mother Jones* 26: 3, 102–103.

Rayson, Ann. 1991. 'Shifting identity in the work of Louise Erdrich and Michael Dorris'. *SAIL* 3: 4, 27–37.

Reid, Dorothy M. 1964. *Tales of Nanabozho*. London: Oxford University Press.

Reid, E. Shelley. 2000. 'The stories we tell: Louise Erdrich's identity narratives'. *MELUS* 25: 3/4, 65–86.

Reid, Jennifer. 2008. *Louis Riel and the Creation of Modern Canada: Mythic Discourse and the Postcolonial State*. Albuquerque: University of New Mexico Press.

Rice, David. 2002. 'Review of *The Birchbark House, Muskrat Will be Swimming, and Rain is Not My Indian Name*'. *MELUS* 27: 2, 246–249.

Rich, Adrienne. 1972. 'When we dead awaken: writing as re-vision'. *College English* 34: 1, 18–30.

Riley In the Woods, Patricia. 2000. 'There is no limit to this dust: the refusal of sacrifice in Louise Erdrich's *Love Medicine*'. *SAIL* 12: 2, 13–23.

Rippley, La Vern J. 1985. 'Ameliorated Americanization: the effect of World War I on German-Americans in the 1920s' in Trommler and McVeigh 1985, 217–231.

Roberson, Susan L. 1998. *Women, America, and Movement: Narratives of Relocation*. Columbia: Missouri University Press.

Rolo, Mark Anthony. 2002. 'The *Progressive* interview: Louise Erdrich'. *Progressive* 66: 4, 36–40.

Roscoe, Will. 1998. *Changing Ones: Third and Fourth Genders in Native North America*. New York and London: Palgrave.

Rosenberg, Roberta. 2002. 'Ceremonial healing and the multiple narrative tradition in Louise Erdrich's *Tales of Burning Love*'. *MELUS* 27: 3, 113–131.

Roufs, Timothy G. 1975. *The Anishinabe of the Minnesota Chippewa Tribe*. Phoenix: Indiana Tribal Series.

Rowe, John Carlos. 2004. 'Buried alive: the Native American political unconscious in Louise Erdrich's fiction'. *Postcolonial Studies* 7: 2, 197–210.

Rowlandson, Mary. 1998 [1682]. 'A true history of the captivity and restoration of Mrs. Mary Rowlandson' in Derounian-Stodola 1998, 1–52.

Ruffo, Armand. 1995. 'From myth to metafiction, a narratological analysis of Thomas King's "The One About Coyote Going West"'. *Aboriginal Peoples and Canada: International Journal of Canadian Studies* 12, 135–154.

Ruoff, LaVonne Brown. 1999. 'Afterword' in Chavkin 1999, 182–188.

Ruppert, James. 1995a. *Mediation in Contemporary Native American Fiction*. Norman and London: University of Oklahoma Press.

—— 1995b. 'Mediation in contemporary Native American writing' in Velie 1995: 7–24.

—— 2000. 'Celebrating culture: *Love Medicine*' in Wong 2000, 67–84.

Said, Edward. 1991 [1984]. *The World, the Text, and the Critic*. London: Vintage.

Sanders, Karla. 1998. 'A healthy balance: religion, identity, and community in Louise Erdrich's *Love Medicine*'. *MELUS* 23: 2, 129–155.

Sands, Kathleen M. 1986. Extract in Kroeber 1986, 269.

—— 2000. '*Love Medicine*: voices and margins' in Wong 2000, 35–42.

Sarris, Greg. 1993. *Keeping Slug Woman Alive: A Holistic Approach to American Indian Texts*. Berkeley: University of California Press.

Sarvé-Gorham, Kristan. 1995. 'Power lines: the motif of twins and the medicine women of *Tracks* and *Love Medicine*' in Pollack 1995, 167–190.

—— 1999. 'Games of chance: gambling and land tenure in *Tracks*, *Love Medicine*, and *The Bingo Palace*'. *Western American Literature* 34: 3, 276–399.

Sayre, Gordon M. 1990. 'Abridging between two worlds: John Tanner as American Indian autobiographer'. *American Literary History* 11, 480–499.

Schirer, Thomas ed. 1987. *Contemporary Native American Cultural Issues*. Sault Sainte Marie, MI: Lake Superior State University Press.

—— ed. 1991. *Entering the 90s: The North American Experience*. Sault Sainte Marie, MI: Lake Superior State University Press.

Schneider, Bethany. 2007. 'Oklahobo: following Craig Womack's American Indian and Queer Studies'. *South Atlantic Quarterly* 106: 3, 599–613.

Schneider, Lissa. 1992. '*Love Medicine*: a metaphor for forgiveness'. *SAIL* 4: 1, 1–13.

Schoolcraft, Henry Rowe. 1997. *Schoolcraft's Ojibwa Lodge Stories: Life on the Lake Superior Frontier*. East Lansing: Michigan State University Press.

Schorcht, Blanca. 2003. *Storied Voices in Native American Texts: Harry Robinson, Thomas King, James Welch and Leslie Marmon Silko*. New York and London: Routledge.

Schultz, Lydia. 1991. 'Fragments and Ojibwe stories: narrative strategies in Louise Erdrich's *Love Medicine*'. *College Literature* 18: 3, 80–95.

Schumacher, Michael. 1991. 'Louise Erdrich, Michael Dorris: a marriage of minds'. *Writer's Digest*, 28–31.

Schweninger, Lee. 1993. 'A skin of lakeweed: an ecofeminist approach to Erdrich and Silko' in Waxman 1993, 37–56.

Seale, Doris and Beverly Slapin eds. 2005. *A Broken Flute: The Native Experience in Books for Children*. Berkeley & Plymouth: Oyate/Alta Mira.

Seeds, Dale E. and John E. Smelcer. 2002. 'The future of Native American literature: a conversation with John E. Smelcer'. *MELUS* 27: 3, 133–145.

Sergi, Jennifer. 1992. 'Storytelling: tradition and preservation in Louise Erdrich's *Tracks*'. *World Literature Today* 66: 2, 279–282.

Shaddock, Jennifer. 1994. 'Mixed blood women: the dynamic of women's relations in the novels of Louise Erdrich and Leslie Silko' in Weisser and Fleischner 1994, 106–121.

Shapiro, Anna. 1996. Review of *Tales of Burning Love*. *Detroit News*, 5 June.

Shoemaker, Nancy ed. 1995. *Negotiators of Change: Historical Perspectives on Native American Women*. New York and London: Routledge.

Silberman, Robert. 1989. 'Opening the text: *Love Medicine* and the return of the Native American woman' in Vizenor 1989c, 101–120.

Silko, Leslie Marmon. 1977. *Ceremony*. New York and London: Penguin.

—— 1986. 'Here's an odd artifact for the fairy tale shelf'. *SAIL* 10: 4, 178–184. First pub. in *Impact/Albuquerque Journal* (8 Sept.), 10–11.

—— 1996. *Yellow Woman and a Beauty of the Spirit: Essays on Native American Life Today*. New York and London: Simon and Schuster.

Sloboda, Nicholas. 1996. 'Beyond the iconic subject: re-visioning Louise Erdrich's *Tracks*'. *SAIL* 8: 3, 63–79.

Smith, Jeanne. 1991. 'Transpersonal selfhood: the boundaries of identity in Louise Erdrich's *Love Medicine*'. *SAIL* 3: 4, 13–27.

Smith, Karen R. 2002. 'Ethnic irony and the quest of reading: Joyce, Erdrich, and chivalry in the introductory literature classroom'. *Journal of the Midwest Modern Language Association* 35: 1, 68–83.

Smith, Theresa, S. 1995. *The Island of the Anishinaabeg: Thunderers and Water Monsters in the Traditional Ojibwe Life-World*. Moscow: University of Idaho Press.

Steinberg, Sybil. 2001. 'PW talks with Louise Erdrich'. *Publisher's Weekly* 248: 5, 64.

Stewart, Michelle Pagni. 2002. 'Judging authors by the color of their skin? Quality Native American children's literature'. *MELUS* 27: 2, 179–196.

Stirrup, David. 2006. '"Songs belong to these islands": mapping the cultural terrain in Louise Erdrich's nonfiction'. *European Review of Native American Studies* 20: 1, 29–34.

Stockham, Alice Bunker. 2008 [1896]. *Karezza: Ethics of Marriage*. Chicago: Stockham Publishing Co., repub. by Forgotten Books.

Stokes, Karah. 1999. 'What about the sweetheart? the "different shape" of Anishinabe two sisters stories in Louise Erdrich's *Love Medicine* and *Tales of Burning Love*'. *MELUS* 24: 2, 89–105.

Stone, Brad. 1998. 'Scenes from a marriage'. *Newsweek*, 131: 12 (23 March), 69.

Stookey, Lorena. 1999. *Louise Erdrich: A Critical Companion*. Westport, CT: Greenwood Press.

Storhoff, Gary. 1998. 'Family systems in Louise Erdrich's *The Beet Queen*'. 39: 4, 341–352.

Stripes, James D. 1991. 'The problem(s) of (Anishinaabe) history in the fiction of Louise Erdrich: voices and contexts'. *Wicazö Sa Review* 7: 2, 26–33.

Suzack, Cheryl. 2008. 'Land claims, identity claims: mapping indigenous feminism in literary criticism and in Winona LaDuke's *Last Standing Woman*' in Acoose et al. 2008, 169–192.

Swain, Gwenyth. 2004. *Little Crow: Taoyateduta*. St. Paul: Minnesota Historical Society Press.

Szanto, Laura Furlan. 2000. 'An annotated secondary bibliography of Louise Erdrich's recent fiction: *The Bingo Palace, Tales of Burning Love,* and *The Antelope Wife*'. *SAIL* 12: 2, 61–89.

Tanrisal, Meldan. 1997. 'Mother and child relationships in the novels of Louise Erdrich'. *American Studies International* 35: 3, 67–79. *Academic Search Complete*. EBSCO. Templeman Library, Canterbury, UK (2 Aug. 2007). http://search.ebscohost.com/login.aspx?direct=true&db=a9h&AN=9711233 074&site=ehost-live.

Tapahonso, Luci. 1993. *Sáanii Dahataal: The Women Are Singing*. Tucson: University of Arizona Press.

—— 1997. *Blue Horses Rush In*. Tucson: University of Arizona Press.

Tatonetti, Lisa. 2007. 'The emergence and importance of Queer American Indian literatures; or, "help and stories" in thirty years of *SAIL*'. *SAIL* 19: 4, 143–172.

Teuton, Christopher B. 2008. 'Theorizing American Indian literature: applying oral concepts to written traditions' in Acoose et al. 2008, 193–215.

Tharp, Julie. 1993. 'Women's community and survival in the novels of Louise Erdrich' in Mink and Ward 1993, 165–180.

—— 2003. 'Windigo ways: eating and excess in Louise Erdrich's *The Antelope Wife*'. *AICQRJ* 27: 4, 117–131.

Tinker, George. 1993. *Missionary Conquest: The Gospel and Native American Cultural Genocide*. Minneapolis: Fortress Press.

—— 1996. 'Spirituality, Native American personhood, sovereignty, and solidarity' in Treat 1996, 115–131.

—— 2004. *Spirit and Resistance: Political Theology and American Indian Liberation*. Minneapolis: Fortress Press.

Totten, Christine. 1985. 'Elusive affinities: acceptance and rejection of the German-Americans' in Trommler and McVeigh 1985, 185–203.

Towery, Margie. 1992. 'Continuity and connection: characters in Louise Erdrich's fiction'. *AICQRJ* 16: 4, 99–122.

Trafzer, Clifford. 1992. '"The world is sacred to a child": American Indians and children's literature'. *American Indian Quarterly* 16: 3, 381–395.

Treat, James ed. 1996. *Native and Christian: Indigenous Voices on Religious Identity in the United States and Canada*. New York and London: Routledge.

Treuer, Anton ed. 2001. *Living our Language: Ojibwe Tales and Oral Histories, a Bilingual Anthology*. St. Paul: Minnesota Historical Society Press.

Treuer, David. 2002. 'Reading culture'. *SAIL* 14: 1, 51–64.

—— 2006. *Native American Fiction: A User's Manual*. St. Paul: Graywolf Press.

Trexler, Richard. 2002. 'Making the American Berdache: choice or constraint'. *Journal of Social History* 35: 3, 613–636.

Trommler, Frank and Joseph McVeigh eds. 1985. *America and the Germans: An Assessment of a Three Hundred Year History* Vol. II. Philadelphia: University of Pennsylvania Press.

Turtle Mountain Chippewa. 1997. 'Tribal historic overview'. *The History and Culture of the Turtle Mountain Band of Chippewa*. Repr. without author credits on the official website. http://turtlemountain chippewa.com/ [last accessed 19.06.05].

Van Dyke, Annette. 1992. 'Questions of the spirit: bloodlines in Louise Erdrich's Chippewa landscape'. *SAIL* 4: 1, 15–27.

—— 1999. 'Of vision quests and spirit guardians: female power in the novels of Louise Erdrich' in Chavkin 1999, 130–143.

—— 2003–4. 'Encounters with Deer Woman: sexual relations in Susan Power's *The Grass Dancer* and Louise Erdrich's *The Antelope Wife*'. *SAIL* 15: 3 and 4, 168–188.

Vecsey, Christopher. 1983. *Traditional Ojibwa Religion and its Historical Changes*. Philadelphia, PA: The American Philosophical Society.

Velie, Alan. 1997. 'Magical Realism and ethnicity: the fantastic in the fiction of Louise Erdrich' in Castillo and Rosa 1997, 57–67.

—— ed. 1995. *Native American Perspectives on Literature and History*. Norman: University of Oklahoma Press.

Vennum, Thomas. 2009 [1982]. *The Ojibwa Dance Drum: Its History and Construction*. St. Paul: Minnesota Historical Society Press.

Versluys, Kristiaan ed. 1992. *Neo-Realism in Contemporary American Fiction*. Amsterdam: Rodopi.

Vizenor, Gerald. 1989a. 'Trickster discourse: comic holotropes and language games' in Vizenor 1989c, 187–212.

—— 1989b. 'Minnesota Chippewa: woodland treaties to tribal bingo'. *AIQ* 13: 1, 31–50.

—— 1991. *The Heirs of Columbus*. Middletown, CT: Wesleyan University Press.

—— 1998a [1984]. *The People Named the Chippewa: Narrative Histories*. Minneapolis and London: University of Minnesota Press.

—— 1998b. *Fugitive Poses: Native American Indian Scenes of Absence and Presence*. Lincoln and London: University of Nebraska Press.

—— 1999 [1994]. *Manifest Manners: Narratives on Postindian Survivance*. Lincoln: University of Nebraska Press.

—— 2001. *The Everlasting Sky: Voices of the Anishinabe People*. St. Paul: Minnesota Historical Society Press.

—— 2006. 'Native American literature: an introduction', catalogue entry for *Ken Lopez Booksellers*. http://lopezbooks.com/catalog/na6/na6–01.html [last accessed 26.06.09].

—— ed. 1989c. *Narrative Chance: Postmodern Discourse on Native American Indian Literatures*. Norman and London: University of Oklahoma Press.

—— ed. and trans. 1993. *Summer in the Spring: Anishinaabe Lyric Poems and Stories, new edn*. Norman and London: University of Oklahoma Press.

Waldman, Carl. 2000 [1985]. *Atlas of the North American Indian*. New York: Chackmark Books.

Walker, Victoria. 1991. 'A note on perspective in *Tracks*'. *SAIL* 3: 4, 37–41.

Walsh, Dennis M. and Ann Braley. 1994. 'The Indianness of Louise Erdrich's *The Beet Queen*: latency as presence'. *AIC&RJ* 18: 3, 1–17.

Walsh, Dennis. 2001. 'Catholicism in Louise Erdrich's *Love Medicine* and *Tracks*'. *AIC&RJ* 25: 2, 107–127.

Warren, William W. 1984 [1885]. *History of the Ojibway People*. St. Paul: Minnesota Historical Society Press.

Warrior, Robert. 1994. *Tribal Secrets: Recovering American Indian Intellectual Traditions*. Minneapolis and London: University of Minnesota Press.

—— Jace Weaver, and Craig Womack. 2006. *American Indian Literary Nationalism*. Albuquerque: University of New Mexico Press.

Waxman, Barbara Frey ed. 1993. *Multicultural Literatures Through Feminist/ Poststructuralist Lenses*. Knoxville: University of Tennessee Press.

Weaver, Jace. 1997a. *That the People Might Live: Native American Literatures and Native American Community*. New York and Oxford: Oxford University Press.

—— 1997b. 'Native American authors and their communities'. *Wicazö Sa Review* 12: 1, 47–88.

Welch, James. 1987 [1979]. *The Death of Jim Loney*. New York and London: Penguin.

The White Earth Reservation Curriculum Committee [Marshall Brown, Jerry Rawley, Georgia Weimer, Everett Goodwin, Kathy Roy Goodwin]. 1989. *White Earth: A History*. Cass Lake: The Minnesota Chippewa Tribe.

Williams, Sarah T. 2008. 'The three graces: a meeting with Louise, Lise, and Heid Erdrich'. *Star Tribune*. 3 Feb. www.startribune.com/entertainment/ books/15083971.html [last accessed 19.07.09].

Williams, Walter L. 1984. *The Spirit and the Flesh: Sexual Diversity in American Indian Cultures*. Boston: Beacon Press.

Wilson, Michael. 1997. 'Speaking of home: the idea of the center in some contemporary American Indian writing'. *Wicazö Sa Review* 12: 1, 129–148.

—— 2007. *Writing Home: Indigenous Narratives of Resistance*. East Lansing: Michigan State University Press.

Winter, Kari J. 2000. 'The politics and erotics of food in Louise Erdrich'. *SAIL* 12: 4, 44–64.

Wittmier, Melanie. 2002. 'Erdrich's *The Last Report on the Miracles at Little No Horse*'. *Explicator* 60: 4, 241–243.

Womack, Craig S. 2000. *Red on Red: Native American Literary Separatism.* Minneapolis and London: University of Minnesota Press.

—— 2008. 'A single decade: book-length Native literary criticism between 1986 and 1997' in Acoose et al. 2008, 3–104.

Wong, Hertha D. Sweet. 1991. 'Adoptive mothers and thrown-away children in the novels of Louise Erdrich' in Daly and Reddy 1991, 174–192.

—— 2000. 'Louise Erdrich's *Love Medicine*: narrative communities and the short story cycle' in Wong 2000, 85–106.

—— ed. 2000. *Louise Erdrich's Love Medicine: A Casebook.* New York and Oxford: Oxford University Press.

Wub-E-Ke-Niew. 1995. *We Have the Right to Exist.* www.maquah.net/We_Have_The_Right_To_Exist/WeHaveTheRight_03TOC.html [last accessed 10.01.09].

Ziff, Larzer. 1991. *Writing in the New Nation: Prose, Print, and Politics in the Early United States.* New Haven and London: Yale University Press.

Index